WATER TOSSING BOULDERS

Katherine Lum with her two daughters, Martha (on left), and Berda (on right), circa 1915. Courtesy of the Lum family.

WATER TOSSING BOULDERS

HOW A FAMILY OF CHINESE IMMIGRANTS
LED THE FIRST FIGHT TO DESEGREGATE SCHOOLS
IN THE JIM CROW SOUTH

ADRIENNE BERARD

Beacon Press
Boston

BEACON PRESS
Boston, Massachusetts
www.beacon.org

Beacon Press books
are published under the auspices of
the Unitarian Universalist Association of Congregations.

19 18 17 16   8 7 6 5 4 3 2 1

This book is printed on acid-free paper that meets the uncoated paper
ANSI/NISO specifications for permanence as revised in 1992.

Text design and composition by Kim Arney

Library of Congress Cataloging-in-Publication Data

Names: Berard, Adrienne, author.
Title: Water tossing boulders : how a family of Chinese immigrants led the
   first fight to desegregate schools in the Jim Crow South / Adrienne Berard.
Description: Boston : Beacon Press, 2016. | Includes bibliographical
   references and index.
Identifiers: LCCN 2015049943 (print) | LCCN 2016012491 (ebook) |
   ISBN 978-0-8070-3353-1 (hardback) | ISBN 978-0-8070-3354-8 (ebook)
Subjects: LCSH: Lum, Martha—Trials, litigation, etc. | Rosedale
   (Miss.)—Trials, litigation, etc. | Segregation in education—Law and
   legislation—Louisiana—Mississippi River Delta—History—20th century. |
   Chinese Americans—Civil rights—Louisiana—Mississippi River
   Delta—History—20th century. | BISAC: SOCIAL SCIENCE / Discrimination &
   Race Relations. | SOCIAL SCIENCE / Ethnic Studies / Asian American
   Studies. | HISTORY / United States / State & Local / South (AL, AR, FL,
   GA, KY, LA, MS, NC, SC, TN, VA, WV).
Classification: LCC KF228.L86 B47 2016 (print) | LCC KF228.L86 (ebook) |
   DDC 344.73/0798—dc23

LC record available at http://lccn.loc.gov/2015049943

When torrential water tosses boulders,
it is because of its momentum.

—Sun Tzu, *The Art of War*

CONTENTS

AS A CHILD GROWING up in New England, I used to listen for hours as my mother told stories in the dawdling Mississippi drawl of her childhood. She learned to hide her accent when she moved north during high school, but her vowels grew long again whenever she took me and my sisters into the backyard to play kick the can. My mother taught us the Mississippi Delta like it was a second language. She slipped back into her accent when she showed us how to cook, how to tell a joke, how to hide between imaginary hedgerows of cotton in a game of blind man's bluff.

This book began as a failed effort to chronicle my own family history in Mississippi. While digging through the archives at Delta State University to research my great-grandmother, I wandered, quite by accident, into a meeting of the Mississippi Delta Chinese Heritage Museum. It was there I overheard a conversation between the university archivist, Emily Jones, and a retired library science professor named Frieda Quon. They were overwhelmed. Dozens of descendants of Chinese immigrants were anxious to have their family histories preserved at Delta State, the only archive collecting material on the Mississippi Delta Chinese.

Leaving the university, I called my grandmother. Although she was raised in the Delta, my grandmother knew next to nothing about its history of Chinese immigration. "We'd go to their stores to cash checks on Saturdays," she told me. That was all she had to say.

After that conversation, my book dramatically changed course. How was it that generations of women raised in the Delta could know nothing about its sizable Chinese population? Through my subsequent research I came across the Lum family. By entering into their world, I was forced to restructure my own. Here was a family of Chinese immigrants living in the segregated South, a third race in a binary racial society, navigating the boundary between black and white. Through the very nature of their racial ambiguity, the Lum family did something remarkable. During the fall of 1924, Jeu Gong Lum filed a lawsuit that would become the first US Supreme Court case to challenge the constitutionality of segregation in Southern public schools.

By the time I discovered it, the story of the Lum family had been lost to history. I saw in its fragments an account of incredible courage, a story about the will to fight, not for victory but for one's own sense of dignity. When I eventually asked the granddaughter of Jeu Gong Lum why her family's story was not in history books, she gave a short, pragmatic response: "Because we lost."

A disservice has been done to history in the omission of the Lum family's story. Those who set themselves against the prevailing current of their times, regardless of the outcome, deserve to be chronicled. What I set out to revive was not merely their story, but their humanity.

I do not take the resurrection of this history lightly and have used my skills as a journalist to give the reader a transparent work of nonfiction. Extensive endnotes will point the reader to how I arrived at various conclusions and re-created various scenes. Some paragraphs will read like fiction, but all dialogue and description has been pulled from the historical record.

Details regarding the weather came from daily reports published in the *Memphis Commercial Appeal*. These reports were not always as descriptive as logs kept by farmers, so for the highly detailed scenes, I have pulled from letters that a planter named Walter Sillers Jr. wrote to his father. In the Sillers family, wealth depended on the cotton crop, which depended on the weather. For this reason, I have chosen to rely on Walter's notes when they differed from the accounts in the *Commercial Appeal*.

Each town described in the book has been re-created through a meticulous three-step process. I began with Sanborn fire insurance maps over which I laid information from census records, which gave me figures like age, race, and profession for nearly every person in every household in each town. After determining the makeup of the town's homes and businesses, I overlaid the map with memories. This I did by matching oral histories to town residents. I used special centennial editions of newspapers and city directories to fill in the gaps between personal accounts. Every room I describe in detail has been visited by me or captured in photographs.

The characters in the book were selected for me, by nature of their relevancy to the court case. It is by luck alone that so much was kept.

Descendants of the Lum family were generous enough to share with me the interviews they conducted with their grandparents, stories passed down through generations, and dozens of photographs and letters that allowed me to supplement archival material with artifacts from their daily lives.

In researching the life of the lawyer who first represented the Lums, Earl Brewer, luck also had a hand. Two of Brewer's three daughters became journalists. Due to their professionalism, I have a detailed record of even the most mundane aspects of their father's life. They studied him as great journalists study their subjects, finding meaning in the quiet moments behind the public persona. It is through their efforts that Brewer appears so vividly in this book.

My research has taken me on train rides through the Cascade Mountains, on winding cliffside drives through Southern California, to church services in Tennessee and family reunions in Texas. I visited archives in Vancouver, Chicago, Washington, and New York. But the most vital part of my research came during the project's final year, when I moved from Harlem to the heart of the Mississippi Delta. Over the course of fifteen months, I came to know the world of my characters. I waded through bayous, wandered along levees, stood in courtrooms, schoolyards, and jail cells. So much of the old Delta remains, touched only by time.

This is the sobering lesson I take from the legacy of the Lum family. Today, the school district where the Lums first filed suit is still segregated. Throughout the Delta, lives are still divided on racial lines by railroad tracks that run both physically and symbolically through the center of cotton towns. Across the nation, school integration has become a bygone promise, made and soon forgotten. School systems from Saint Louis to Saint Petersburg remain segregated. In restoring *Gong Lum v. Rice* to its rightful place in history, I hope to shed light on a crisis that, nearly a century later, has yet to be resolved.

A NOTE ON TERMINOLOGY

IN ORDER TO AUTHENTICALLY re-create the world in which the characters in this book lived, I have chosen to adopt the language of their time. The words "colored" and "Negro" are used as the primary identifiers for African American characters. The word "Mongolian" is sometimes used to refer to the book's Chinese American characters. This is a narrative device deliberately intended to transport the reader into the reality of the era.

SEPTEMBER 15, 1924

AS WITH ALL RUMORS, the stories grew over time, in the long months between June and September, when the air is so thick that gossip is all that circulates. The new students wouldn't bathe. They didn't have money to buy books. They didn't care about learning. They had so many brothers and sisters, their mothers didn't even know their names.

Of all the kinds of people who lived in Bolivar County, it was the children of country folk that Martha Lum knew the least about. Occasionally they came to Rosedale's downtown, as if to study it, fumbling through the magazine racks at the local drugstore. After getting their fill, they returned to wherever it was they came from, their bare, sun-blistered feet parading them home.

Word had filtered back to town that the country folk had been holding meetings all summer at Al Gervin's store. Gervin's place was the type that existed only out of necessity, as there was nothing surrounding it except farmland and swamp. The store served a small population of farmers and river dwellers, white families who survived on whatever their hands could pull from the fertile fields and mud-soaked coves of the Mississippi Delta.

The cotton market crash had hit them harder than most, and seeing as they were Mr. Gervin's only customers, he took a hit right along with them. The farmers were not prone to organizing. They usually kept to themselves. So when the first meeting was held on the last day of June, and all those people came up from the woods beside the river, it was clear that something important was being discussed. While most people didn't know exactly what was said, there was talk it involved money and the school district. The townspeople whispered that Mr. Gervin and all the other farmers would be sending their children to be educated in Rosedale.

If the rumors were true, the first day of school was going to be a spectacle, and Martha prepared herself accordingly. She strapped on a pair of polished patent-leather shoes and slid into a freshly pressed dress. Martha was tall for the age of nine and a half, but carried herself gracefully, even in the arms, which seemed to have undergone a dramatic growth spurt in recent months. There was a delicate elegance to Martha that expressed itself along the soft curves of her eyes, nose, and chin. Her coal-black hair was cropped into a bob, revealing a slender neckline.

Mornings had their own rhythm at the Lum household on the far end of Bruce Street. At eight o'clock, the Peavine train rumbled under the floorboards of the second-story apartment built over the Lum family's grocery store. The crowded apartment provided optimal views of the railroad and all of its curiosities. When the circus came to town, it was as if a menagerie was delivered to Martha's bedroom window.

Next came the whistle for the Rosedale Compress Company. The shrill call was the same winnowing melody as the signal for the *Kate Adams*, a local showboat named after the wife of a beloved Confederate major. The plant's manager, William Priestly, believing the sound would increase morale, had hired a steamboat manufacturer to replicate and install the *Kate Adams* whistle inside the compress. Rosedale was now in its third year of hearing the morning blast, and most of the novelty had worn off.

Classes began at eight thirty, which gave Martha and her older sister enough time for the quarter-mile walk to school. There were two routes the girls could take, and one was decidedly more interesting. The first went north along the train tracks, past the lumberyard and the sprawling fields of white cotton that blended into a pale sky beyond. Late-August rains made the bolls open early, and farmhands were already weaving between the rows, twisting their fingers into the spiny brown seedpods.

The more interesting route took the girls through the colored section of Rosedale, which spilled west onto Bruce Street from the tracks on the east side of town. Most Negro children didn't go to school, and those who did started only after the cotton was harvested, which was not until November. Their schoolhouse was more than a mile south of town, with its white clapboard walls running parallel to the cotton rows alongside the Rosedale gin. Many of the children didn't know their birthdays or how to read, but Martha was friendly with them anyway. The Lum family grocery served mostly colored folk, so Martha learned to get along.

After crossing Bruce Street, with its empty juke joints and pool halls sagging with the weight of daybreak, the girls were on Main Street. There, in the center of town, was Rosedale's new courthouse. It was located directly in the middle of a central square, where Court Street ran westward over Main Street toward the Mississippi River. The remodeled building was designed to look modern, a streamlined, single-story accolade to a new era of justice in Rosedale. There was a new district attorney, a new county attorney, a new probate judge, and a new clerk. All that remained of the old county courthouse was its cornerstone. The two slabs of granite sat like grave markers beside the gleam of the new district court.

At the end of Court Street was the Colonial Inn, a towering, white brick structure with four columns that extended the entire elevation of the hotel. Inside its elegant facade, the inn was a home for recklessness. Visiting salesmen and cotton buyers would gamble, drink, and fight under the building's plaster pillars. So near to the levee, the Colonial was a frequent stop for whiskey boats, or "blind tigers" as the locals called them. Mississippi bootleggers outfitted small riverboats with casks of illegal corn whiskey and docked them behind the inn.

The most famous blind tiger belonged to Perry Martin. Eight miles northwest of Rosedale, on an island in the middle of the river, Perry ran the largest whiskey-producing operation in the whole United States. Every variety of alcohol was considered contraband by the US government, and Perry Martin's whiskey was no exception. He populated his island with an unruly throng of outlaws and fugitives. Rosedale mothers warned their children that just over the levee walls was whiskey territory, and nobody entered those woods without express permission.

Continuing north along Main Street, at the intersection of Main and Clark, was the Talisman Theater. John Lobdell purchased the building in 1916 and, eager to believe that a theater—and through it the town—manifested the chivalry of ancient Scottish noblemen, named the place after a nineteenth-century novel by Sir Walter Scott.

Just past the Talisman was the local hat shop. Two spouseless Swiss sisters managed the millinery, Rosa and Mollie Oberst. In the spring, when the sisters held their annual sale, society ladies in hobble skirts and side-laced heels teetered in the street, mud shoe-top deep, to get a glimpse of the merchandise.

A block and a half north was the Rosedale Consolidated High School, built directly beside the Episcopal church that had been there since the Federals intervened after the war. Set against a dusty churchyard with tufts of scorched grass, the redbrick building looked like a Spanish cathedral. The school used to be located in a two-story white frame house up on Levee Street, near the mansions of the aristocrats, who included Senator William Beauregard Roberts, the first man in Rosedale to own a motor boat, an automobile, and a radio.

The new brick schoolhouse was built after 1920, when Henry McGowen, the mayor of Beulah, petitioned to expand the county school district to include Beulah and Malvina. With taxes from an expanded district, the Rosedale Consolidated School was created. McGowen then became the first president of the school's board of trustees, and his sister-in-law, Mrs. Rae Wolfe, became the school's first teacher.

At the beginning of every year, Miss Rae, as the children called her, presented her class with a giant posterboard creation, designed to resemble the limbs on a tree. She then assigned each student a red, hand-cut paper apple with his or her name on it. To climb a limb, she explained, a student had to earn one hundred points on the weekly spelling exam. With each perfect score, the apple moved closer and closer to the top of the tree. If a student failed, their apple fell to the ground and had to make its ascent all over again.

Martha's name was always hovering somewhere in the upper branches of Miss Rae's misshapen tree. She was one of the top students in her class, even after the teachers decided she should skip a grade. She'd spent the last year in the same grade as her older sister, Berda. Unlike Martha, Berda was a rebellious child. Once, in third grade, she was nearly expelled for stabbing a girl with a pencil. Berda started fights even when she knew she was licked. She called it courage. At Rosedale Consolidated, it was considered "a discipline problem."

Like two wings on a bird, it was their opposite nature that made the sisters inseparable. Each relied on the other to make sense of a childhood trapped somewhere in the margins between colored and white. Martha understood that Berda's pride in heritage did not come from what she learned in history class. The Lum girls were raised daughters of an ancient nation called China. Berda was taught to stare at the moon and see a rabbit, while her classmates looked up and saw an old man.

As she entered Rosedale Consolidated for the first time in months, Martha adjusted to the sights, sounds, and smells of school. The new country students padded down the halls in an ungainly procession as teachers corralled boisterous children into classrooms. The stark scent of chalk mixed with sweet talcum powder and cologne. The first day of school offered a momentary opportunity for reinvention, as each student funneled everything they wanted to be into one morning.

Under the guidance of a new principal, Mr. J. H. Nutt, Rosedale had recently passed its accreditation requirements. This meant that the school's graduates were now guaranteed acceptance into every state college. It was a huge achievement for the county and would explain why Mr. Gervin and all the other farmers wanted to send their children to Rosedale. The new facility was now one of the top-ranked schools in the state.

Before taking the position as principal, Mr. Nutt spent a summer in the suburbs of Chicago. He and his wife developed an affection for the area. Mrs. Nutt told one reporter that, while in Illinois, her husband had grown accustomed to the suburban "middle class, native-born, Protestant American whites in the school system and in the community." Rosedale, by contrast, had a sizable population of blacks, Italians, Russians, Poles, Syrians, Mexicans, and Chinese. Hardly the white suburbs of Chicago.

Out of the relatively diverse student body at Rosedale, only four Chinese pupils—the Lum sisters and two other girls—were summoned to Mr. Nutt's office at noon lunch hour on the first day of class. Mr. Nutt had requested to speak with them in private. He explained in a conciliatory tone that an order had been issued by the school's board of trustees, under the recommendation of the state superintendent of education, to bar all children of Chinese descent from the premises. The girls were colored, he explained, and therefore not welcome on school grounds.

His words hung like smoke in a closed room. The backwater children, barefoot and illiterate, now crowded the halls of Rosedale Consolidated, while Martha, a straight-A student, was no longer welcome there. Quietly, the sisters collected their knapsacks and walked home along the same route they had always taken. On schedule, the twelve-thirty train, local from Vicksburg, roared past Bruce Street and the girls entered the grocery.

Once safely inside the walls of the store, the sisters told their parents about the events of that morning. As they repeated the school board's order, a stillness settled over the family. There was a decision to be made. Its outcome would alter the course of history. Within a Chinese grocery, next to a railroad track, on the colored side of a small Mississippi town, the seeds of a revolution were stirring. In the afternoon hours, one Monday in September, the Lum family decided to fight.

PART ONE

MEN WHO ENTER THESE PLACES

MARCH 31, 1904

Mr. L. T. Plummer
Chinese Inspector in Charge
2 River Street
Chicago, Ill.

Dear Sir:

We have recently had information that Chinese smuggled into the country from Canada, and who were destined for Chicago, almost invariably went to either 296 or 299 South Clark Street, and there is another place in the same vicinity, in a basement, of which I have not the number. The modus operandi, as I understand it, is that they are smuggled across the river and then they either take a freight out on the Wabash as far as Montpelier, or they drive along that line some distance, and then get aboard of the Wabash trains. Their favorite route, I understand is the Wabash.

These Chinamen are always accompanied by one or two white fellows, and sometimes a negro, and they get off the train at or near Ashley, where, I am told, the train is made up again for Chicago. Sometimes they go as far as the stockyards, but, as above stated, they ultimately work into one or the other of these places, and I believe they generally arrive in the early morning. I would suggest that you might shadow these places for some time, and if you ever see these Chinamen conducted through by the smugglers, arrest them on sight.

There is no doubt but that you would be able to distinguish these newcomers from the frequent habitues of these places. This winter all the

Chinamen whom we have caught—and there have been quite a few of them—have been most invariably dressed with caps, heavy rubbers or arctics, and overcoats, such as you would not see a Chicago Chinaman wearing. This might give you an idea of the green men who enter these places. All of the above is only offered as a suggestion for the good of the service, and for what action you may see fit to take in the premises.

Respectfully,

H. E. Tippett
Chinese Inspector in Charge
Port of Detroit

CHAPTER I

WINTER, 1904

A THIN RAY OF light moved over the silent ice like a pendulum. Its motion was metered, and though it made no sound, the light left echoes of silver mist above the Detroit River. Jeu Gong Lum stood at the bank of the frozen causeway. Beneath his feet, winter mud splintered into needles. In China, rigid earth like this would grow nothing, but in *Gam Saan*, vibrant cities sprang up from hardened riverbeds. In constant rotation, the beam emanating from the Detroit River lighthouse stretched out over Lake Erie, then turned northward to the glimmering city of Detroit. From the city, the finger of light spun east across the river, illuminating where ice had buckled under itself, casting up walls of ivory.

A furious wind ripped through the channel. Dressed in a thick wool cap, heavy rubber boots, and a large overcoat, Jeu Gong braced himself against a cold that he had never experienced in his twenty-odd years of life in southern China. In the distance, at the end of the canal, giant steamships trailed smoke over Lake Erie. The cold would not last much longer. Jeu Gong had only to make it to the other side of the river, across the ice, to America.

In China they called it *Gam Saan*, Gold Mountain, where fortunes were as easily made as picking gold off the street. Under the shade of banyan trees, villagers told stories of a world where wealth fell into young men's palms. Jeu Gong's brother, Gow, had already made the journey. He was somewhere over the frozen river, in a city called Chicago.

Jeu Gong waited for a signal. This was a new kind of waiting. A patience stronger than the wait that came for harvest, when the rice fields of Sun Wui ripened in succession, a patchwork of jade over forested hills. This wait was with him when he boarded a steamship in Hong Kong, when he crossed the Pacific Ocean, when he tasted nothing but waves while the moon waned twice. The wait was there when he arrived in Canada and moved from the dockyard to the freight train. When the train coughed and lurched forward, threading through mountainside tunnels, peak rising beyond peak as dark bands of forest fell below.

The wait was with him as he passed sawmills, coal mines, and slate quarries. Each with its own town, a main street and a string of electric lights. Each with its own station stop, where worn men with rucksacks were waiting just like him. The wait crossed with him over ravines, walls thousands of feet high, angry rapids breaking below. The wait coiled through gorges and crops of rock with trees clinging to crumbling stone. The wait was there when the mountains gave way to a great plain of earth. The sky grew longer and Jeu Gong and his wait watched its ragged winter clouds. From the plains came the lakes, each one larger than the last. And Jeu Gong and his wait left the train and stood at the bank of a river, on the shores of America, ready to cross.

Just over the water was a freight train bound for Chicago. Jeu Gong was to arrive at the city stockyards at dawn. He would leave the train and hide inside the pulse of a thriving city. He would fill his empty pockets with silver and become to his family a *Gam Saan haak*, a son of Gold Mountain. But first there was the ice. He had to walk quickly, so as not to be detected, but if he moved too fast he might fall through. Trapped under the water, Jeu Gong would sink deeper and deeper into darkness. A stone tablet, reserved for his grave in Sun Wui, would remain blank, his name unwritten in the land of his ancestors, all memory erased as his body turned cold and white like ash, disappearing at the border of *Gam Saan*. With one brave step, Jeu Gong moved onto the ice.

The waters Jeu Gong grew up on were nothing like those he stood on now. Never still, the rivers were like veins that moved life in Sun Wui. The Xi River to the east and the Tan to the west wound southward through the narrow valley of Yinzhouhu, before reaching the sea through the Ya Men Inlet. Between the two rivers, an elaborate network of waterways and bridges connected hundreds of villages.

Streams and tributaries, fed by generations of rain, linked together the threshing grounds and fishponds of ancient courts. The same waters connected the new shantytowns of migrant farmers, their straw huts strung along dikes where fan palms and citrus orchards grew. It was a vibrant place that stirred in Jeu Gong's memory; one that smelled of tangerines and mandarin oranges, of mulberry shrubs and sugarcane, all feeding from the same rich soil.

The rivers carried flower boats with blackwood tables and chairs inlaid with mother-of-pearl. The elegant rafts were home to *haam sui mui*, the saltwater girls, beautiful women who entertained only the wealthiest of men. At night the vessels drifted along the river, lit by a myriad of lanterns, casting reflections onto the churning water.

There were the large junks that traded with Hong Kong, Macao, and the West, their decks laden with fine silks and woven baskets. There were the gunboats from Canton that protected the white men and traveled the river searching for pirates. There were the missionary boats that first arrived when Jeu Gong's father was a boy. The sailors spoke in broken Cantonese and gave away pictures of a dying man hung from a crosspiece.

Beside the large boats of the Westerners were the small boats of local fishermen, provision boats selling ginger root and melon seed, cakes and dried shrimp. There was the hot-soup boat with its raging fire and the boatman who carefully dipped his clay bowls into the river before filling each one with boiling water, rice, fish, and finely chopped carrots.

There were the duck farmers who traveled in ships with large, overhanging sides that rattled with feathers. In daylight, the men let their merchandise off to feed. At dusk, the farmers released a bamboo gangway and the birds rushed back onboard, not wanting to incur a beating for being last in line. And all of the boats came and went from the dry docks at the mouth of the river, the great ports that sprouted from tiny fishing villages.

On the riverbeds grew fruit trees and vegetables and beside them were rice fields that stretched as far as Jeu Gong could see. In the distance, the terraced hillsides of Wuchow lay barren, for there was no one left to work the land. When the rebels came they had moved on water. The river carried them down from the hills. They killed the men and their wives. They killed the children. The river, swollen from spring rains, swiftly lifted the bodies of Wuchow and the boats of the rebels who murdered there. For fifty years, the land remained uncultivated, the memory of massacre made visible with every empty harvest.

These were the waters of Jeu Gong's youth. Now they carried nothing but news of war and famine, of all that had been lost. The waters emptied into a sea that brought him to this frozen shore. One day Jeu Gong would return to them. He would come home to a towering mansion with hundreds of *mou* of fields. With this land, he would provide freely for his family, never again letting hunger gather in great knots in his stomach. All that was to be lay just across the river. With deliberate steps, careful not to break the ice, Jeu Gong walked between the past and *Gam Saan.*

Between 1882 and 1920 an estimated 17,300 Chinese immigrants entered the United States by crossing the Canadian and Mexican borders illegally. The most numerous and earliest crossings occurred along the Canadian border, which proved the least expensive point of entry. In 1903 the Bureau of Immigration estimated that it cost Chinese immigrants $300 to sneak across the Canadian border into the United States. During the same period, it cost more than twice as much to purchase the identity papers and supporting evidence required to attempt entry through more official routes.

While less expensive, crossing through Canada was much riskier. Charging little money up front, sometimes only twenty dollars, smugglers along Canada's border catered to the poorest Chinese émigrés, often choosing profit over their clients' safety. "Of all the contraband, it is quite possible that human beings are the most valuable," read an article in the *Vancouver Daily World* detailing the smugglers' tactics. "The greatest risk is taken to get them past the barrier of regulations which forbid their entry into other lands than their own."

When Jeu Gong took his first step onto Canadian soil, he placed his life in the hands of a smuggler, as hundreds of other Chinese immigrants had done. These strangers were fishermen, saloonkeepers, elevator operators, and pool sharks. They held unskilled, low-status, transient jobs that garnered little pay and even less respect. So the men moonlighted as human traffickers in a growing underground trade along the American border.

They joined an existing network of outlaws who specialized in transporting drugs and liquor into the United States. New on this list of contraband was the Chinese immigrant. Stowed between chests of opium and stolen silks, thousands of Chinese immigrants found themselves on south-bound freighters, headed for America.

Low-skilled laborers were not the only ones tempted by the financial windfall that smuggling could bring. In fact, many smugglers were also immigration inspectors and policemen, double agents reaping the benefits of both a government salary and an illicit trade. The rewards could be enormous in an era when the maximum salary for a Buffalo police patrolman was $900 per year and an immigration agent made at most $17.50 per week. The world of smuggling was much more lucrative.

According to newspapers from the Great Lakes region, smugglers received between $50 and $125 for each immigrant who successfully reached New York or Chicago. One immigration inspector, Thomas Thomas, estimated that individual smugglers brought five or six immigrants to the border once or occasionally even twice a week. Assuming Thomas's information was correct, one smuggler could earn between $250 and $750 every week, and twice that on occasion. In one week as a smuggler, a police patrolman had the potential to make what it would take a year to earn as a cop.

Immigration inspectors were more likely than police officers to be drawn into the world of illicit border crossings. This was likely due to the fact that inspectors had access to classified information regarding the US government's antismuggling operations, making the job of outwitting the government relatively simple. Not all inspectors were crooked. There was a certain personality type drawn to the life of a smuggler, the type of person who embraced risk.

Edward Baltz was a smuggler and inspector for the Great Lakes region between 1902 and 1904. Before working for the Department of Commerce and Labor, he performed in carnivals, parachuting from a balloon to thrill the "rubes at the county fairs." In 1904 Baltz was implicated in a plot to traffic Chinese along the border and was dismissed from the service. Another inspector, David Hoover, was a deputy collector of customs stationed along the Montana boundary, when he was arrested in 1906 on the charge of smuggling Chinese into the States. A former police chief from Kalispell, Montana, Hoover had been a customs collector since his station was first established in 1901. During his five-year tenure, Hoover was said to have joined a "big organization to smuggle Chinese and opium" into the country. W. B. Greene, a former railroad conductor from Jamestown, New York, served as the immigration inspector for Montreal before he was charged with "conspiracy to smuggle Chinese" while acting as an employee of the immigration service.

Such widespread corruption was due in part to the fact that border enforcement was a relatively new concept. Until the turn of the twentieth century, the US-Canadian border had existed as a kind of porous, suggestive demarcation between the two countries. That relationship changed with the advent of America's restrictive immigration policies during the late nineteenth century. In 1894 the United States entered into a contract with Canadian transportation companies. Known as the Canadian Agreement, the contract granted US inspectors the right to enforce US immigration laws on steamships and passenger trains within the boundaries of Canada. The agreement effectively extended America's anti-immigrant policies into the northern half of the continent. This meant that those wishing to bypass the border patrol had to evade not only US law enforcement, but hundreds of conductors, captains, and servicemen throughout North America's vast transportation network.

In many cases, corrupt agents were able to entice transit workers into becoming smugglers themselves. John Yanner and William Bies were working as cooks on the Rock Island Railroad when they were arrested in Chicago for smuggling Chinese immigrants in iceboxes installed on the line's dining cars. "In many instances," read an article detailing their arrest, "Chinamen had almost frozen to death in the refrigerators." Yanner was a suspect in the murder of a Chinese man found dead near Kansas City whose nameless, frozen body, the prosecutors argued, had been tossed from a moving train.

Crossing into the United States over a vast, unpatrolled border meant that there was little chance of rescue if a smuggling operation went wrong. Those Chinese who made the decision to immigrate during the turn of the twentieth century were taking an enormous gamble, one that could easily result in death.

Every act of legislation aimed at restricting immigration only heightened the danger for Chinese immigrants. Smugglers were forced to take greater risks with their human cargo and faced lesser sentences if something went wrong. Illegal Chinese immigrants were quite literally treated as commodities, both by the law and the smugglers who circumvented it.

At the frontier along the shores of Lake Erie, where Jeu Gong attempted passage over the Detroit River, crossings typically occurred at night, when visibility was near zero. In spring and summer months, traffickers loaded the Chinese immigrants into overcrowded rowboats, dropping them at points along the American shore, a particularly hazardous operation given the river's treacherous currents. In the winter, traffickers took an even greater risk, forcing their cargo to walk over frozen waterways.

A 1912 report by one US immigration inspector details the harrowing journey a group of immigrants and their smugglers made across ice. "The first three Chinese persons named admitted to crossing from Canada into the United States by walking on the ice which covered the Detroit River," the inspector wrote, after profiling six Chinese men held in US custody. "When arrested, the clothing of two of the Chinese persons was soaking wet, as well as the clothing of one of the whitemen [sic], showing that while crossing the ice, they had evidently broken through and fell into the water. This fact gave rise to a rumor that several of the party had fallen through the ice, and were drowned. After consulting with the District Attorney, it was thought advisable to investigate the rumor that certain Chinese had drowned." Little came of any such inquiry, as no further reports were filed about the incident.

Hundreds of Chinese immigrants sought entry in other ways that proved just as deadly. In 1909 the bodies of ten Chinese immigrants were delivered, sealed in barrels, to an address on Mott Street in New York. According to the report, "the trainman failed to give them water and food en route" and "they arrived to their destination dead." A similar fate met four Chinese men found frozen in a boxcar in 1914.

Despite the risks, a relatively low cost of entry and the convenience of Canada's burgeoning transportation network provided incentive enough for many Chinese immigrants to cross along America's northern frontier. In 1891 the Canadian Pacific Railway Company joined the Pacific Mail Steamship Company and assigned three steamers to sail between Hong Kong, Japan, Victoria, and Vancouver. The partnership created a pipeline between North America and the Far East. Through the Canadian Pacific Railway, Chinese immigrants could purchase one ticket for passage across the Pacific Ocean and the American continent, without ever having to navigate the transfer from steamship to train. Immigrants like Jeu Gong were able to ensure their journey from Hong Kong all the way to the northeastern coast of Canada under the umbrella of the CPR. The relatively unregulated transpacific network created a new brand of hysteria in the United States, fear of "the illegal foreigner."

The influx of Chinese immigrants did not go unnoticed by the American public. In 1891, the year of CPR's partnership with the Pacific Mail Steamship Company, O. L. Spaulding, acting secretary of the Treasury, complained that "an increasing number of aliens are now landing at Canadian ports and then entering the United States by Rail, thus practically avoiding all effective scrutiny."

That same year, *Harper's Magazine* published an exposé written by Julian Ralph, a tall, stocky thirty-eight-year-old reporter for the *New York Sun*. Titling the piece "The Chinese Leak," Ralph, himself the child of immigrants, explained in detail the "wily" strategies used by Chinese to enter the United States from Canada. Citing figures even Ralph qualified as possibly being inaccurate, the article depicted the Canadian frontier as a region rife with illegal immigration—to the tune of fifteen hundred Chinese immigrants per year.

"The prairie, the plains of the western provinces and the thick-clustered mountains of British Columbia are repeated in our Minnesota, North Dakota, Montana, Idaho and Washington," he wrote. "Geologically and naturally there is no difference between the countries; the boundary line is an arbitrary mark. . . . There is no part of it over which a Chinaman may not pass into our country without fear of hindrance; there are scarcely any parts of it where he may not walk boldly across it at high noon."

While exaggerated, Ralph's assertion of a porous northern border spoke to national concerns about patrolling such a vast region. In 1902 the total force of immigration inspectors numbered only 66, which included inspectors for both the northern and southern borders. Even if the full immigration force were stationed near Canada, it would not be sufficient to protect an area 3,987 miles long. The next year, the number of inspectors was increased to 116, mostly along the US-Canadian border.

Policing the border was not only a matter of manpower; there was also the logistical challenge of creating the government organizations and policies necessary to curb Chinese immigration, both legal and illegal.

For the majority of Chinese immigrants seeking entry into the United States during the turn of the twentieth century, crossing the border illegally was their only option. On May 6, 1882, President Chester A. Arthur had signed into law the Chinese Exclusion Act and with it fostered the creation of the nation's first "illegal" race. For the first time, federal law proscribed entry of an entire ethnic working group, the Chinese, on the premise that their presence in America "endangers the good order of certain localities within the territory."

The act effectively halted all Chinese immigration for a minimum period of ten years, barring most Chinese from entering the United States and forbidding all federal, state, and local courts from admitting Chinese to citizenship. Only six categories of Chinese immigrants were allowed to enter the country: teachers, students, tourists, properly certified returning laborers, merchants and their family members, and diplomats and their families. These six categories were carefully crafted, designed by legislators to exclude the largest population of Chinese citizens, the working class.

The sole voice in opposition to the exclusion bill was a Republican senator from Massachusetts named George Frisbie Hoar. Hoar argued that the act was nothing less than the legalization of racial discrimination, a charge that would have resonated in a Senate that legislated the end of slavery.

"The old race prejudice, ever fruitful of crime and of folly, has not been confined to monarchies or to the dark ages," Hoar castigated his fellow senators. "Our own Republic and our own generation have yielded to this delusion and paid the terrible penalty. . . . What argument can be urged against the Chinese that has not been heard against the negro within living memory?"

Hoar's remarks fell on deaf ears and, with the passage of the act, America entered into the era of Chinese exclusion. The result of such restrictions, as historian Erika Lee noted, was that "Chinese border crossers became the public image of a new type of immigrant—the 'illegal' . . . merging the illegal aspect of their migration with coexisting charges that Chinese were either cunning criminals or 'coolies' whose immigration constituted a harmful invasion of inferior and unassimilable aliens." The exclusion act, renewed and amended in 1892, 1902, 1904, 1917, and 1924, ushered in immigration restrictions based on race and nationality that would endure for more than half a century.

Jeu Gong was crossing into an America that defined itself by what it was not, crafting its identity around those it excluded. The nation's immigration policy created invisible borders, much larger than physical ones, that narrowed desirable races into subgroups eligible for citizenship. There was a new sense that the American identity deserved protection, that it was somehow under threat, and government agencies were created and funded to aid in such protection. The era, as historian Roger Daniels wrote, was "a time when nativism and racism gained strength and acceptance at all levels of society."

In the year following Jeu Gong's departure from China, one million immigrants would leave their homelands for the United States, the most in the nation's history. As America's immigrant population grew, so did resistance. Murders of Chinese miners were frequent in the West during the late nineteenth century. In Wyoming, twenty-eight Chinese men were killed and fifteen injured in the Rock Springs Massacre of 1885. In 1887 a band of six white men gunned down thirty-four Chinese immigrants in Hells Canyon, Idaho. Greek immigrants were beaten and their homes burned by mobs in Nevada, Utah, and in Nebraska—the site of the most notorious of the attacks, the Greek Town Riot of 1909. During the riot, three thousand men set fire to the Greek enclave in South Omaha, resulting in the death of a child and displacing the city's entire Greek population.

In 1891 eleven Italian immigrants were murdered by a lynch mob in New Orleans. Dozens of Slavic and Polish coal miners were killed and wounded by a Pennsylvania militia during a labor dispute in 1897. In 1913 a Jewish man in Atlanta named Leo Frank was convicted, on dubious evidence, of raping and murdering a thirteen-year-old girl. After several appeals, the Georgia governor lowered Frank's sentence from death to life in prison. On the night of August 16, 1915, white citizen vigilantes took Frank from his cell and hung him from an oak tree at sunrise.

Each wave of violence unearthed something deeply troubling about American society. The country had developed a delusional self-image, one of racial purity and hegemony, an industrialist white nation destined for progress. In reality, the country was witnessing an unprecedented surge in diversity, as families from every corner of the globe flocked to the United States to supply its growing demand for labor.

Throughout this period of heavy immigration, there was a second immigrant narrative, one hidden in boxcars and stowed in rowboats. The stories of these immigrants were not documented, even within families. Fathers never told their sons about the weeks spent in the dark cargo hold of a steamship, that they crawled for twelve hours along riverbeds, that they taught themselves not to be hungry, not to breathe, not to sleep. It was as if their gateway to America vanished upon arrival, as if history covered its tracks.

As Jeu Gong set out for *Gam Saan*, a metalworker was engraving a bronze plaque on the pedestal of the Statue of Liberty. Fourteen lines of a sonnet, written by an American poet. Its tenth line would become an anthem: "Give me your tired, your poor, your huddled masses yearning to breathe free."

Some thirty miles east of the statue, with much less fanfare, another monument was nearing completion. At Cold Spring Harbor on Long Island, construction was almost finished on a new, state-of-the-art laboratory. Built with a hefty donation from Andrew Carnegie, the Station for Experimental Evolution was one of the first American institutions to study genetics. Heralded as the future of biological science, the laboratory would become the headquarters for the eugenics movement.

A campaign to classify races by means of a hierarchy, eugenics would provide scientific justification for segregation, mass sterilizations, and the exclusion of an entire immigrant population. It would grow to influence all levels of society, from public policy to children's books. A sanctioned form of racism, eugenics served as the scientific articulation of white supremacy and the politician's strongest weapon against immigrants.

In the forested fringes of Detroit, along the south shores of Lake Erie, Jeu Gong stowed himself on a Chicago-bound freighter. He had grown accustomed to the lilting groan of train against track, and although the country was new and exciting, the ride was quite similar to what he'd experienced over the past several weeks.

Once in Chicago, Jeu Gong continued on. He could have stayed in the city, finding work in a Chinese restaurant or laundry, living with his brother or anyone else who would take him in. But there was a phantom that chased Jeu Gong from the moment he crossed the ice. It followed him the way shadows chase swallows at dusk. Jeu Gong had become a man he could no longer change or escape. He was a criminal, stealing a place for himself in a new nation.

A city was too risky, too many ears listening and eyes watching. He would go south, to farmlands, timber mills, and cotton fields. He had a relative in Mississippi who ran a small grocery store. There would be work for him in Mississippi, and he would be free from the fear of detection. He would hide in a place where no inspector would ever think to look. And so, with only a vague idea about where he was going, Jeu Gong boarded a southbound train.

Carved into frozen valleys, the tracks seemingly willed the land to wake in their path. As the train moved southward, giant snowdrifts turned to scant patches of ice on gray earth, and the drumbeat of the rails continued. Soon the tracks curved to meet a bend in a great river.

When the natives spoke of this river, they talked about it the way the men of Jeu Gong's village spoke of war. It was to be both feared and respected. If it was not seen, it was felt, an ever-present force shaping all it touched. Life survived beside it and beside it life would end. The river ruled its people, seething behind mounds of earth, remote and intimate all at once.

From the flat land that spilled from its banks grew small towns with clapboard churches, central squares, and stone monuments to buried soldiers. The streets were christened with the names of fathers and grandfathers who followed those dead men into battle. Streams and creeks unfurled from the great river, with curious names like Tallahatchie, Sunflower, and Rattlesnake. Webs of pale moss hung from cypress trees that grew on their flooded banks. In a canopy of gray, the virgin swampland wore the veil of a widow, living and dying at the same time.

Beside the tracks were the fields, dormant in winter frost, that still held captive the creatures who worked them. Their skin was as dark as the soil they tended, as if over years of sowing and harvest the earth had stained them. These were tenant farmers, who owned neither the fields they planted nor the narrow shacks they lived in.

Though an ocean away, this world was ruled much like Jeu Gong's. All wealth belonged to the men who owned the land, and they governed the society that drew life from it. In leasing the fields to farmers, the rich men gave up none of their power. They would always have the laborers, chained to the fields for them to control. With a rumbling cadence, the train growled to a halt beside a wooden platform. Jeu Gong had arrived at his new home, a place they called the Mississippi Delta.

An alluvial plain, the Yazoo-Mississippi Delta was forged by the tides of the Mississippi River, its rich soil created from centuries of sediment. Throughout hundreds of years, the river deposited layers of silt over a stretch of land some seven thousand square miles in breadth, from Memphis, Tennessee, to Vicksburg, Mississippi.

With slightly over 50 percent of the region's rainfall occurring between December and May, when the river was at its highest, the flooding that created the Delta remained a part of the natural, recurrent life cycle of the land. For the people living along the banks of the Mississippi, high water was a season all its own. To them, the river was a swift, feral force that "coils and returns on itself in great loops and crescents," as William Alexander Percy, the son of a Delta planter, wrote. "Every few years it rises like a monster from its bed and pushes over its banks to vex and sweeten the land it has made." The Mississippi's vernal ebb and flow gave birth to fresh silt and from it grew dense woodland and swamp. Percy called it the "land of unbroken forests," a thick tangle of water oak, pecan, cypress, and sweetgum trees, whose roots clung to soil more valuable than gold.

The Delta was settled during the 1830s, after the Choctaw Nation, under orders from President Andrew Jackson, was driven from its land. Forced from their home, the Choctaw left behind a vast territory of woods and undergrowth. Young sons of Southern oligarchs brought their slaves to the Delta to carve cotton fields from wild brush. Whole forests were leveled by thousands of slaves. By 1850, across the Delta, slaves outnumbered whites five to one.

As a consequence of its creation, the Delta became a bastion for the institution of slavery—for slavery was the system upon which its economic foundation was laid. In his desperate search for liberty, Jeu Gong had arrived in a place still clinging to the memory of slavery. It was this very memory, the white man's resolve to resurrect an antebellum South, that drew Jeu Gong's forebearers, the Delta's first Chinese immigrants, to Mississippi.

. . .

At the dawn of the nineteenth century, enterprising Westerners, with the help of Chinese middlemen, began the importation of Chinese "coolie" labor to the Caribbean and South American regions of the plantation world. Serving as surrogates for African slaves, Chinese were first shipped to Trinidad in 1808 and then on to countries throughout Latin America.

The so-called "coolie" market expanded rapidly, developing trade centers in major New World destinations such as Cuba and Peru. On vessels registered to the United States and modeled after the slave ships of the Middle Passage, American brokers in ports throughout southern China carried more than six thousand Chinese laborers, their bare chests painted with letters marking their destinations, to sugar plantations in Cuba or deadly guano pits in Peru.

"It was a brutal and infamous system that in some ways was worse than slavery," wrote the historian Roger Daniels. "Some employers literally worked their coolies to death." Other Chinese slaves, often indenturing themselves for the price of passage, were transported to Chile, Ecuador, Panama, and Mexico. One United States congressional report noted that the "coolie trade . . . seems to have commenced about the time when the laws against the prosecution of the African slave trade were enforced with the greatest stringency."

Following the Civil War, Southern whites sought new ways to replace slave labor and ensure their economic, political, and social dominance of the South. As early as 1866, editorials in Southern newspapers discussed the possibility of importing Chinese as a source of agricultural labor in the region.

On June 22, 1869, an editorial in the *Memphis Daily Appeal* proposed a meeting to discuss the means by which landowners could obtain Chinese laborers. Less than a month later, on July 13, about five hundred delegates from Alabama, Georgia, Kentucky, Mississippi, South Carolina, Louisiana, Arkansas, Tennessee, Missouri, and California, representing planting, railroad, and business interests, flocked to the Greenlaw Opera House in Memphis for the inaugural Memphis Chinese Labor Convention.

Isham Green Harris, a lawyer and former congressman from Mississippi, served as chairman of the convention. Under his guidance, the event generated widespread publicity and triggered a new national interest in importing Chinese labor. Following the convention, an American could scarcely pick up a newspaper without reading about some new plan to import Chinese workers into the United States.

"A number of Chinamen have already been introduced to the South, and the planters are exceedingly well pleased with them," read an article in the *New York Times*. "They are not only patient and faithful workers, but they seem well adapted to the climate and industries of the South. The Mississippi Valley could feed and pay a hundred million of these Mongolians, and China has a hundred million that she could very easily spare."

The notion of introducing an entirely foreign source of labor to replace slavery captivated industrialists and alarmed advocates for the working class. One month after the Memphis convention, American labor leaders such as Susan B. Anthony and William Jessup gathered in Philadelphia for the third National Labor Congress, where they discussed Chinese immigration for the first time in the congress's history. The acting president, a New York tailor named Henry Lucker, condemned the coolie trade, calling it "a revival of the slave system." The importation of Chinese workers, he argued, "is not for their advantages socially or morally, but has for its only object the damnable one of cheapening American labor and to eventually force the workingman into a condition worse than slavery."

Despite such concerns, efforts to introduce Chinese into the South increased between 1869 and 1871. Southerners deluged Chinese slave brokers with requests for laborers. Nathan Bedford Forrest, president of the New Selma, Marion, and Memphis Railroad, a former Confederate general and the first grand wizard of the Ku Klux Klan, offered $5,000 to procure a thousand workers from China to lay track across Tennessee.

As increasing numbers of Chinese laborers arrived in the South, planters soon discovered the newly imported men were deserting the fields. It quickly dawned on the Chinese that their social and economic position as foreigners left them unable to compete with the black labor they had been hired to replace. By the fall of 1871, one year after their arrival, most of the Chinese imported to work New Orleans's Millaudon Plantation had left. Of the 141 originally brought there, only 25 remained.

Fleeing the plantation, many Chinese immigrants became itinerant peddlers, traveling to communities throughout the South, selling teas and trinkets. Others looked for work as house servants, farmers, storekeepers, physicians, clerks, and cooks. Ultimately, the Southern experiment to supplant slave labor was a failure. But what remained was a lasting sentiment against Chinese immigration, under the veil of national unity.

"When the paroxysm of humanitarianism which followed the abolition of slavery in this country had subsided," read a 1905 editorial in the *Washington Post*, "and the Chinese problem arose to be reckoned with, our people began to realize that charity begins at home. . . . The exclusion policy is not based on race or national prejudices. It was established, after long and serious consideration and debate, as necessary to the peace and welfare of the nation."

With the help of his relative, Jeu Gong found a job at a small general store, earning enough to send money home. Whatever success he found, however, he was never fully at ease. There would always be someone hunting him. So he strove to blend in, to draw no attention to himself. He dressed as the *lo fan*, the white men, dressed. He walked the way they walked and ate the way they ate. He learned to call them "sir" and "ma'am," even the children. Yet as close as Jeu Gong came to the *lo fan*, he always lived at a distance from them. Chinese could not buy property to live as the *lo fan* lived, so they settled into the edges of *lo fan* towns, building homes in the backrooms of their businesses.

In his new life in *Gam Saan*, Jeu Gong did not forget where he came from. He found a community of Chinese men who were just like him, still connected to the abstract place that was their homeland. For although they had cut their queues, and changed their names to John and Charlie, and spoke of cotton as they once spoke of rice, these men shared the same ache for a nation that was swiftly drifting from memory. In this painful transition from Chinese to American, Jeu Gong found brothers.

J.K. Young ran a Chinese grocery just south of Memphis in a river town called Tunica in Mississippi. He was a slight man, just over five feet tall, with oversized glasses, boyish features, and abnormally large ears. J.K. could hardly be considered handsome, but he carried himself like a prince. On the occasion that someone of importance, or anyone with a camera, stopped by the store, J.K. outfitted himself in a white button-down shirt and a bow tie. This happened more often than one would expect, because J.K. was the regional expert on nearly everything and a leader within the community of Delta Chinese.

A self-taught scholar, J.K. could speak, read, and write English. He served as a kind of interpreter for Jeu Gong. There were many things about America that J.K. understood. Even J.K.'s name was telling of his wisdom. In fact, "J.K. Young" was not his real name. Believing that the *lo fan* would prefer to do business with a man named Young, J.K. never told the white merchandisers and bankers that his actual surname was Joe. He never explained that the Joes were the first Chinese in the Delta, that his ancestors had likely arrived long before those of the white men who called him a foreigner.

It was the language of unsaid things that J.K. knew best, the language that all Delta people spoke. Contracts were written in nods and handshakes, the correct gesture at the correct time. J.K. knew whom to befriend and whom to ignore. He knew how to find the things that Jeu Gong longed for from home: tea, soap, incense, dried fish, plums. J.K. knew where to go to treat a toothache or a backache. He knew how to sign his name in English with long, graceful strokes and read the labels on tin cans and boxes. J.K. was also the first to know about what was happening back home. He sat on a bench behind his grocery, reading the headlines, sharing whatever news the paper contained . . . REVOLUTION AGAINST GOVERNMENT GAINS HOURLY THROUGHOUT CHINA . . . DISLOYAL TROOPS MURDER HUN-DREDS . . . MUTINEERS SHOUT VENGEANCE ON MEMBERS OF THE RULING FAMILY . . . DOWN WITH MANCHUS . . . 300 SUPPORTERS OF THRONE SLAIN IN HANKOW THIS MORNING . . .

Even as the old country fell into civil war, J.K. retained the sense that home would always be China. Because of this, he remained single. Like many of the young men who visited him, J.K. intended to wait and return to China to find a wife. Some men did not wait, and for this they paid a great price. There were laws in Mississippi that barred Chinese men from marrying white women. Yet no law prohibited marriage between Chinese and blacks. The men who married outside of their race, choosing to live with black women, were exiled by the Chinese community. Although blacks and Chinese were relegated to the same neighborhoods and each occupied a lower social status than whiteness, the few Chinese men to cross the color line were excommunicated, forgotten by the very people they once considered family.

Like every other immigrant group to arrive in America, the Chinese in Mississippi distanced themselves from blacks in an effort to better align themselves with the white power structure. They developed a double-edged identity, adopting the customs of whites while refusing to associate socially with blacks.

Despite their status as outsiders, the Mississippi Chinese were able to achieve a higher social standing than their black neighbors and customers. In fact, it was their outsider status itself that mitigated against their being classed as black in America. "They cling," the novelist James Baldwin later wrote of immigrants, "to those credentials forged in the Old World, credentials which cannot be duplicated here, credentials which the American Negro does not have."

For Jeu Gong, who by now was in his midtwenties, crossing the color line meant forfeiting all prospects of elevating his station in Southern society. He would have to find a Chinese wife, which would be harder for him than it was for merchants like J.K. Young. Jeu Gong came to America on foot, without papers or any semblance of citizenship. J.K. was successful and spoke English. He had all the money and expertise required to cross effortlessly into the United States. If J.K. wanted to go to China and return with a wife, he could. Jeu Gong was not so fortunate. He would have to find his bride in America.

There was talk of a servant girl who lived in Gunnison. She cared for the Wong family's two young sons and worked in their grocery. Her name was Katherine, an American name, a name that did not spend its childhood barefoot, bent over rows of dry earth, harvesting sweet potatoes. In China she was Hang Toy, an orphaned peasant. In America she was Katherine Wong, adoptive daughter of a wealthy merchant.

Jeu Gong began courting Katherine shortly after her eighteenth birthday in December 1912. Within a few weeks, she was pregnant. Katherine was bound by Chinese custom to serve the Wong family until the age of eighteen, so with Jeu Gong's promise of marriage and a child growing inside her, she left Gunnison.

Jeu Gong and Katherine married on the second Tuesday in June. They wed using their formal Chinese names and, in this way, Lum Dock Gong and Hang Toy Wong began their lives together. They opened a small grocery store south of Gunnison, in the plantation town of Benoit.

Although it was June, Benoit's farmers had yet to sow their crops. The river had grown high with winter rains, and in January a levee broke ten miles to the north, flooding the town. Rooftops drifted from homes. Bloated cattle floated over fields. Negro tenant farmers, who lost everything, built camps along the levees. Even as the land dried out, water rushing down Benoit's avenues in retreat, the destruction from the flood remained.

Still, Katherine and Jeu Gong fashioned a life for themselves in the small Delta town. Katherine was quick to befriend the *lo fan*. She seemed at home in their world, maybe because there was no home for her in China, no family to write to on thin sheets of rice paper the way Jeu Gong did. She prayed to a long-haired god and read the King James Bible. She fried chicken and catfish. She smoked cigarettes and laughed at her own stories.

After the floodwaters receded, the shadows lengthened and the air grew colder. Bare branches thrashed against gray autumn skies and a child stirred in Katherine's belly. Harvest came and Jeu Gong and Katherine worked until they were numb with exhaustion. When they fell asleep, side by side at the back of the store, they dreamed in different languages.

CHAPTER II

AUTUMN, 1913

BERDA WAS BORN IN the Year of the Ox, during the fall of 1913, in the months before Europe went to war with itself and drew the whole world in with it. She came into being at the back of a grocery, in a dark, damp cellar, between the storeroom of a Russian merchant and an Italian butcher.

The construction of her defenses began early, probably from the day she was born. Dr. Edwin Martin arrived on horseback from his home on the east side of the tracks. As one of only two doctors in Benoit, he had witnessed more death than birth given the region's thick swamps and malaria-ridden bayous. Holding the leather strap of a medical bag, he sidestepped sacks of cornmeal, sugar, rice, and flour, making his way to the back of the grocery. He found Katherine, her short crop of hair damp with sweat.

Merely a child the year before, eighteen-year-old Katherine was now a mother. From his bag of instruments, Dr. Martin removed a sheet of paper. He noted that the child, a daughter, was born alive on October 22, 1913, and scratched out the nationality of the mother and father. Katherine told the doctor that she was from Canada. Jeu Gong said he was born in California. Each parent did this to protect the infant, upon whose future they rested their own. In the stillness between their child's breathing was the urgency of all they would do for her, to give her a life they could not yet imagine. And so it was, the arrival of their first child, a daughter, an American.

They named her Berda after Berta Beadel, a young woman who lived in a mansion on Sycamore. Mrs. Beadel's husband was a traveling salesman, and in his absence, during the long weeks spent alone, she devoted herself to the betterment of the community. The women of Benoit lauded her commitment to "charitable and worthy causes." One such cause was bringing the word of God to the Lum family.

On Sundays, Mrs. Beadel accompanied the Lums to church, a one-room wood-frame structure that served the town's Presbyterians, Baptists, and Methodists, each pastor taking the pulpit in rotation. The Benoit Union Church, as it was called, was inconveniently located directly behind the town's largest ginnery. In autumn, during the cotton harvest, the congregation was forced to sing over the clanging iron jaws of the gin. "Come home, come home," Mrs. Beadel howled beside Berda on an old, splintered pew. "Ye who are weary come home."

Katherine understood that the drafty shack of a chapel offered her family another kind of ascension—a baptism into high society. In naming her daughter Berda, Katherine laid claim to an aristocracy, one created by those of old Southern lineage, who for generations had prayed together in the same clapboard churches.

When it came time for Katherine to name her second child, she chose to call her Martha, after a kind woman who lived next door named Martha Bonds. When, a few years later, Katherine gave birth to a son, she would name him after the town's mayor. And in this way, the Lum children were christened into a culture that was not fully theirs. Nor was it that of their parents. They were part of the first wave in a generation of Delta children born from immigrants.

They would learn English and speak with a Southern drawl. They would drink Coca-Cola and play baseball. They would attend school and pledge allegiance to the United States of America, reciting the words from memory the same tired way their parents recited stories from the old country. Their childhoods, unfolding in the tense space between two worlds, represented the end of one South and the beginning of another.

The change began during the first decade of the twentieth century, when plantation owners experimented with importing immigrant laborers to replace black sharecroppers, large numbers of whom were leaving the South to find work in Northern cities.

In 1905 as many as five hundred Italian immigrants worked on plantations in Washington County, Mississippi. In Bolivar County there was also an influx of Italians, as well as Chinese, Russians, Austrians, and Romanians. Yet the harsh conditions and poor pay proved to be unsustainable for the new immigrants. Like the black sharecroppers they had come to replace, the immigrants asserted their limited autonomy by moving from one plantation to another, jumping from place to place unpredictably and often without clearing up their accounts.

Many immigrants unwittingly found themselves among the swelling ranks of convict laborers in the Mississippi and Arkansas Deltas. In 1908 a German citizen named George Scharmer was arrested for trespassing when he jumped a train in Malvern, Arkansas. He was sentenced to four months of hard labor at a plantation in Drew County and was still there at harvest time nearly a year later.

The story of Joseph Callas, a Russian Jew arrested for vagrancy in Little Rock, drew national attention. Marched to a field at gunpoint, a burlap sack tied to his back, Callas picked his first boll of Delta cotton in the presence of an overseer with a three-foot-long whip and a pack of bloodhounds. "We were put to different works," he wrote in *Collier's* after his release in 1909. "We gathered cotton, we dug ditches, tilled the ground, built fences around the fields. . . . There was not one day in which someone was not flogged. Two or three were flogged each day, and sometimes the number rose to ten."

In 1914 twelve unsuspecting Hungarian immigrants from New York City, who spoke no English, were taken from a train station in the Yazoo Delta, stripped of their belongings, and forced to work at a lumber mill. When several tried to escape, they were arrested and returned to the mill.

Although they spoke different languages and came from vastly different cultures, each immigrant group arrived in the Delta with the same stigma of subservience that adhered to the black laborer. For those who intentionally came to work on plantations, like the Italians of Washington County, the reality of their situation dawned on them quickly. "Realizing that such treatment was similar to that accorded blacks, they soon became resentful," wrote the historian James Cobb, "having grasped quickly the mores of a society where the actual physical cultivation of cotton bore the stigma of 'nigger work.'"

Some immigrants gave up plantation life altogether and opened businesses with the little money they had managed to save while sharecropping, or with the sale of stolen cotton bales to black market barges along the Mississippi. Their loss of immigrant labor rankled the Delta's white planters.

In 1907 a plantation owner from Greenville named LeRoy Percy told the state bar association that white Mississippians might be caricatured "as standing with both heels firmly planted in the earth, and with both hands firmly clasping the coat tails of the fleeing negro, in one breath upbraiding him for worthlessness and inefficiency and in the other vowing that no other laborer should be allowed to replace him."

It was this failed effort to replace the Negro workforce that created one of the most fascinating ethnic enclaves in America. Having left the cotton fields, dozens of Chinese laborers, the most sizable cluster of Chinese Americans anywhere in the nonmetropolitan South, opened groceries in small towns throughout the Mississippi Delta.

Their enterprise was a new one, created by the liberation of four million slaves. With the abolishment of slavery, and the advent of tenant farming, Southern blacks had newfound earning power, however small, and the ability to become a consumer market. Yet due to segregation, a white storeowner would not sell goods to black sharecroppers. The only way a sharecropper could purchase goods was through his local plantation commissary.

In an act of defiance toward plantation rule, black sharecroppers began asserting their liberation by purchasing goods away from the commissary, at groceries run by Chinese families in town. "It seems as if there was a ready-made niche for the Chinese grocer in the Delta," wrote historian James Loewen. "A slot which existed for reasons intrinsic to the social system, and which for similar reasons could not be filled by persons produced by that system."

While groceries provided black sharecroppers a new level of financial independence, the motives of the Chinese grocer, in most cases, were purely based on profit. He treated his customers equally, regardless of race, because they were paying customers. As one grocer recalled, "We have to treat colored and white alike. The American money, they don't make special for colored, special for whites."

In one respect, the Chinese were directly responsible for giving black sharecroppers the ability to live separately from the plantation. Yet, in another way, they profited from a highly stratified society, which placed their consumer base on the bottom rung. For better or worse, the blacks and Chinese had a symbiotic relationship within the segregated South.

·   ·   ·

Saturdays were the busiest day for the Lum family. The grocery served as a meeting place, where tenant farmers from nearby plantations gathered on milk crates outside the store to eat sardines and crackers, drink beer, and visit with one another. On Saturdays, the only day of the week they could rest, the sharecroppers came into town, loaded onto train cars and mule-drawn wagons.

As soon as Martha was talking, she was taking orders. Next she was opening soda bottles and cleaning spills. Sometimes, while running errands, parents would leave their children at the grocery, giving Martha and her sister temporary playmates. For a few precious hours, the shy, barefooted visitors gained entry into Martha and Berda's world.

Always there were the smells, cornbread and buttermilk, garlic and ginger, fresh longbeans and green onions. The scents filtered into the store from the kitchen out back and mixed with the tobacco smoke and dip jars, stale sweat and laughter emanating from the men out front. There were the smells that made a throat grow whiskers, fuming from gas cans and jugs of turpentine, shoe polish and tar. And there were the sweet smells of Mary Janes, peppermints, Whitman's chocolates, Wrigley's gum, Tootsie Rolls, butterscotch, and caramels.

As evening set in, and sharecropper children left the store with candies pressed onto the roof of their mouths for safe keeping, Martha and Berda, Jeu Gong, and Katherine made sure the money was taken in and counted. The bills were sorted, change rolled. And on Monday, they rose early, walking to the bank on the corner of Main and Richardson to deposit the weekend's earnings.

Both the grocery and the bank faced east. When dawn came, a gold haze settled over the fields along Main Street, its alchemy interrupted only by a freight depot. The shadowy depot served the Gibson Cotton Gin, arguably the most successful business in town. It boasted two cottonseed warehouses, an iron conveyor belt, and four Munger gins with eighty saws each.

In autumn, the grinding wail of the machinery overtook Main Street. Beneath clouds of coal smoke, wagons from local plantations delivered billowing piles of cotton to the Gibson gin. There it was vacuumed from the wagons through a suction pipe and run through the Mungers, which, by means of narrowly spaced teeth, removed the seeds from the fiber.

The cotton was then funneled into a compressing room, where it was pressed into bales, wrapped in burlap, and bound together with steel bands. From there, the bales went right out onto the gin's own platform, the train depot that faced the Lums' store. Then the Yazoo and Mississippi Valley Railroad shipped the bales south to New Orleans or north to markets in Memphis and Chicago.

Even with its cutting-edge cotton gin, Benoit was a timeworn town. Main Street, with its rough assembly of decaying brick storefronts and mud-caked windows, was home to an old hotel, two drugstores, a bank, a telephone company, and a few scattered groceries and meat markets. As with all Delta towns, life was injected into Benoit from outside forces, firms across the Atlantic pricing cotton futures, Northern capitalists seeking short-staple for their mills, the boll weevil, the railroads, the rains, the levees, the soil. From its very inception, Benoit was at the mercy of an expanding, industrialized world.

Benoit began life in the year 1889, with the coming of the Yazoo and Mississippi Valley Railroad. There was never any plan to run track through the plantations south of Rosedale, but James Richardson, the largest individual cotton grower in the world at that time, offered the railroad free use of his land if, in turn, the company built him a station.

James was the eldest son of Edmund Richardson, a planter whose holdings at one time included banks, steamboats, and railroads. He owned three-dozen cotton plantations and had a controlling interest in Mississippi Mills, the largest textile plant in the Lower South. His New Orleans–based brokerage house, Richardson and May, handled more than 250,000 bales of cotton every year.

Edmund Richardson was not always so prosperous. By the end of the Civil War, he had lost almost his entire net worth, close to $1 million. So in 1868, Richardson struck a deal with the federal authorities in Mississippi to contract labor from the state penitentiary, which was overflowing with ex-slaves, and work the men outside prison walls. He promised to feed and clothe the prisoners, and in return, the government agreed to pay him $18,000 a year for their maintenance.

The contract struck between Richardson and the State of Mississippi began an era of convict leasing that would spread throughout the South.

Before it was over, a generation of black prisoners would suffer and die under conditions that were in many cases worse than anything they had ever experienced as slaves. Confining his laborers to primitive camps, Richardson forced the convicts to clear hundreds of acres of dense woodland throughout the Yazoo Delta. When the land was cleared, he put prisoners to work raising and picking cotton on the plowed gound.

Through this new system, Richardson regained his fortune. By 1880 he had built a mansion in New Orleans, another in Jackson, and a sprawling plantation house known as Refuge in the Yazoo Delta. When he died in 1886, he left his holdings to his eldest son, James.

As an inveterate gambler and drunk, James decided to spend his inheritance building a new town, developed solely as a center for sport. He bought racehorses and designed a racetrack. He built five brick stores and four homes. In 1889, when the station stop was finally completed for his new city, James told the railroad to call the town Benoit, after the family auditor. James's sudden death in 1898 put an end to his ambitions for the town. But decades later, a Richardson Street still ran through Benoit, westward toward the river, in crumbling tribute to the man.

With hundreds of miles of new track, poured over acres of fertile land, the Yazoo and Mississippi Valley Railroad changed the very fabric of Delta society. It opened up the region to international trade with large port cities like New York and New Orleans and created a direct line to burgeoning Midwestern cities like Chicago and Detroit. The railroads brought the world to the Delta and the Delta to the world. The station stops and tiny towns that sprang up around them, however, disrupted the region's traditional social structure.

Until the final decade of the nineteenth century, there had been only one society in the Delta—plantation society. Its structure was rigid, with boundaries that were drawn in the very blood and marrow of those who lived within its confines. "The plantation tended to find its center in itself," wrote the journalist and historian W. J. Cash, "to be an independent social unit, a self-contained and largely self-sufficient little world of its own." At the dawn of the twentieth century, that little world was under threat by virtue of its own expansion.

After the railroads, the factories followed, and the Industrial Revolution of the North spread southward, along the veins of progress and industry it had constructed. Its steel spikes and wooden ties served as bedrock for hundreds of cotton mills, seed oil plants, and lumberyards, supplying markets across the nation and throughout the globe.

With laborers no longer dependent on a plantation economy, the physical and social order of the past faced extinction. Fueled by greed and the desire to expand their empires, planters inadvertently set the stage for their own demise. "To accept Progress at all was manifestly to abandon the purely agricultural basis from which the Southern world, and ultimately the Southern mind had been reared," wrote Cash. "To bring in the factory, to turn to the creation of industrial empire . . . would be to bring in the machine and the town, [which] would naturally be to bring in the laws of the machine and the town."

With their hegemony in jeopardy, the planters moved from plantation to town, laying claim to a new, mechanized frontier. By the early 1900s many of the Delta's plantation homes were abandoned, their owners moving into mansions on spruce-lined streets. Such relocation assured that the South's social hierarchies would remain intact, even as its economic landscape was transformed.

The new mills functioned under the same social order as the plantation, each factory built inside a series of small private villages. Just as the plantation provided meager provisions for its slaves and tenants, the mills owned the beds on which their workers slept, the streets on which they traveled, and the land on which their houses stood. They provided commissaries, from which a workman could get advances on rations against his future earnings. In the mill town, just as on the plantation, the laborer was stripped of all autonomy, every aspect of his life controlled by his employer.

Still, from Mississippi's Piney Woods and Red Clay Hills came the poor yeoman farmers, to work the mills as they had once worked the land. Families moved from fields they had worked for generations. Children as young as six and seven, boys and girls, and their pregnant mothers, labored in the cotton mills. By the hundreds they migrated to factories, accepting wages barely half the pay at Northern mills.

They rose before dawn to man the machines, some so young they carried boxes on which they could climb to reach the spindles. "I have known mills," wrote the clergyman Edgar Gardner Murphy in 1904, "in which for ten or twelve days at a time the factory hands—children and all—were called to work before sunrise and dismissed from work only after sunset, laboring from dark to dark . . . finding their way with their own little lanterns through the unlighted streets of the mill village, to their squalid homes."

Industrialization, which drove the creation of Benoit and the Delta towns surrounding it, spread rapidly throughout the South. In just one decade, the number of cotton mills multiplied dramatically. Between 1900 and 1910 the South had come to operate more than 39 percent of the nation's mills, more than the entire country had in 1880.

Yet with the factories came tax subsidies and with those subsidies came paved roads and water systems and electric lights. Most importantly, for the Lums and other immigrant families, the tax revenue brought public education to the Delta and other farming regions across the South. By 1914, a year after Berda was born, every Southern state had some sort of uniform school system, and virtually every rural community had a schoolhouse. In total there were nearly eight million pupils in the public schools of the South—for the first time, almost as many in proportion to the population as the rest of the country.

Benoit's two-room schoolhouse was as much a source of pride for the community as the town's gin and lumber mill. Martha Bonds, Martha Lum's namesake and godmother, was the school's longest-serving teacher. She had no children of her own, so the town's scattering of pupils substituted as her makeshift family. Mrs. Bonds lived with her husband on Main Street, next door to the Lums, beside the hotel.

Mr. Bonds, twenty years his wife's senior, had left his position as a dry goods salesman to work in the town's lumberyard. The couple's most prized possession was a jewelry stand from the Coghill family of Virginia that was over one hundred years old. The antique looked as if it came from another, more graceful, time, from one of the books written by Englishmen about elegant love affairs and palace gardens. There, beside the jewelry stand, in the guardianship of her godmother, Martha learned all the things a lady should be.

Until Martha was old enough to attend school, her childhood was spent with Mrs. Bonds or at her family's grocery store, where she studied the cycle of seasons and the lives of the customers who depended on them. The winter months were the hardest. By the end of January, most of the croppers were out of harvest money, so the Lums were forced to extend credit until planting season. Without any profits, the family barely sustained themselves through winter, rationing their modest income for basic necessities.

At last, March would arrive, its rains turning the fields into bogs. Inside Benoit's clapboard church, congregants prayed the levees would hold. When the fields began to dry, and leaves burst into spring, hyacinths thrusting into bloom, the men began breaking up the soil. They left their cabins before dawn to hook their plows to their mules and turn up the land. Just as the men labored, the Lums labored with them, opening the store well before the day's first light. They sold the blades, bolts, straps, feed, and ties with which the men could furrow the earth.

By early May the fields were ready to plant. The men would dig narrow trenches in the mounds they made and, at every pace, drop in cottonseed. Once the plants sprouted, the men would bring their families to the fields. Together, in the stifling heat, they chopped weeds with long-handled hoes, in a syncopation all their own.

At the end of spring, a light-hued blossom grew from the cotton stems. It stayed only a few days before darkening, wilting, and falling beside the young stalks. Then the summer arrived and with it the storms that came without warning, crackling along a low sky. Tiny green pods appeared at the base of the faded cotton flowers. The pods, filled with seeds, would swell with fleecy fibers during the summer months. In late August, when the air moved through the trees slow as butter, the bolls split open and the fields erupted into white.

Again, the men took their families to the land. They moved together through the cotton rows, long burlap sacks dragging behind them, sometimes so heavy the straps would draw blood. By November, all of the cotton had been harvested and the men were paid a share of the crop. Whatever they made would have to last through the winter, until the earth was ready again for planting.

Until Martha was school age, she observed the seasons in much the same way the tenant farmers did. When they had money, her family had money. When the crop yield was poor, Martha was poor. The ebb and flow of the land and its production was her only method for keeping time. Then, when Martha turned six, school began and time was measured in semesters. Spring planting and fall harvest were eclipsed by writing exercises and arithmetic. She studied distant worlds outside her own, with ancient kings and great armies. The two crowded rooms that made up Benoit's schoolhouse were an escape from everything Martha had ever known.

The school was located on the far west side of town at the end of Richardson and Adams Streets, where they ran at right angles to Second Street. Beyond Second, the town gave way to farmland and the levee. None of the streets were paved, and when the rains came in spring, mud spilled all the way from the bayous down to the shops on Main Street. Martha and Berda would have to trudge west three blocks along Adams or Richardson, up toward their swamp of a schoolyard.

Adams Street, lined with symmetrical shotgun shacks, belonged to the Negro tenant farmers. Most of the farmers came from somewhere else, another county, maybe even another state. It was in their nature to move often, always following the best wages and crop shares, but they were quick to make a home from their cabins of rough lumber, with walls beaten and weathered as reeds. In town, the farmers joked that they could "study astronomy through the openings in the roof and geology through holes in the floor."

There was only one room to each house. The room had a fireplace for heat and one or two windows for light, but the landlords didn't waste money on glass, so the houses were shuttered when the weather grew cold. In the winter, when temperatures dipped near freezing, the children patched up the drafty walls of their cabins with newspapers. If it was an especially cold winter, they pulled up fences from their yards to burn for fuel.

Richardson ran on a parallel course beside Adams Street, but despite their proximity, the two streets were worlds apart. Richardson, on its path west toward the school, was lined with humble vistas of shoe repair shops and hardware supply stores, but as the street arched slowly toward the river, the porches of regal mansions blossomed in perfect rows behind wrought iron fences. The hum of Main Street quickly faded as magnolias unfurled over manicured lawns.

The children in these houses played games of lost legacy. They were raised on stories of life before the war, reminiscences of "Christmas on the plantation . . . [when] there was a big tree with strong branches, lighted with many candles, and on or under it, wonderful presents . . . There were the breakfasts with the hot rolls, as light as sea foam; the beaten biscuit, white as snow; the corn muffins; the broiled chicken; the eggs; the hominy; the waffles; the coffee and cream. . . . Comfort and even luxury were visible in every room of this rambling plantation house."

The children of Richardson Street clung to distant memories. To play their games was to act out their legends, to resurrect their past.

Martha and Berda passed their mansions on the way to school. The looming residences belonged to their classmates, but the sisters were not welcome there. Confined to the bustling, crowded streets of town, Martha and Berda returned each day to where the immigrants lived, beside the line of track that had brought their father south. Night after night, they awoke to the roar of a steam train clattering past, bearing another future, another legacy to be constructed behind other brick storefronts.

Inside, the infants, cradled by wooden crates, carried with them the expectations of an entire generation. These children, sunburned and threadbare, born on the rich soil of a foreign land, inherited only the debt they owed their own future. Martha and Berda, the daughters of Delta immigrants, were to make the hardships of their ancestors worthwhile.

In the cramped room behind her family's grocery, Martha made good on this promise. Under the yellow glow of kerosene, she learned to read and to write, to keep the books for her father's business. Yet beneath that dedication was a deep and incurable loneliness. Martha would never be one of the charmed ones, the golden people, the *lo fan*, the children of Richardson Street. There was no Lum family Bible, linking generations of blood to Mississippi land. Martha's heritage slept behind a grocery every night. She could trace her lineage only in the creases of her father's eyes, the dark stages where scenes from distant places flickered and were never explained.

If her family had been different, maybe she would have been invited to dine at the long, elegant *lo fan* tables. She could have attended their picnics and visited their wealthy relatives in New Orleans and Memphis. She could enter through the front doors of their hotels without the paralyzing fear that she was not welcome, that girls like her had to enter through the back. Sitting in rows of desks, inches from Martha, was the world of the *lo fan*, a world of privilege more distant to her than China. And in this exile, quietly practicing her penmanship, Martha developed a strength of character that would one day threaten the very structure of Southern society.

CHAPTER III

WINTER, 1919

MOONLIGHT LEAKED THROUGH THE gaps in the door onto the dirt floor and cold walls of the grocery. Sunday nights were always the quietest, and now they belonged to Jeu Gong. Katherine insisted the store remain closed one day per week, out of respect for religion. While he accepted Katherine's belief in divinity, Jeu Gong himself had no interest in Christianity. He never attended church services. He wasn't baptized. Religion for Jeu Gong was a pact that he made with himself long before he arrived in America, that he would one day provide for his family. Six years ago they had come here to Benoit, raised two daughters, and Katherine was now six months pregnant with a third child. The promise he made himself was almost realized—almost.

Katherine was growing sicker every day. Living as they did, in a single room behind the store, her illness had become a family burden. The girls, even in their childish ignorance, saw that their mother was tired, sleeping at odd hours, complaining of headaches.

Even if Jeu Gong knew of a cure, he could not give it to her. There was no money left. His store, which once overflowed with customers stocking their wagons with salt meat, molasses, flour, lard, beans, tobacco, coffee, snuff, and sugar, was now silent. His patrons were all gone. It was a deceptive stillness that settled into the moonlit cracks of the grocery that winter night. Jeu Gong, a businessman on the brink of bankruptcy, was bearing witness to an exodus.

.   .   .

January was "movin'" month for sharecroppers. The departures often took place on Sunday nights between eight and midnight. They never told anyone they planned on leaving. They just disappeared. They packed their lives into burlap sacks and suitcases and boarded northbound trains.

A report by the US Department of Labor estimated that as many as 350,000 black laborers left the South during one eighteen-month period between 1916 and 1917, nearly a third of them from Mississippi. An investigator visiting Washington County at the end of 1917 found two hundred abandoned houses in just one town. Under the cover of darkness, in the biting chill of a winter Sunday, Jeu Gong's customers were leaving the Delta, each in their own way, headed for a place where the future looked brighter.

As immigration plunged by more than 90 percent during World War I—from 1.2 million in 1914 to 110,618 in 1918—Northern industries such as steel mills, railroads, and packinghouses sent recruiters throughout the South to find black laborers to replace a dwindling European workforce. In 1917 the United States instituted the universal draft, further depleting the North of white labor.

To fill the jobs left vacant in Northern cities, some 550,000 blacks left the South during the decade of World War I, more than all those who had left in the five decades following the Emancipation Proclamation. As the migrants settled into their new lives in the North, reports of higher wages, more schools, and better living conditions traveled south. As one woman wrote back to a friend in Mississippi, "Honey, I got a bathtub."

Such accounts passed from one person to another, culminating in a vision of a promised land. This vision was then projected onto the pages of the black press, as newspapers like the *Chicago Defender* and the *Pittsburgh Courier* were borne southward, distributed by railroad porters. By 1919 the *Defender* was circulated in 1,542 towns and cities across the South, including rural Delta communities like Tunica, Mississippi. "Our problem today," read an editorial in the *Chicago Defender* in August of 1916, "is to widen our economic opportunities, to find more openings and more kinds of openings in the industrial world. Our chance is right now."

Local white leaders blamed the *Chicago Defender* for encouraging sharecroppers to demand better working conditions and political freedoms. One Delta paper argued that by instilling the notion of equality, the *Defender* was directly responsible for the violence directed against Southern blacks. "The negroes who are making money out of this newspaper," the article read, "are paving the way for ignorant Southern negroes to go to their graves."

Measures were quickly taken throughout Mississippi to outlaw the distribution of the *Defender* as well as the *Crisis,* the magazine of the newly formed National Association for the Advancement of Colored People. In 1920 the state passed a law making it a misdemeanor to "print or publish or circulate" literature favoring social equality. Shortly after the law was passed, E. R. Franklin of Holmes County, Mississippi, received six months in prison and a $400 fine for selling the *Crisis* at his store.

Despite the risk, hundreds of thousands of Southern blacks managed to circulate the literature throughout the South. "Subscribers passed the publications among their fellow lodge and church members," wrote the historian Nan Elizabeth Woodruff, "while the literate read to the illiterate. Thus rural black people, like industrial workers of an earlier time, had ways of transmitting information they deemed relevant to their community's survival."

The most famous and arguably most successful transmission of such information was through song. Music journeyed south from recording studios in Northern industrial centers, including the earliest iterations of what would hold the ultimate appeal for migration, the blues.

Blues pioneer and Mississippi native Charley Patton recorded his classic "Pea Vine Blues" in 1929 for Paramount Records. The song, played with the driving pulse of a moving train, referred to the Delta's main rail line, the Peavine, which carried sharecroppers away from plantations to Northern cities. The lyrics were a message, clear to all Delta residents who heard Patton's call: "I think I heard the Peavine when it blowed. . . . I'm goin' up country, Mama, in a few more days."

The railroads, which first fueled and then solidified the South's place in the global economy, had now become the mode of exodus for hundreds of thousands of Southern blacks. The tracks that coursed through the Delta, giving life to towns like Benoit, were now ferrying its labor force—and its economic foundation—northward. The planters feared that their fields, which they had seen parched by drought, drowned by rain, swept by fire, beaten by hail, and eaten bare as bones by boll weevils, would not survive without the Negro to tend to them.

They vowed to stem the tide of out-migrants by whatever means necessary. In the Delta city of Greenwood, white law enforcement officials dragged black passengers off of outbound trains, often taking the train's porters as well. In order to avoid confrontations with whites at a train station farther south of Greenwood, in Greenville, a number of local blacks walked twelve miles east to Leland to board the train north to Chicago.

After the United States entered World War I, Southern landowners had a new means of ensuring their laborers remained on plantations—the threat of the draft. In the summer of 1918 the army's provost marshal, General Enoch Crowder, issued a "Work or Fight" order to all local exemption boards, allowing them to draft men who were not engaged in employment.

Crowder's order essentially federalized the local vagrancy laws that were already pervasive throughout the South. It was now up to the small-town sheriff, mayor, constable, and justice of the peace to identify "vagrants" and turn them in to the local exemption board to be shipped off to war. In the Delta, local defense councils adopted an identification system that required all blacks to carry a card listing their place of employment. The defense council requested national support in forcing "our negro labor to stay on the job six days in the week or they will be inducted into service."

When the black men drafted into war eventually returned home, they were met with rabid hostility from local whites. "What did they do to the niggers after this first world war?" recalled a black sharecropper named Nate Shaw. "Meet em at these stations where they was gettin off, comin back to the United States, and cut the buttons and armaments off of their clothes, make em get out of them clothes, make em pull them uniforms off and if they didn't have another suit of clothes—quite naturally, if they was colored men they was poor and they might not a had a thread of clothes in the world but them uniforms—make em walk in their underwear."

In the spring of 1919, a band of white men in Blakely, Georgia, confronted a black soldier named Wilbur Little as he returned home from his tour of duty in World War I. When they ordered him to take off his uniform, he refused. A few days later, a mob attacked Little at a celebration for his achievements during the war. He was found beaten to death on the outskirts of town, still wearing his uniform.

In the Mississippi Delta, a black coast guardsman returning on leave to visit his mother in Greenwood was stopped in Tchula and arrested for "trespassing without money." When it was discovered that he did, in fact, have money, the charge was changed to vagrancy. He was sentenced to thirty days of hard labor at a cotton plantation. Thirty-six days later, he was released, having been beaten on several occasions with a "seven pound strap," once for writing a letter to his commanding officer.

The social and economic forces pushing blacks out of the Delta were also acting upon the Lum family, but in an entirely different way. At the outset of World War I, inflated wartime cotton prices gave sharecroppers unprecedented earning power. For the first time in history, thousands of Southern blacks were purchasing luxury items such as automobiles, radios, Victrolas, and pianos.

The Lums and other merchant families found themselves the beneficiaries of a rising black middle class. The Lums purchased a car and traveled to other towns. Katherine bought furs. The children wore new shoes. But the family's newfound wealth did not last long. Soon, landowners began refusing laborers their share of the crop yields, often employing intimidation and violence. Within a few short years, tens of thousands of blacks escaped Mississippi and moved north.

As their customer base dwindled, the Lums were forced to supplement their income by taking in boarders. Katherine, in ill health and preparing for the birth of her third child, made room for two more residents in their home behind the grocery. Fifty-year-old Bartlett Dabney, along with his younger sister Cammie, boarded with the Lum family. Bartlett owned a general store in town, but his business, too, was failing, and with it his ability to afford his farmhouse outside Benoit.

The Dabneys of Benoit were a strange breed. For one thing, none of them ever married. Bartlett's younger brother, William, owned a drugstore in town and devoted his life to his business. Bartlett, by contrast, moved often and changed professions regularly. He worked in cotton sales at the Speakes Plantation just outside Benoit. He then became a postmaster and then a farmer before trying his hand at operating a general store.

At the time he made the move into town, Cammie was living with him, so she accompanied him into the Lum household. As Bartlett struggled to save his store, Cammie helped Katherine around the house. Berda was now of age to attend school and Martha was both mobile and curious. The girls required a tender hand and watchful eye that their ailing mother struggled to give to them. Cammie became the nurse the family so desperately needed. She cooked meals and washed laundry. She entertained the children and recalled memories of her own youth, now distant after forty-eight years.

Likely inspired by her father, who ran his own medical practice, Cammie devoted her life to caring for others. As a young woman, Cammie had moved alone to Memphis to work at a sanitarium geared toward curing addiction. Working as the clinic's stenographer, she transcribed hundreds of patients' stories, typing the details of their troubles with alcohol, opioids, and pills.

The Dabneys did not live with the Lums for long, but Cammie's nurturing presence was a welcome one for the family, helping them through a difficult time. Eventually, she became the proprietor of Benoit's hotel and her bachelor brothers moved in with her.

In the winter before her son was born, Katherine told her husband she could no longer live in Benoit. The cramped, dirty quarters had taken a toll on her health. Jeu Gong agreed to sell the store and purchase property a few miles north, in Rosedale. Even as he made this promise, Jeu Gong understood that owning a grocery in Rosedale was a dream his family could not afford. Still its blaze of electric lights stood on the horizon, a world of potential. It was in Rosedale where Jeu Gong and Katherine were determined to build their future.

On January 21, 1919, Jeu Gong purchased a plot of land next to the railway depot on the east side of Rosedale. The barren lot, scraggled with brush, belonged to the Radjeskys, a family of Jewish immigrants from Germany. Katherine had known the family for most of her life. The patriarch, Jake Radjesky, was something of a real estate mogul in Gunnison, where Katherine had been raised. He was one of the town's first settlers, buying up property while land was cheap. He owned the town's livery stable, hotel, and mercantile business.

Jake's relationship with Katherine's family went all the way back to China. He testified on behalf of Katherine's adoptive father, Don Chuck Tai Wong, when Don first decided to immigrate to the United States with his wife and children. The Radjeskys had since moved to Memphis, but Jake's wife, Annie, still owned a parcel of land in Rosedale. She was eager to sell the property to Katherine, whom she called Katie.

When all of the details were finalized and contracts drawn, Jeu Gong was able to purchase the quarter-acre plot for a thousand dollars, paying one dollar as a down payment. One of Mississippi's most powerful men, a lawyer, cotton planter, and state representative named Walter Sillers Jr., loaned Jeu Gong the rest of the money, at a rate of 6 percent interest.

Sillers had been a member of the state legislature since 1916. He also served on the town's board of supervisors, the levee board, and as chief attorney for the city. His father, Walter Sillers Sr., also practiced law and served in the state legislature during Reconstruction. Minus a brief stint working in the state capitol, the elder Sillers had lived within the boundaries of Rosedale all his life. Even when federal troops invaded during the Civil War, Walter Sillers Sr. did not leave the city.

As a ten-year-old boy, Walter had sat in the schoolyard and watched Confederate cavalrymen, including his father, prepare for battle. "When troopers began to drill," he later wrote, "every school boy was equipped with a uniform and a little sword, and a juvenile cavalry organized.... After months of drilling, the Bolivar Troop was ordered to war, and our little company accompanied them to the river landing, where they embarked."

During the war, young Sillers Sr. and his mother hid in an abandoned plantation on the outskirts of town and foraged the woods for food. When the Federals took Vicksburg, Walter Sr.'s father was taken prisoner, executed, and buried in an unmarked grave. After the war, Walter's brother tried to recover their father's body but returned to Rosedale with nothing. These stories Walter shared with his son, who strove to honor his father's memory. For Walter Sillers Jr., the town of Rosedale, and by extension the entire South, was as much a philosophy as it was a place. His contract with Jeu Gong was conditional, that the Lum family uphold the values of the Southern way of life.

In March 1919 Katherine gave birth to a son. She named him Hamilton Biscoe Lum, after Benoit's mayor. It was a vow to herself and her only son that the future held greatness. There was now a boy to carry on the family name in America.

In keeping with tradition, Biscoe was baptized in the manner of all Chinese sons. The family celebrated his arrival with a great banquet known as the *hone aun*, or red egg ceremony. Katherine and her young daughters prepared a feast of eggs, hard-boiling and delicately wrapping them in thin, red calligraphy paper until the kitchen overflowed with bright pink chicken eggs. Then they prepared the *tay doy*, tea pastries, molding rich confections called moon cakes out of sweet bean curd.

The relatives arrived bringing *lee shee*, red envelopes filled with "lucky money." Katherine's adoptive brothers were in attendance. Her brother Ben lived behind a grocery in Rosedale, with his wife, Susie, and their son Alex, who was recently given a *hone aun* of his own. Biscoe's grandparents, Don Chuck Tai Wong and Lung Jin Foon Wong, who first brought Katherine to America, had planned to move back to China in the winter but delayed their voyage just long enough to attend the banquet. Following the ceremony, the Wongs sold their store in Gunnison and moved back to their native country, never to see Katherine or her children again.

While many of Katherine's relatives came to congratulate her, there was only one relative who arrived for Jeu Gong, his eldest brother, Gow. They had not seen each other in over a decade, not since Jeu Gong crossed the US border. They had each fashioned vastly different lives for themselves, Jeu Gong as a grocer in Mississippi and Gow as a laundryman in Michigan. Yet both men had started American families.

Gow brought a son with him, whom Jeu Gong now met for the first time. Gow's son, Lee, spoke fluent English, unlike his father, whose tongue snapped awkwardly across the foreign syllables. As relatives filtered out of the grocery, each leaving behind gifts and well wishes, Jeu Gong informed Katherine that Gow and his son would be staying in Benoit. They, too, would live at the grocery. Lee would work the register and Gow would learn about the grocery business from Jeu Gong.

Katherine could have told her husband that she was too weak to care for others, that there were no beds to spare with the Dabneys boarding in the home, but Gow and Lee were family, and family provide for one another. So the two men moved in behind the store, sleeping on mattresses along-side Cammie and Bartlett Dabney, Martha, Berda, Jeu Gong, Katherine, and baby Biscoe.

The girls called their uncle Ah Bok, the respectful term for a father's older brother. Gow commanded this respect. He was much older than their father and did not have a wife's touch to temper his rough disposition. He spoke with his brother in Cantonese about the things they used to have in the old country. His son, Lee, shared stories of life in the North, of snow and ice and towering buildings that almost touched the sky. There were cinemas and opera houses where a Chinese man could enter right through the front door. There were parts of the city where everyone spoke Cantonese, even the same Sze Yap dialect that Gow spoke with his brother.

For Berda, who was about to begin primary school, the stories were mesmerizing. In learning about cities, Berda developed a yearning for a world outside the Delta and a wanderlust that would stay with her all her life. Martha was far too young to make sense of the stories. She clambered about the store with childish buoyancy, leaving the duty of listening to her sister.

As much as Jeu Gong enjoyed the company of his brother, Gow's stay was unsettling. Jeu Gong had traveled south to avoid the immigration officers of the North. In a big city, there are many eyes watching. Gow brought those eyes with him. And with them, he brought the threat of deportation into Jeu Gong's home.

What if his brother had been followed? What if the inspectors came to the grocery? How could Jeu Gong protect his family? Who would care for them if he was sent back to China? If Jeu Gong were taken, he would likely be detained and questioned about his brother, how they came to America, if they were native citizens. He must know the answers to every question.

With a little money Jeu Gong managed to save, he purchased coaching papers. The papers provided a series of responses to questions that an inspector would likely ask during an interrogation. To protect his family and his brother, Jeu Gong memorized the details of an American childhood he had never experienced in a place he had never been.

Where were you born?

We were born in San Francisco.

Where were you born in San Francisco?

I was born at the corner store 803 at Grant and Clay Street, room 5, second floor, above the grocery and store Chang Jan. On the left, 805, was Chang Tai, a grocery and clothing store.

Where were you born?

We were born in San Francisco, 803 Grant Avenue, corner of Grant and Clay. Downstairs was the Chang Jan grocery store. They also sold books and metal utensils. We were born in room 5 on the second floor Chang Jan. On the left at 805 was Chang Tai, a grocery and clothing store.

Where did your father work in San Francisco?

He was manager at the Chang Tai store at 805 Grant Avenue.

Where did you go after the San Francisco earthquake?

We lived with our parents in Oakland at 31 Eighth Street, corner of Eighth and Harrison. On 4th month, 19th day, Kuang Hsu 15, my brother and I went to Chicago.

The list of questions ended with a warning, cautioning that the inspector would likely ask about Gow and what Jeu Gong knew of his activities in the North.

There needs to be remarks about you two separating in Chicago and your meeting again:

My brother and I were in Chicago barely a week when we separated. I went to the South to look for work. We did not communicate for many years because I worked at many different places. It was not until the end of the World War when he visited me that we met again.

"Further words of advice," the letter concluded:

In case immigration officials were to investigate, be sure to memorize what we discussed above. . . . You can tell them what you did in the South after you and Gow Lum separated in Chicago. After you have read and committed to memory what's in these papers, you should put them away in a safe place so they will not be seen by any white person. Otherwise, it could lead to serious problems.

Over time, Gow grew restless and returned to the North and Jeu Gong's fear of deportation gave way to a new fear, the loss of his wife. Katherine had been in poor health during her pregnancy, but she'd survived Biscoe's birth. Now many months had passed, and her condition only seemed to grow worse. Every remedy failed as her body grew weaker. One room was too small for a family. Katherine needed a new home.

Whenever Jeu Gong could get away from the store, he went to his small plot of land at the far end of Bruce Street, beside the train depot, in Rosedale. He cleared brush from the lot to lay the foundation, cutting back grasses and cane scrub that grew near the tracks. Over several years, gradually purchasing labor, mortar, and brick, Jeu Gong built a new home for his family.

The first floor included a cashier's counter, behind which were rows of dry goods and farm supplies. At the rear of the grocery was a kitchen. In the yard behind the house, Jeu Gong planted a garden. There was an opulence in the kind of plants that Jeu Gong could coax from the soil, thick curls of longbean sprouts, glittering purple eggplants, green celery and bok choy, fragrant ginger root, squash, tomatoes, cucumbers, and snow peas. Through his garden, Jeu Gong gave life to memory, now oceans and decades away.

Katherine designed the second floor of the house, which would serve as the family's living quarters. It included eight rooms, far more than the family required, but Katherine wanted to be able to welcome guests. Hoping to spare visiting Chinese the humiliation of being rejected from local hotels, Katherine decided their grocery would be a place for all Chinese families, not merely her own. Finally, in 1923, four years after Jeu Gong signed the papers on his plot of land, the Lum family moved to Rosedale.

CHAPTER IV

SUMMER, 1923

BRUCE STREET WAS SO alive it had its own heartbeat. Its rhythm came from the fast crack of billiard balls at Charlie Green's pool hall and the midnight laughter burning like pipe tobacco in Lottie Jeritt's rooming house.

The street's loudest pulse was the quaking meter of steel on steel, as the steam train known as the Owl shuddered to a stop in the dead of night. A handful of dedicated men, eyes blurry with either sleep or drink, would stand by the station, waiting for the next morning's papers and news from Bolivar County's great beyond.

The pace never slowed on the colored side of Rosedale. It was as if its very motion kept it alive. The Lums' grocery was located on the corner of Bruce and Railroad Streets, next to the rail line. On one side of the grocery was the train depot and on the other side were two cobblers, a barber, a restaurant, and a laundry.

Just south of the train depot, a short walk along the tracks, was the town's ice plant. There, great slabs of ice were loaded into insulated boxcars. Fishermen, boots caked with the mud of the Arkansas, White, and Mississippi Rivers, heaved crates of buffalo and catfish onto waiting trains. Packed tight with ice, the fish then shipped up to Chicago, as many as three express carloads a day.

Whether it was the vibrancy of the town or the new house, Katherine's health began to improve almost immediately. By harvest season she was strong enough to work long hours at the grocery, from well before sunrise until long after sundown.

Throughout most of the year, the family's customers came in from Scott Plantation, a cotton farm controlled by the Delta and Pine Land Company.

The corporation owned eighteen plantations and most of the cotton land within the county.

During harvest, when the grocery was busiest, the Lums served new customers, day laborers who came looking for better wages from as far as the Red Clay Hills or plantations in distant Delta counties. The migrant farmers arrived with the first burst of the cotton boll and left immediately after the crop was collected.

By September, when harvest was well under way, Martha and Berda woke early each weekday morning to help in the store before walking to school. The girls were in Miss Rae's third- and fourth-grade classroom at Rosedale Consolidated High School. The sprawling redbrick structure was an object of regional pride. The district had consolidated its education funds to construct the new facility.

The consolidated school was not designed for the city's current residents, but rather the residents Rosedale's leaders hoped to attract. With the exodus of thousands of black laborers, planters feared they would be unable to secure a strong workforce. By 1920 landowners began to consider recruiting white labor.

Mrs. Walter Sillers Sr. was one of the first in the Delta to suggest replacing black sharecroppers with white laborers from Mississippi's Red Clay Hills. In an essay for the Bolivar County Daughters of the American Revolution, she advocated dividing plantations into thirty-acre plots and leasing the land to white farmers.

The survival of the region, Mrs. Sillers claimed, relied on recruiting "Anglo Saxon stock from the hill sections." She insisted that such a project was essential to ensure that "this fine race of people may be kept in ascendancy in this nation." Her son Walter served on Rosedale's school board.

One of the chief ways to lure farmers from the hills to the banks of the Mississippi River, Walter Sillers Jr. and other Delta planters decided, was to build modern consolidated schools throughout the region. The beautiful brick buildings would impress poor yeoman farmers, whose children likely studied in one-room shacks, if they studied at all. After several county meetings, it was decided that Rosedale Consolidated High School would be constructed and serve as the district's recruiting grounds for a new white workforce.

Immediately following the school's opening in 1923, Rosedale's principal and board of trustees made an application to the state accreditation commission. If Rosedale received accreditation from the commission, its graduates would be accepted to state colleges without examinations, further increasing the district's appeal for white farmers.

In order to meet the commission's standards, the school was expected to fulfill a series of fourteen requirements, including maintaining a full library and a nine-month scholastic calendar, hiring teachers with four-year college degrees, and enrolling students who exhibited "good intellectual and moral tone with stability of character."

Seeing as the school had opened just months before, it was unlikely that Rosedale would meet the stringent requirements of the accreditation commission with its first application. But on November 26, 1923, a few days before the commission met to decide the school's fate, Walter Sillers Jr. sent a personal letter to Mississippi's superintendent of education, Willard Faroe Bond.

"We of Rosedale are very interested in the progress of our school and in having it meet the standard of this Commission," he wrote. "We trust that you will see that this gets due consideration at the meeting. . . . I assure you that [Senator] W. B. Roberts and the other good citizens of Rosedale will appreciate whatever you may do for us." By springtime, Rosedale Consolidated was approved for accreditation.

On April 16, 1924, nearing the end of Martha and Berda's second semester at Rosedale, Jeu Gong and Katherine ushered their daughters out the door for their first class photo. The event was particularly momentous, because it was the school's inaugural year. The teachers led forty third- and fourth-grade students onto the front steps of the new building, filing the children into four rows, one for each step.

The boys sat in the back two rows, the older ones dressed in white collared shirts and neckties. The younger ones wore shorts, belted high over their waists, and long dress socks that covered their dust-scrubbed legs, an assortment of ruddy knees visible in the gaps between socks and shorts.

The girls wore loose-fit, hand-sewn dresses, some decorated with bits of lace around the neckline and cuff. Each girl sported the same boyish bob that seemed torn from the pages of *Motion Picture* magazine. Martha and Berda sat next to one another in the front row, Martha with her long arms dangling by her side and Berda locking her fingers impatiently over her lap. Wriggling in place, the children tried to remain still long enough for the photographer to take an image that would capture history.

. . .

As Martha and Berda posed on the front steps of Rosedale Consolidated High School, a thousand miles away, at the Capitol Building in Washington, DC, two cousins were locked in a battle that would determine the fate of every immigrant in America.

Inside the Senate chamber, Senator David Reed, a Republican from Pennsylvania, had just proposed an amendment to an act that he recently authored with Congressman Albert Johnson. The tentatively titled Johnson-Reed Act was the single most restrictive immigration legislation ever introduced to Congress.

The two men wanted to reform the country's immigration system to operate strictly on the basis of quotas. The cap for the number of citizens admitted from each foreign nation would be determined based on the racial makeup of the United States in 1910. Using census figures, a national immigration bureau would determine how many countries were represented in the bloodline of "American stock." Those figures would dictate the number of immigrants permitted into the United States from each foreign country. The goal was to preserve the nation's current ideal of American Anglo-Saxon homogeneity while slowing the influx of migrants from southern and eastern Europe.

Congressman Johnson, chair of the House Committee on Immigration and Naturalization, who helped draft the act with Reed, sought guidance for designing his quota system from a researcher named Harry Laughlin. A stolid man with a rare, faint smile, Laughlin was the nation's leading eugenicist. He was the first and only director of the Eugenics Record Office located in Cold Spring Harbor, New York. Frequently making trips to Ellis Island with his colleague Charles Davenport, Laughlin studied arriving immigrants to construct a hierarchy of national origins.

According to his findings, the unfit and insane constituted an excessively large proportion of the national populations of Russia, Poland, Italy, and the Balkans, which also happened to be the birth countries of an increasing percentage of America's new immigrants. By drafting policy that reflected his research, Laughlin had the opportunity to legitimize the field of eugenics on a national scale. If the bill passed, it would give credence to Laughlin's life work.

At noon on Wednesday, April 16, 1924, the bill was in its later stages of development, but still nowhere ready for a vote. What was up for debate was an amendment proposed by its author, David Reed, to include a provision that would exclude from entry any alien who, by virtue of race or nationality, was "ineligible for citizenship."

The existing laws prohibited only people of Asian nationalities from American citizenship. This meant that if passed, Reed's amendment would all but end immigration from East Asia and the Indian subcontinent. Asians as a whole would no longer be admitted into the United States as immigrants. Reed's amendment was met with widespread approval as senator after senator took to the floor to support the new measure.

"Mr. President," Senator Walter George, a Georgia Democrat, proclaimed in a lilting drawl,

> when we think of the Chinese and the Japanese . . . we must think of them, Mr. President, as children of a very old civilization. . . . We have in America a peculiar government, a self-government that is peculiar to the people of America. That government has many great excellences, but it has no excellency that makes it fit and proper for every race of man. . . . So I think that in the broader question involved in this immigration measure before us, we must of necessity keep in mind the ease or difficulty with which separate races and the nationals of other nations can be assimilated. . . . I believe that amendment is a good amendment and it is a wise amendment.

Other senators joined in a chorus of agreement; one even suggested barring immigration altogether for a period of five years. As afternoon faded into evening and it appeared the amendment would pass, James Reed, a Democrat from Missouri, took the floor from his cousin David.

Described by those who knew him as "vigorous" and "alert," with a bellowing voice and an "acid tongue," James lived to wage wars no one believed he could win. He was a slender man, with a wide face and penetrating eyes that carried an unmistakable gravity. His cousin David was full of social graces, described by others as "charming, handsome and adroit." As one writer recalled of David, "he came as close as any opponent ever had done to outwit" his cousin James.

James was the only senator to vote against the Emergency Quota Act of 1921, which enacted strict limits on immigration. While James fiercely opposed every aspect of David's bill, the fight was far more than political. It was personal. In a rivalry of kinship, James set out to dismantle his cousin's amendment.

"Mr. President," he began in a measured tone, "at this late hour in the discussion of the bill, with full knowledge that probably every Senator has made up his mind on the subject, and with but few members of the Senate in the chamber, I do not presume to think that I shall change a single vote, or that my remarks will have any other present effect than to register my own views regarding the character of legislation. I shall try to do that briefly."

James then proceeded to break apart the logic behind David's amendment, explaining the country's history as an immigrant nation, that every person, regardless of origin, is both a physical and financial asset to the United States. He pointed out that every person in the room was in some way the descendant of immigrants, that he had known many immigrants in his life and seen their children grow into honorable citizens.

"They were regarded as a scourge," James said, his voice thick with passion. "Yet I lived to see the sons and daughters of those people enter the public schools and I entered with them. . . . The fact that a man happened to be born on the other side of the red line of the map does not make his presence here any less valuable. . . . I do not expect to stop this craze: I do not expect to arrest this movement: But I say that it is one of the narrowest and most contemptible movements that ever cursed the American people."

As the sky grew darker and the sun began to set over the Potomac River, James turned to his colleagues and gave one final plea.

"This movement is but a part of a general swing. We are going to exclude everybody; we are going to keep this country just for ourselves, we think: But we are simply denying ourselves the wealth of the world, the splendid men and women who want to come to this country and live under our flag and become a part of this great people. You may do it; you doubtless will do it."

Before the end of the session, a vote was taken. David's amendment passed by a margin of 71 to 4. Then, a month later, the Senate passed the Immigration Act of 1924 in its entirety.

On July 1, President Calvin Coolidge signed the measure into law. With the act's ratification, the country was set on a course to, by its own definition, "maintain the racial preponderance of the basic strain [of] our people" and "stabilize the ethnic composition of the population."

The act proved so restrictive for Asians and eastern Europeans that in 1924 more Italians, Czechs, Yugoslavs, Greeks, Lithuanians, Hungarians, Poles, Portuguese, Romanians, Chinese, and Japanese left the United States than arrived as immigrants. More than just crafting legislation, David Reed, Albert Johnson, the Sixty-Eighth Congress, and President Calvin Coolidge institutionalized America's virulent nativism to an extent that would prove catastrophic for generations of immigrants.

The three women living in Jeu Gong's house scurried about at such a frantic pace, it seemed they might be preparing for the German invasion. In reality, it was the first day of school.

The date was September 15, 1924, and Jeu Gong was downstairs in the grocery, seeking shelter from the storm rolling through the apartment above. Berda, true to form, made no attempt to hide her displeasure. She could just as well have been preparing to enter purgatory. Martha, on the other hand, was dressed and ready, eager to meet her new classmates and teachers.

Katherine needed to be sure the girls looked clean and presentable. The impression her daughters made on their first day was crucial. Katherine's motivations were not those of a matriarch, but of a commander. The girls were unaware that the mother who brushed their hair and straightened their collars was indeed preparing them for battle.

For the past several weeks, Katherine had been hearing rumors about a new policy that would bar Chinese children from attending Rosedale's school. The district was experiencing an expansion and the school had made numerous changes in faculty, the most significant being the promotion of a new principal, a man named J. H. Nutt.

Even with all the changes, Katherine found it hard to believe that the school board would actually implement a policy strictly designed to exclude her daughters. The only way to test the board would be to send her girls to the front lines. It was a risky move. If Martha and Berda were turned away, Katherine's family would face a dangerous choice.

She knew all too well the type of violence inflicted on those who tried to change the social order of the Delta. Over the past few years, Katherine had heard accounts of night riders burning homes and businesses all over the county. The increase in violence was a direct response to black laborers' rising demands for equality, an equality that Katherine, too, sought. She was not ignorant as to the risk. Local planters like W. B. Roberts and Walter Sillers Jr., whom Katherine often saw at church, were involved with the Ku Klux Klan and used the association as a tool for maintaining control and influence over the town.

Along with their lives, the Lums' livelihood would be at stake. One step too far and Sillers, who mortgaged their store, would cut their credit line. The town's white officers could demand their immigration papers. They could arrest Jeu Gong and separate him from his family for life.

Still, if Katherine did not send her daughters to school, she would be admitting defeat before the battle had even begun. Jeu Gong needed convincing, but eventually he sided with Katherine that Martha and Berda should attend the first day of classes. Maybe, deep down, Katherine knew the girls would be turned away. For in that moment, they would finally have a reason to take a stand.

As Martha and Berda left for school, their parents offered them a warning: On this day, they would have to remember to stay strong, no matter what happened. Then they sent the girls out onto Bruce Street and into the most important morning of their lives.

Jeu Gong was uneasy. If he had had more time, he might have told his children a story, the story of the Lum name and the lesson behind its Chinese character. If he was sure they would understand, he could have sat them down and shown them how to draw the brush strokes, two strong lines with interlocking branches, the two trees that once bore the weight of a child's future.

He would have begun the story this way: "Three thousand years in the past . . ."

During the Shang Dynasty, a king named T'ai-ting had a son named Pi-Kan. Pi-Kan was a virtuous child, with a fierce sense of purpose. After leading a good and noble life, Pi-Kan was honored as a member of the royal house and became an advisor to his nephew, the king, Chou-hsin. Chou-hsin was a cruel and tyrannical king. He inflicted tremendous suffering upon his people. When other loyal advisors went to the king and begged him to change his ways, Chou-hsin ordered their executions. Eventually, all of the king's imperial advisors were dead. Only Pi-Kan remained. Pi-Kan continued to plead with the king to correct his ways, but the king only grew angrier and angrier.

Then Chou-hsin came up with a plan to eliminate Pi-Kan. Under the pretext of curiosity, the king asked Pi-Kan why the hearts of great sages possess seven channels, while the heart of a common man does not. Pi-Kan did not know the answer, so the king requested that Pi-Kan offer him his heart. And so, the evil king pulled the heart from his last detractor. When the news of Pi-Kan's death reached his pregnant wife, she feared for the safety of their unborn child and fled into the forest to hide inside a cave. When it came time to give birth, Pi-Kan's wife was alone. She used the last of her strength to walk from the cave into the woods, where she found two adjacent trees. Gripping their limbs for support, she brought Pi-Kan's son into the world. Cradling him on the silent forest floor, she named her newborn son Lum, or "trees," after the branches that held her when she was weakest. The child would grow to see the evil king overthrown. A new ruler would take the place of Chou-hsin and invite the child into his court, where he would honor the name Lum as royalty and celebrate the strength of a family whose faith brought justice to the kingdom.

The two girls returned to the grocery at half past twelve. Together, they recounted the conversation that had taken place with Principal Nutt. His tone had been pleasant, cordial, even polite. He cited a decision made by a man in Jackson named Attorney General, who had never met Martha and Berda but saw the girls as a threat.

"As to whether or not Chinese children should be excluded," the man had decided, "courts have held in an almost unbroken line that the words 'white person' were meant to indicate a person of what is popularly known as the Caucasian race."

Principal Nutt said the arrangement was outside of his control. The school's board of trustees had come to a consensus on their own. He was sorry. He had to follow orders. He told the children to return home. Chinese students were no longer welcome at Rosedale Consolidated.

The girls were confused. There was no problem with their attendance the year before. What had changed? Over the course of one morning, the sisters moved from one side of the color line to the other. Could they see their classmates again? Would they be welcome in church? If the children could no longer attend the white school, then they could just as easily be excluded from all of white society. The world they once inhabited had disappeared within the length of a conversation.

In a desperate attempt to avoid discrimination against her family, Katherine vowed to do everything in her power to keep the girls enrolled at Rosedale's white school. "I did not want my children to attend the 'colored' schools," Katherine told a reporter years later. "If they had, the community would have classified us as negroes." Katherine witnessed on a daily basis the injustices faced by blacks in the Delta. A lifetime inside a grocery had furnished her with decades of stories, revealed in hushed voices, about indignities too painful to imagine. She knew that such a classification would have instantly disenfranchised her family.

For Katherine to send her children to the colored school would be to yield to the trustees, to agree with them that her daughters were not worthy of the privileges afforded to whites. Katherine spoke with her husband. She had heard of a lawyer who'd helped another Chinese child once, but the case was stalled in court. Maybe this man would help Martha and Berda.

Even if Jeu Gong had protested, explaining the risks the family faced if they took legal action, it would not have done any good. Her mind was made up. When Jeu Gong married Katherine, she took the name Lum. Once, there were two trees that held a mother as she gave birth to a child who would one day challenge an empire.

Jeu Gong slid his arms into a pressed shirt with a high collar and fastened the buttons with metronomic precision. He stood beside his wife looking refined, stately, polished. High cheekbones carved a delicate contour across Jeu Gong's face, meeting his hairline at the ear. His straight black hair had been trimmed short with a razor, some places cropped shorter than others, but the hair above his forehead he let grow and wore it as long as his fingers. When he finished dressing, Jeu Gong ran his hands through his hair, restraining stray strands with pomade.

With the engine idling, Jeu Gong climbed into the passenger side of the car as Katherine took her place in the driver's seat. Katherine was the motorist in the family; Jeu Gong had never learned to drive. He was content to sit beside his wife as she pressed her palms against the wheel, a cigarette laced between her fingers.

For what must have been hours, the Ford lurched back and forth beside the levee on a trail that ran from Onward to Moon Lake, the old cart path carving a parallel course beside the Mississippi River and the Yazoo and Mississippi Valley Railroad line. As the landscape gently unfolded into fertile flatlands, painted white with harvest, the levee rose beside Katherine, a steady, snaking bulwark against the great surge of river behind it.

The drone of the Clarksdale Gin Company was audible to them long before they glimpsed the pitched metal roof of the cotton gin rising on the southern edge of town. Inside the gin, black laborers churned cotton bolls into soft white fibers that clung to the ginnery rafters like cobwebs. Soon rows of brick storefronts and gravel-lined streets came into view. Katherine and Jeu Gong had arrived in Clarksdale, home to one of the most famous lawyers in the state.

Jeu Gong had no way of knowing what the lawyer would say. In all likelihood, Jeu Gong and his wife would be turned away before they even had the chance to meet him. Jeu Gong was painfully aware of how little money they had and how much it would cost to bring the case. The couple had tried to raise funds from other Chinese families, families whose children had also been barred from the school, but no one wanted to take the risk. There was too much at stake.

The other families tried to convince Katherine to back down, telling her it was better not to burn bridges. She had good standing in the community. She belonged to the Methodist church. Her family ran a business. Why jeopardize everything for a battle they could not win? But for Katherine this was more than just her family's struggle. It was larger than any one person.

So on a September afternoon, Katherine and Jeu Gong drove to Clarksdale to meet a lawyer and offer him next to nothing to take a case he would likely lose. They had no strategy, but the law offices of Brewer & Brewer seemed like a good enough place to start. Standing beside one another in the fierce heat of a Delta fall, the Lums knocked on the door and quietly waited for an answer.

*Governor Earl Brewer standing beside a levee in the Mississippi
Delta, circa 1912. Photo by Milton McFarland Painter Sr.
Courtesy of the Archives and Records Services Division,
Mississippi Department of Archives and History.*

PART TWO

WIN OR LOSE IT ALL

CHAPTER V

AUTUMN, 1924

A WAVE OF FRESH cigar smoke crested over a well-dressed Chinese couple as Earl Brewer, Esq., opened the door to his office at 301 Yazoo Avenue. The lawyer greeted his two guests, ushering them through the foyer of an office that looked to be a combination of library and billiard room. Files and documents lay strewn about on tables, and layers of smoke hung in the air.

Brewer was a giant of a man. His hulking figure tapered up to a large head with a wide jaw. He was older than his two visitors and certainly not handsome, but his mannerisms betrayed an intense and youthful disposition. Unaccustomed to entertaining guests, at least not lately, he had let his hair grow long, into a wiry gray mane that fell just above his broad shoulders. His voice, weathered by constant smoking, was deep and gravelly.

Every aspect of Brewer's appearance showcased the ways in which age will sink into a man. At fifty-five, Brewer had creases across his forehead and ridges under his eyes, eyes that a younger, more successful version of himself used to shade with the broad brim of a Stetson hat.

He could no longer keep pace with the children darting along Clarksdale's sidewalks, playfully calling him Governor. His fitness was now maintained by conducting morning calisthenics on the lawn. The limited routine consisted of bending over several times, with noticeable effort. His wife had begun to suggest that he reserve his exercising for indoors.

Due to a steady wave of misfortune, Brewer was down to his last few clients and therefore his last few dollars. Ever since the value of Delta farmland had begun to plummet, compensation for Brewer's legal services typically came in sacks of cowpeas and soybeans. Anyone who needed his help was usually too poor to ask for it, and when they did, the bill was rarely paid. The Chinese couple standing beside Brewer was no different. They had no money, but what they did offer was infinitely more valuable: a case that could rescue his career. Gazing at the young couple, the lawyer was aware he needed these clients far more than they needed him.

If the woman felt out of place inside the smoky haze of Brewer's office, she did not show it. She was a pleasant and easy conversationalist. Had Brewer been a man to take note of such things, he would have recognized her beauty. She had finely cut features, their clear, elegant lines enhancing her soft brown eyes beneath the smooth ivory of her forehead.

She introduced herself as Kate, but Brewer took to calling her Katie. She explained that the family's local school district had recently decided to bar her two daughters from Rosedale Consolidated High School. The school officials had justified the children's exclusion by saying they were simply following a state mandate. The Chinese, the order stated, were not white and therefore not permitted to attend white schools.

The trouble, Katie explained, was that her daughters were already attending Rosedale's white school when they were kicked out. While Berda, Katie's eldest child, cared little for studies and was often caught skipping class, Martha, her second daughter, was an avid reader and had every intention of graduating college. Katie and her husband owned a grocery business. They paid taxes. They went to church. Katie's husband had built the family's house himself, pouring all they had into its construction. They couldn't just pack up and move to another town. Rosedale was their home.

Her husband said little, no doubt due in part to his wife's frenetic pace of speaking. His name was Jeu Gong, but to accommodate Brewer's American ear, Katie referred to him simply as J.G. He was only a few inches taller than his wife, but he had a broad build and carried himself with a stately stoicism. Behind thick, wire-rimmed spectacles, his face betrayed its age as little as it betrayed anything else.

Brewer continued his conversation with Katie until he knew enough of the facts to be able to build a case. The family didn't want to sue for damages. Katie was very clear about that. The only reason they came to Brewer was to get the children back in school. A victory for Katie and J.G. would simply be a return to how life had been before the girls were ejected from Rosedale Consolidated on September 15.

This left Brewer with limited options. He would have to confront the entire school board and likely the state board of education as well. There were dozens of people involved in enforcing the new policy, and Brewer would have to go up against every single one of them. Fortunately for Katie and J.G., Brewer was ready for a fight.

Just weeks before, Brewer had conceded defeat in a humiliating Senate race against one of the most established politicians in the state. Envisioning a historic political comeback after decades out of the public sphere, Brewer decided to run against Mississippi's incumbent senator, Pat Harrison. Following the announcement of his candidacy, Brewer became the laughingstock of the country.

"Nobody in Washington gives Brewer even a look in," declared the *New York Times*. "For Harrison, one of the most popular men in Congress, is just as popular in his home State."

Even the local papers derided him.

"It is very unbecoming of Earl Brewer, alleged candidate for the United States Senate against Pat Harrison, in his tactics of attempting to belittle the brilliant Mississippian," read an editorial in a Bolivar County newspaper.

We say attempting to belittle him advisedly, for the reason that nobody is paying any attention to Brewer, except to condemn him for his actions, and if he is affecting Harrison at all by his activities he is helping him. As a matter of fact, Brewer ought to withdraw from the race. He hasn't got a ghost of a chance. But, come to think about it, it is every man's inalienable right to run [for] office, and we guess Brewer is just simply exercising this right. That's about all it amounts to anyway.

Even before the final votes were tallied during the third week of August, headlines throughout the nation announced that Brewer had lost in a landslide. He returned to his law practice in Clarksdale the embarrassment of Mississippi.

Brewer needed this case more than he was willing to admit. He told Katie and J.G. that he would represent them in their lawsuit and sent them back out the door with a final burst of cigar smoke. It was time for him to mount another comeback.

. . .

Dusk was thickening as Brewer sped his horse between the rows of cotton along Cassidy Bayou. A luminous haze blanketed the quiet field, cut from the curves of the Tallahatchie River. Beyond the field, the river churned, brown and sluggish. A breeze passing through its dense swamp carried the faint smell of honeysuckle mixed with the musk of sunflowers growing on a flatter shore. At the water's edge were muddy coves where willow saplings flickered their shadows onto the sand.

Sundown was quitting time. As the end of the day neared, a single field hand would begin a song. Then, hoes beating the earth in unison, the other hands would join in the singing. As dusk settled in red along the procession of cotton, an aching hymn would mount over the still air. *Just a few more weary days and then, I'll fly away. I'll fly away. I'll fly away.* They were calling out to one another, but deep inside, they were calling to God.

The rhythm of his horse's hooves kept pace with the pound of harvest. Brewer rode until the wide stretch of cotton became a white blur. This was his land, and he charted its boundary with a fervor he felt only here. The plantation, into which Brewer had poured his life savings, was a badge of pride, a symbol, an idea much greater than the land itself.

Its furrowed fields tugged at a piece of Brewer's history, a time in his life very few people knew or understood. The soil stirred memories of a young man, barely sixteen, a burlap pick sack strapped to his shoulders, harvesting cotton in the blistering heat of a Delta summer. He was alone and a long way from home, far from that small plot of farmland on a hillside in Carroll County, the place where Brewer was raised.

Brewer was born in the blaze of August in a single-story farmhouse in Midway, Mississippi, in 1869. His father, Ratliff Rodney Brewer, was a captain in the Confederate Army. After the war, tired and defeated, Ratliff returned home to his wife, Lizzie, on an old mule he borrowed from a Union soldier. Their war-ravaged cabin looked nothing like the home he had left just years before. Lizzie comforted Ratliff with the promise that they would rebuild, and the two began to farm again as they prepared for the birth of their first child, Eloise. After Eloise came Earl, their first son, then Claude, Helen, King Ratliff, who died in infancy, John Dodridge, and baby Melinda, better known as Mel.

As the eldest son, Brewer was taught by his father to work the land. Together they raised alfalfa, crimson, and red clover hay. They planted and harvested crops of corn and peas and beans. They raised and slaughtered hogs. Brewer learned to feel the pulse of the seasons. The family survived on what the soil gave them, their vitality and purpose rooted in the earth beneath their bare feet.

In the fall of 1881 Ratliff became ill and died soon after. Brewer was twelve years old. He buried his father in the same land the man had taught him to till. After his father's death, Brewer assumed the responsibility of the household, raising extra crops to pay off the family's debt on the property. Brewer's younger brother Claude was of age to farm, but walked with a crutch and was too weak to perform hard labor. So Brewer farmed the land with his mother, who taught him passages from the Bible as they worked. Brewer would later say it was his mother who proved to be the greatest influence on his life. He would quote her in courtrooms as often as he quoted the law.

By 1884, at the age of fifteen, Brewer had managed to pay off all the debt on the farm. When his older sister, Eloise, married, bringing her new husband to live with the family, Brewer asked his mother's permission to leave home. The widow told her young son to travel, to broaden his understanding of the world, to see if he could get an education for himself. Unable to bear the pain of saying goodbye to his siblings, especially his brother Claude, Brewer snuck away early one morning before daybreak. He wandered west toward the Delta, eventually reaching a bend in the Mississippi River known as Friar's Point.

Two years earlier, a violent storm had caused the levee there to burst open, flooding a vast region of Delta farmland. The break was the result of heavy rains that had lasted for more than five months, causing over a hundred similar breaks in levees throughout the Mississippi River valley. Water inundated twenty-two thousand square miles of alluvial plain and displaced a population of over four hundred thousand people.

Destitute, without homes and land to farm, thousands of people across the flooded region made appeals to the federal government for aid. On August 2, 1882, the US Congress gave the Mississippi River Commission its first federal funding. The River and Harbor Act appropriated $4.1 million for improvements of the river's levee system, of which an estimated

$155,000 was allocated to build thirty-four miles of levee between Friar's Point and Sunflower, Mississippi.

Arriving at Friar's Point in the summer of 1884, Brewer quickly found work repairing the levee for a small monthly salary.

The brutality of levee work deeply affected the young man. During the late nineteenth century, the majority of the levees in the Lower Mississippi valley were built by means of the convict leasing system. Under that system, black men and women, working in chains, under the crack of a bullwhip, were forced to haul dirt, trees, and stones to form the new embankments.

For months, the fifteen-year-old farmboy moved great mounds of earth alongside prisoners, many of whom were worked to death, their bodies buried in the very levees they built. After that first summer, Brewer asked Thomas Aderholdt, his overseer, if there was other work to be had in the county.

Aderholdt offered Brewer a job picking cotton on his family's farm in Friar's Point. Brewer was a fast worker and was soon gathering bolls by the hundreds. If he awoke before dawn and worked until nightfall, he could earn decent enough wages, more than he'd earned on the levee. As Brewer bowed to collect the bolls, knotting his fingers between sharp pods of cotton, he swore to himself that he would one day return to this place a wealthy man, that he would own some of the Delta for himself.

When spring came, Brewer drifted west. He worked at a sawmill in Arkansas and herded cattle on a ranch in Texas. Then, in 1887, his sister's husband died, and Brewer returned home to once again work the farm with his mother. For five years he cared for his family. Then, at the age of twenty-three, he borrowed $400 from a local storekeeper and enrolled in a two-year law course at the University of Mississippi. He completed the degree in six and a half months.

In 1893 Brewer opened a law practice in Water Valley, Mississippi, with his classmate Julian Wilson. Water Valley served as the local headquarters of the Illinois Central Railroad, a powerful corporation that wielded a monopoly over the state's transportation system. As Mississippi's largest cotton freighter, the company's interests generally coincided with those of most Delta politicians, to the detriment of rail line laborers seeking better working conditions and wages from their employer. By locating their practice in Water Valley, Brewer and Wilson became the primary legal advocates for thousands of Mississippi rail workers and their families.

Realizing the limits of what he could accomplish as a lawyer, Brewer decided to run for the state legislature. He billed himself as a candidate who could not be bought, and charged the political leadership of the Delta with corruption, claiming that it had allowed the Illinois Central to avoid paying taxes by falsifying state records, assessing the company's value at $11 million when it was really worth $58.5 million. Brewer also took on the railroad, accusing its executives of using physical intimidation and bribery to gain favorable treatment from politicians and the press.

Brewer's bold campaign proved successful, and in 1895 he was elected to the Mississippi State Senate. During his first year in politics, Brewer married Minnie Marion Block, a high school student from Water Valley. Ten months after the wedding, their first child was born, a daughter named after her mother and grandmother, Minnie Elizabeth. When Minnie was three years old, Brewer was appointed district attorney for Mississippi's newly created Eleventh District in Coahoma County. He moved his family to Clarksdale and bought a house at 41 John Street, where they would reside for another thirty years.

In 1911 Brewer decided to run for governor. He was unopposed in the Democratic primary, and easily won the governorship in the 1912 election. Newspapers scoffed at the "barefoot ploughboy from Carroll County" who had been raised by a single mother and worked on the levees and in the fields with Negroes. He advocated stronger labor laws and railed against corporate wealth. If ever there was an outsider in Mississippi politics, it was Earl Brewer. Only now, he was the state's governor.

During his inaugural address, Brewer set his sights on a complete moral reform of the state, to outlaw drinking and gambling, to raise the age of consent, to adopt labor laws that protected women and ensured collective-bargaining rights for industrial workers. But the real reform, the one that was closest to his heart, was not mentioned in his speech. Brewer, haunted by ghosts from his childhood, planned to reform the state penitentiary system. In a silent, radical pact, Brewer vowed to abolish convict leasing.

By the time Brewer took office in January 1912, Mississippi prison inmates had been used to build public works for nearly half a century. Following Emancipation, the Mississippi legislature passed a series of acts known collectively as the Black Codes. The laws, copied in half a dozen other

Southern states, listed specific crimes applicable to the "free negro" alone, such as: "mischief," "insulting gestures," and intermarriage with whites, which carried the penalty of "confinement in the State penitentiary for life."

At the heart of the codes was the Vagrancy Act, which guaranteed planters a continued supply of black labor by requiring that "all free negroes and mulattoes over the age of eighteen" carry written proof of employment. Those found to be "vagrants" were fined fifty dollars. If they could not afford the fee, the ex-slaves worked off their fine picking cotton, scrubbing floors, and hauling lumber. The new laws ensured that the region's Negro population remained in chains, as every offense against a white citizen became an offense against the state.

"In slavery times," one freedman recalled, "jails was all built for the white folks. There warn't never nobody of my color put in none of them. . . . They had to work; when they done wrong they was whipped and let go." Following Emancipation, the pattern was reversed. Free from the bonds of slavery, thousands of men and women across the South entered the criminal justice system.

Mississippi's first Negro convicts were put to work building track, but as the railroad boom trailed off in the mid-1880s, most convicts were transferred to the emerging Yazoo Delta to clear land and build levees and infrastructure for future cotton plantations.

It was this state-sponsored resurrection of slavery that the fifteen-year-old Brewer encountered at Friar's Point as a levee worker in the spring of 1884. And it was the atrocities of the convict leasing system he witnessed firsthand that stayed with him. Men who tried to escape were "whipped 'till the blood ran down their legs" and returned to the chain gang with metal spurs riveted to their feet to keep them from running. Laborers collapsed from sunstroke, dysentery, and gunshot wounds. They died from exhaustion, from malaria, from consumption. They died from the very chains that bound them, from shackle poisoning caused by the constant rubbing of leg irons against bare flesh.

"It is not the shame or the hard labor to which we object," wrote a levee worker from Okolona, Mississippi, in 1884. "It is the slow torturous death inflicted by the demonic-like contractor who takes us to the Yazoo Delta to 'wear our lives away.' It is fearful, it is dreadful, it is damnable."

In 1904, shortly after Brewer was appointed Clarksdale's district attorney, a Democrat named James Kimble Vardaman was elected governor.

Just prior to Vardaman's election, the state legislature had purchased more than twenty thousand acres of Delta farmland in Brewer's neighboring Sunflower County. Once in office, Vardaman oversaw the construction of a prison on the site. The convicts would be worked almost exclusively for the production of cotton. He created the post of penitentiary superintendent to manage the expansive penal farm. The superintendent lived in a Victorian mansion beside the cotton fields and was referred to by convicts as "master."

Vardaman's farm, which he named Parchman, was soon generating more revenue than any other state institution. But no government regulation accompanied the rapid increase in the production of state cotton. When Brewer came into office in 1912, thousands of bales of cotton were being sold to foreign markets, as trustees of the state penal board pocketed the profits. Brewer's first move as governor was to conduct a thorough investigation of Parchman and the state's penitentiary system.

Once rumors began to spread about the investigation, the president of the prison board, C. C. Smith, threatened Brewer. He warned the governor that if he did not drop the case, the Democratic Party would crush him. When Brewer pushed forward with the investigation, Smith made good on his word. The legislature held an emergency meeting and refused to allocate funds for the investigative committee. Unmoved, Brewer continued to finance the investigation through his own private accounts.

In August 1912 he traveled to Europe and spent a month tracking the sale of state cotton to firms across the Atlantic. When he returned, Brewer had gathered enough evidence to charge C. C. Smith with embezzlement. As the case went to trial that fall, Brewer received a series of death threats. One was particularly jarring. It warned Brewer to keep an eye on his third and youngest daughter, Claudia, who was attending elementary school in Jackson. Claudia was assigned a bodyguard, a convict named Henry Trott, who worked in the mansion. "For over a year, a trusty negro convict accompanied me," Claudia recalled, "everywhere I went."

In times of great struggle, Brewer turned to his faith for guidance. He knelt by his bedside each morning and called to his daughters. Together, they prayed. "Ere we leave our room this morning, we shall think to pray and sue for loving favor as our shield today."

Smith's eventual conviction was hardly a victory for Brewer. He was fighting for a greater cause, for divine justice. Such an aim would require personal suffering, the suffering of the righteous for their faith. He was waging a battle that would test his very creed. "I beg to thank you for your very interesting letter," Brewer wrote a friend in Coldwater, Mississippi. "And note what you say as how many matters have come to vex me lately. Since you mention Job and how near he came to giving up the fight, you will remember that in the end he was greatly prospered. I am in the penitentiary fight to stay until it is over and my only desire is see every guilty man punished and all innocent men exonerated."

Brewer questioned the legality of the prison-labor system. He wrote to the state's attorney general on April 3, 1913, to ask "whether the Board of Trustees of the penitentiary can work the State convicts on the levees of the Mississippi River." He wanted it to be unlawful, to be condemned, to be stopped. He wanted the penitentiary board to pay for sins they had committed in the name of progress, in the name of the state. Instead, Brewer received a response as heartless as the acts he had witnessed on the levee.

"The board of trustees have full power to place convicts on the levees," wrote the attorney general, Ross A. Collins, "provided they do not keep them there for such a length of time as would prevent the proper cultivation and growing of a crop, and under the condition that they shall be under State management. It is my opinion that the board of trustees has the power to send as many convicts as the necessity requires, subject to the conditions above."

By the summer of 1913, Brewer, with the help of the William J. Burns Detective Agency of New Orleans, was able to prosecute eight prison officials on charges of thievery, graft, and embezzlement. Despite the convictions, Brewer's fight was far from over. He came into the investigation with one singular goal and he would not stop until it was accomplished. He was determined to end the cruel abuse of convicts in Mississippi.

"It is freely predicted that the scandal has far from reached a climax," read an article announcing the convictions. "Governor Brewer has headed the investigation and brought charges before grand juries. . . . He now is investigating stories of serious conditions at the State prison farms."

Since beginning the investigation, Brewer had spent most of his time questioning cotton buyers. He visited foreign firms and tracked cotton bales from Memphis to London. He spoke regularly with wealthy planters and statesmen, but rarely did Brewer interact with the prisoners themselves.

On February 12, 1914, Brewer left his office inside the Capitol to spend the day interviewing prisoners at Parchman farm. He was joined by Dan Lehon, the southern district manager of the Burns Detective Agency and several of his associates. On that cold morning in February, Brewer understood that the board's greatest crime was not theft, but brutality.

The Parchman interviews lasted late into the day. Investigators spoke with commissary clerks, reverends, doctors, and prison workers. They learned how the farm functioned, how rules were enforced, how secrets were kept. "He held a gun in one hand and strapped me with the other," one inmate told the detectives. "I says, what made you whip me? . . . And he says, well, you talked to that god damned committee."

At 3:25 in the afternoon, Brewer met an aging inmate named J. G. Bennett. Bennett began the interview by making small talk with one of the investigators named Detective Johnson. Then Johnson asked about the routines on the farm, the seasons, the crops, and Bennett's tone changed, as if a stone had settled inside him.

"The day before Thanksgiving would be picking day," Bennett began. "And [the cotton] would be weighed on Thanksgiving morning."

Johnson asked Bennett to tell him about the man doing the weighing, a farm manager appointed by the board named Mr. Stubblefield.

"He whipped nine men for not picking 150 pounds," Bennett responded, describing Stubblefield. "He whipped everybody . . ."

"What time of year was that?" Johnson asked.

"That was Thanksgiving Day."

Brewer needed to uncover evidence that would point to the theft of state cotton, so the detectives interviewed one of the farm's bookkeepers. The sergeant, who had been keeping a partial record of the board's affairs, testified that he did in fact have evidence, but all of his books were kept at his house outside the farm. The detectives requested he return with the records on a future date. The sergeant agreed. That night, at his home, he lit a fire. Then he systematically tore the leaves from every file and cast them into the flames. When all of the records were burned, the bookkeeper committed suicide.

As Brewer closed out his term as governor, he was left with the burden of his failure. Every man he convicted was eventually pardoned. The penitentiary system was no more regulated than when he first took office.

Brewer had always lived his life according to the belief that true righteousness rested in the rule of law. He read the Bible and the legal code in
tandem, as though one could not exist without the other. "Zion will be
redeemed with justice," God told the people of Jerusalem.

Brewer wanted justice, but there was no judgment a jury could render
that would fix a system so wholly broken. Once so full of hope, Brewer left
office a defeated man.

During one of his last exchanges as governor, Brewer corresponded with
a Jewish immigrant from Russia named Phillip Seigel. Seigel had been
arrested on vagrancy charges in Vicksburg and put to work on a nearby
farm. While in the custody of the state, Seigel was severely beaten. After
his release, he contacted the governor, detailing his abuse.

"It is against the law for the superintendent of the county convicts to
brutally whip or mistreat prisoners in his care," Brewer wrote in response.
"It is a matter for investigation by the grand jury and he could be convicted
for brutality."

Rather than show gratitude, Seigel's reply was an indictment against all
Brewer held dear. He questioned the very bedrock upon which Brewer had
built his life.

"Your honor," wrote Seigel. "How could I explain my self to the grand
jury about them mistreating me or make it known to any of the grand jury
when I come out of the county farm I did not have money to go home?"

How can the rule of law govern society, Seigel asked, when the justice
system itself has been corrupted? How can you ask a man to stand before
the very jury that placed him in chains and beg for sympathy? What do
they know about this suffering?

"If the grand jury should happen to call for me, would I be protected by
the law from being hurt or arrested again?" he asked.

Seigel told Brewer he would not testify before a grand jury. He would
not place his faith in the courts. There was no ruling that would restore
what had been taken from him. The American dream had been beaten
from his flesh and no lawyer, no judge, no jury could bring it back.

"How could a man stand gettin whipped and not to wriggle and beg for
mercy?" Seigel concluded. "The more he begs the harder he parts the 4 in.
leather on the body. I know it with the experience which he made the blood
come of my body. . . . I thought to myself if you call that justice or law of

the civil country of liberty, a man better go to Europe. They don't beat up a prisoner like they did me."

An immigrant came to America and was placed in chains. He wanted his governor to know that this America, the one he witnessed on the county farm, was not worth all he had sacrificed to reach these shores. A decade later, Brewer had not forgotten Phillip Seigel. His unfinished wars, waged inside a marble citadel, followed him back to an old law office in Clarksdale. By taking this case, the case of the Chinese girl, Brewer would fight for the tacit promise made to every immigrant arriving at the nation's gates, that they would find democracy on the other side.

As Brewer's horse slowed, its coat stained with rich soil, the aging man looked upon his land. The Delta had taken everything from him. Brewer was one of many cotton planters caught in the extreme deflation of 1920. During World War I, both the price and production of cotton increased, adding extra value to the worth of Delta farmland. Then, at the close of the war, both the value of the land and the price of cotton began to decrease in conjunction with one another.

The effects were devastating for planters and sharecroppers alike. Brewer had wagered everything he owned, and then some, in investments in the Delta's cotton fields. When the crash hit, Brewer was forced to borrow $375,000 from the Canal Bank and Trust Company of New Orleans to pay off his other debts. When Brewer's loan payments began to dwindle, the bank sought to relinquish his collateral, which consisted of the deed to Brewer's land and his only stable income.

The collapse of Brewer's estate provided the editors of the *Clarksdale Register* with endless amusement, which they masked in an air of sympathy. "The Register learns with regret that Hon. Earl Brewer has been forced into financial embarrassments," read one article from late February 1924. "The slump came in 1921 and tied up everything he owned, including his home. . . . The bad conditions have overwhelmed him, and as a result of it his creditors on these endorsements have taken judgments against him. . . . We hope that the clouds will yet clear away and that this man will not be crushed by the noble efforts he has made." The article was recirculated in several other papers throughout the county. Brewer came to read it in a newspaper edited by his own daughter, his eldest, Minnie Elizabeth. Even the bonds of family were broken in the crash.

Turning his back to the fields, Brewer followed the road that led home to Clarksdale. The air was cooler now, brought up from the draws and low places by the night. Occasionally the dancing lights of a motorcar would plunge past and the thin white path of the road would swell with dust. Then it would settle again and Brewer could see where the familiar low country unfolded gently, receding from the riverbanks as if it had been smoothed out by the tide. Beside the road, the warm shadows of poplars pointed the tired man home.

Brewer entered his mansion at 41 John Street with an air of resignation. Nothing had changed since the morning. Hardly anything changed anymore. After the children left, Brewer and his wife sank into the routine monotony of the life they once dreamed for themselves. Brewer stood gazing at the Persian rugs, the chandelier, and the Spanish tapestry chairs—all the same. The table lamps, flaunting their Victorian fringe, still rested on burnished brass bases. The gilded grandfather clock stood in its corner as usual.

At the end of the hall, opposite the front door, a wide master staircase spread into the edges of the room. Mrs. Brewer and her three daughters used to make entrances there, blooming forth in elegant evening gowns before crowds of dignitaries and celebrities. Now only the weight of Brewer's footsteps echoed through the house.

On the right side of the reception hall was the dining room, where the colored servants were readying the table for dinner. The banquet area was as large and empty as any other room in the house. Polished wooden chairs lined the walls, relics from a time when guests would arrive in droves.

A wide chiffonier sat plumb against the wall opposite the doorway. Its engraved drawers rang with the soft clatter of silver. Hanging over the table, the stained glass of a mosaic lamp cast a dull glow over the room. At the dinner table, Brewer and his wife brought their hands together in prayer. Bowing his head, Brewer recited the words his mother had spoken each night at the small table she shared with her six children: "Our Heavenly Father, we thank thee most kindly for this and every blessing in life. We ask it in Jesus' name. Amen."

. . .

After decades, Brewer still didn't tire of going to his office. Anyone unfamiliar with the bedraggled lawyer would assume that he was drowning in cases, for there was no other explanation for why a man his age would continue to keep such hours. The reality was that, until recently, Brewer barely had any kind of caseload at all. Still, he enjoyed his routine and kept it despite the dearth of casework. Each morning, he strolled into town, passing the picture theater, the boarding house, the filling stations and dress shops. As Clarksdale came alive, Brewer entered the small corner office he had maintained for nearly twenty years.

The office was located at the intersection of Yazoo and Third Street, directly across from the New Alcazar Hotel. The hotel, named after the Spanish word for "fortress," was an elegant, four-story structure, built during the fleeting period of prosperity when escalating crop yields and wartime cotton prices created a new class of royalty in the Mississippi Delta.

The hotel's marble-clad lobby was lit by a giant skylight that towered over a second-floor mezzanine, which contained a restaurant, a kitchen, and a ballroom. Now, years after the cotton market had collapsed, the hotel served as an extravagant mausoleum for all the grandeur the town once promised itself. Brewer's office, inside the aging brick walls of a bank, faced the facade of Grecian friezes that lined the Alcazar. His fortune had been built and lost in the shadow of a castle.

Stationed at his desk, Brewer turned to the case of the Chinese girl. He paused to light a cigar, which soon became another cigar followed by another. The smoking helped Brewer think. He wasn't going to be able to file a civil suit. The couple was not seeking damages. This left Brewer little room to make a deal with the few local judges who still regarded him favorably. Brewer's recent failed race for the Senate had significantly lowered his social standing. Now was not the ideal time to be asking favors. Maybe it was better this way. All or nothing.

Brewer's first order of business was to figure out exactly who the defendants would be. Any person responsible for keeping the child out of school qualified as a defendant, meaning Brewer would have to go all the way up to the state level. It so happened that the state superintendent of education had a long and bitter history with the onetime governor.

Willard Faroe Bond had been appointed by Brewer's greatest rival, Theodore Bilbo. Tapping Bond for superintendent of education was one of Bilbo's first actions as governor of Mississippi, after he was elected in a landslide victory in 1916. Two terms later, Bond still held the post, despite the fact that Bilbo was no longer in office.

Before Bilbo became governor, the short, paunchy man with round glasses and an even rounder face had served as Mississippi's lieutenant governor under a relatively unknown Progressive named Earl Brewer. From the very beginning of Brewer's administration, Bilbo worked to build allies in the legislature, eventually turning the entire legislative apparatus against its executive.

By the end of Brewer's governorship, the two men did not speak to one another. It was understood by every Mississippi politician that to align oneself with Bilbo was to markedly side against Brewer. Bond was deeply aligned with Bilbo.

Bond was born the only child of a poor housekeeper in Stone County, Mississippi, during the winter of 1876. In 1881 his mother, Nancy, died suddenly, leaving her son orphaned at the age of five. Since the boy had no other living relatives, he was left in the care of his mother's employer, a farmer and stockman named Loamie A. Batson. Batson readily accepted the child as his son, but more bad luck befell the boy when his guardian died in 1882, just months after the death of Bond's mother.

In his will, Batson stipulated that his adoptive son would receive $500 for his future education and would be placed under the care of Batson's younger brother, Lewis Cass. With the generous funds left to him by Batson, Bond attended various rural schoolhouses and eventually graduated from Purvis High School in 1897.

In the fall of 1898 Bond entered Peabody College for Teachers in Nashville, Tennessee. He boarded with a gregarious twenty-one-year-old named Theodore Bilbo. Bilbo was also studying at Peabody, but was on track to become a Baptist preacher. After Bond received his bachelor's degree in 1902, he was hired as the superintendent of a boarding school in his hometown of Wiggins, Mississippi.

One year into the job, Bond received a strange request from his old classmate. Theodore Bilbo had struggled in his courses at Peabody and eventually left Nashville to return to his home county and go into politics.

By 1903 Bilbo had been defeated in his campaign for circuit clerk and was ready to try his hand at teaching, an occupation in which he had no experience. In the manner of an old friend requesting a favor, Bilbo asked Bond for a job at Wiggins.

Out of loyalty, Bond offered Bilbo and his wife, Linda Gaddy, positions teaching at the school for a salary of $55 per month. Despite the benefits of his new employment, Bilbo did not last long at Wiggins. He was dismissed during his second year on charges of seducing an orphan girl in the dormitory. Upon his dismissal, Bilbo worked at the local drugstore for several months before entering Vanderbilt Law School in 1905.

Bond, on the other hand, remained at Wiggins for close to a decade, until he was hired to teach history and Latin at the newly established Mississippi Normal College in Hattiesburg in 1912. Four years into his tenure at Hattiesburg, Bond heard again from his old friend Bilbo, who had recently been elected governor.

Bilbo was facing allegations of immorality, as the seduction charges from his short career as a teacher had resurfaced during the campaign. Bilbo offered Bond the position of state superintendent of education, and Bond quickly accepted his offer, in turn proclaiming Bilbo innocent of all charges. A lifetime of trading favors had landed both men in two of the highest positions of power in the state.

Brewer was not a man to hold grudges, but he did have a long memory. Bond was as close a friend as Brewer's enemy ever had. He decided the best course of action for the suit was the one that would hit Bond the hardest. Brewer would file a writ of mandamus. The writ was essentially an order demanding the local court prosecute an individual, or in this case individuals, for violating the constitutional rights of another citizen. If successful, Mississippi's school board would be forced, under court order, to permit Martha Lum into Rosedale Consolidated High.

Of course, the case ran the risk of being thrown out immediately. If the defendants could argue that there were no constitutional grounds for Brewer's suit, his case would never even go to trial. It was a risky move, but a dramatic one.

Once a writ is filed, the court must summon every named defendant, sending an officer of the law to their doorstep. The day after Brewer filed the suit, police would visit the homes of politicians all over the state. Bond would answer his door at the capital one bright autumn morning to find the Hinds County sheriff serving him a summons to face trial for violating the United States Constitution.

As for which part of the Constitution the men would be charged with violating, Brewer chose to build his argument around one amendment, the Fourteenth. This was the first time Brewer employed the Fourteenth Amendment so strongly in a suit, and his interpretation of its statutes was a stroke of brilliance. With the Fourteenth Amendment as his brick and mortar, Brewer would build his case.

Drafted by the Joint Committee on Reconstruction following the Civil War, the Fourteenth Amendment was created with the lofty promise of granting the rights of citizenship to every person born in the United States. Its goal was to ensure that the nation's four million recently liberated slaves would be afforded the same rights as their fellow United States citizens.

The notion of turning a massive population of slaves into equal members of American society was as radical a concept as the creation of the Constitution itself. But the Congress that shepherded the passage of the Fourteenth Amendment was the same Congress that saw the nation shattered by civil war. For those men to guarantee the rights of citizenship to freed slaves was to make sense of a devastated nation and to bring justice to one of the largest injustices the country had ever known.

At the opening of the Thirty-Ninth Congress on December 4, 1865, Congressman Thaddeus Stevens, a prominent Radical Republican from Pennsylvania, introduced a resolution to establish a joint congressional committee on Reconstruction. The committee would be tasked with outlining the means by which the nation would restore unity and guarantee the protection of freed slaves. Along with proposing the new committee, Stevens also proposed a constitutional amendment declaring that "all national and state laws shall be equally applicable to every citizen, and no discrimination shall be made on account of race and color."

Congressman John Bingham of Ohio was in favor of the measure, and within twenty-four hours wrote and introduced a more comprehensive amendment based on Stevens's suggestion. On December 13, 1865, Stevens's proposal for a joint congressional committee on Reconstruction was approved, and fifteen men from both the House and the Senate, including

Stevens and Bingham, got to work drafting versions of a constitutional amendment that would guarantee the rights of citizenship to freed slaves.

In the end it was Bingham's final proposal, submitted to the committee on February 3, that laid the foundation for what later became the first section of the Fourteenth Amendment. The language, which was approved by the committee a week after it was introduced, read, "The Congress shall have power to make all laws which shall be necessary and proper to secure to citizens of each State all privileges and immunities of citizens in the several States; and to all persons in the several States equal protection in the rights of life, liberty and property."

On May 10 the House passed the Fourteenth Amendment by slightly more than the required two-thirds majority in a vote of 128 to 37, sparking applause in the House galleries as well as on the floor. Then the amendment opened for debate in the Senate, where Senator Jacob Howard of Michigan began the discussion by suggesting that the Fourteenth Amendment pass, but with an added citizenship clause reading, "All persons born or naturalized in the United States and subject to the jurisdiction thereof, are citizens of the United States and of the States wherein they reside." Scarcely had Howard finished introducing the amendment when a senator from Pennsylvania with a penchant for controversy took the floor.

Edgar A. Cowan of Westmoreland County, Pennsylvania, was selected as an elector for his state in the volatile presidential election of 1860. As the nation erupted into civil war following Lincoln's election in November 1860, Cowan's stubbornness and unwillingness to negotiate made him extremely unpopular both in his home state and in Washington.

According to one of Cowan's biographers, "few men in our Congress at any time have so completely lost the confidence and support of those who elected them." An article published in the *Pittsburgh Gazette* in the spring of 1862 read, "Among the members of the large convention of Republicans which met in this city on Monday, there was not a man that had a word to say in defense of Edgar A. Cowan in the Senate of the United States. There was a universal feeling of execration against the ingrate who had so basely deceived his political friends who had elevated him to a seat so much beyond his capacity."

Despite widespread unpopularity, in 1864 Cowan was elected to the Thirty-Ninth Congress, and on the afternoon of May 30, 1866, took the Senate floor in an attempt to break apart the proposed Fourteenth Amendment and Howard's notion of citizenship.

"The honorable senator from Michigan has given this subject, I have no doubt, a good deal of his attention," he began. "And I am really desirous to have a legal definition of 'citizenship of the United States.' What does it mean? What is its length and breadth? . . . Is the child of the Chinese immigrant in California a citizen? . . . If so, what rights have they?

"Now, I should like to know," Cowan continued. "Because I have been puzzled for a long while and have been unable to determine exactly, either from conversation with those who ought to know, who have given this subject their attention, or from the decisions of the Supreme Court, the lines and boundaries which circumscribe that phrase, 'citizen of the United States.'"

Cowan's quandary was not addressed, and the next day the Senate approved the amendment by a vote of 32 to 10. Two years later, on July 9, 1868, an amendment to the United States Constitution was ratified that read as follows:

> All persons born or naturalized in the United States, and subject to the jurisdiction thereof, are citizens of the United States and the States wherein they reside. No State shall make or enforce any law which shall abridge the privileges or immunities of citizens of the United States, nor shall any state deprive any person of life, liberty or property without due process of law, nor deny any person within its jurisdiction the equal protection of the laws.

Had Senator Cowan been more popular, his issue with the amendment's vague definition of citizenship may have resulted in an entirely different Fourteenth Amendment, one that outlined the status of immigrants and their respective constitutional rights. Instead, Cowan was silenced and the amendment passed, leaving his question to be answered more than a half century later by a man named Earl Brewer, as he fought for one of the most disenfranchised of citizens, the nine-year-old daughter of Chinese immigrants.

. . .

Earl Brewer poured himself a glass of milk. A curl of smoke issued from the stub of a cigar in an ashtray on the desk in front of him. Brewer rarely wrote down early drafts of his arguments or speeches, preferring instead to sort out the words by talking to himself. His voice was low and gruff and hardly carried above a whisper. He told his colleagues it was because he wanted to save all his bellowing for the courtroom. In reality, a doctor in Memphis told Brewer his throat was as tanned as leather. The smoking had taken its toll.

Sometimes when Brewer struggled with stringing words together, he left the confines of his office and made his way down Second Street, crossing the bridge over the Sunflower River, and headed north along Oakhurst Avenue toward the Oakridge Cemetery. It was there, pacing back and forth between the rows of headstones, that Brewer could gather his thoughts.

The case, he decided, should begin with Martha. The entire suit depended on the character of the child. She was an exemplary student and of pure Chinese descent, no mixed blood. Brewer had to make her seem just like any other white child in the state. He had to humanize her.

Martha Lum is of good moral character and is a good, clean, moral girl between the ages of five and twenty-one years and a native born citizen of the United States and the State of Mississippi, and that as such citizen and educable child it becomes her father's duty under the law to send her to school. And that she is an educable child of the said district and desires to attend the Rosedale Consolidated High School.

Brewer's long stride slowed when he was deep in thought. The residents along Oakhurst Avenue had grown accustomed to seeing the large man treading through the town's burial grounds, muttering in a half-audible drone. One by one, he passed the grave markers, the procession of lives once lived in Clarksdale: *To the memory of my husband, Rev R. P. Mitchell, whose body now sleeps in the cemetery . . . Here lies Frank N. Alford. Corp. in U.S. Army . . . Our baby, Bertha A. Prichard, blessed are the pure in heart . . .* Finally, Brewer came to the wide block letters etched into marble on a headstone on the north side of the cemetery, a life he knew better than all the rest.

MOTHER. MARY ELIZABETH BREWER. BORN SEPT. 27, 1841. DIED JAN. 14, 1920.

A lifetime had passed since Brewer had toiled in the fields beside his mother, but he had always stayed fast to his principles as the world changed around him. His country now dreamed of the fast life, propelled by celebrity, riches, and cosmopolitan ideals. His three little girls were now rouged young women, who bobbed their hair, drank, and danced to jazz music. He still advocated for progressive reform, but his policies were now branded Bolshevism, as newspapers and politicians traded on Americans' fears that the communist revolution in Russia would spread to the United States. He watched as his old colleagues fanned the flames of postwar nationalism, promoting the rise of nativism and violent hostility toward immigrants, blacks, Catholics, and Jews. All across the country, the ranks of a reawakened Ku Klux Klan surged to five million strong, capitalizing on national anxieties about threats to true Americanism.

In the fall of 1924, at the very moment Brewer decided to represent the Lum family, the KKK was at the height of its power, a potent force in both local and national politics. The year had been a triumphant one for the Klan, culminating in the recent passage of the Johnson-Reed Act. Its restrictive immigration quotas had codified the very nativism they espoused. With the rise of such extremism, there was no use for Brewer to retain any of his old political ties. Earl Brewer the politician was dead, but Earl Brewer the crusader was just coming to life.

> She is advised that notification had been issued by Mr. W. F. Bond, State Superintendent of Education of the State of Mississippi, to the superintendent, Mr. J. H. Nutt, and to the Board of Trustees, whose names are above set forth, to deny her this right solely and exclusively on the ground that she is of Chinese descent, and she is therefore discriminated against directly and denied the valuable right and privilege which she is entitled to, as a citizen of the State of Mississippi, on account of her race.

This case, unlike Brewer's previous cases, would have to hinge almost exclusively on the Fourteenth Amendment. While the original intention of the amendment was to guarantee freed slaves the "privileges and immunities" of citizenship and "equal protection of the law," Brewer expanded its definition to include children of immigrants. Taking the argument a step further, he established that Martha's right to attend school was also guaranteed by Mississippi's constitution.

According to the state's compulsory-education law, it was illegal for a child between the ages of five and eighteen to be kept from school. When Martha was barred from Rosedale High, Brewer contended that she was in fact denied her constitutional right as an American and a Mississippian.

> Said consolidated high school, is denying her, a native born resident citizen of the United States and the State of Mississippi, the privileges and immunities of her citizenship. . . . On account of her race or descent she is being denied the equal protection of the law, and contrary to the provisions of the constitution of the United States. . . . Your petitioners are entitled to have a writ of mandamus issued from this Court commanding the defendants and each of them to admit the said Martha Lum into the said school as a pupil and to desist from discriminating against her on account of her race or ancestry, and to accord to her the same rights and privileges accorded to other educable children.

Whether Brewer was ready or not, he would have to file the case quickly. September was drawing to a close and the court went into recess in October. Under pressure to file a case that Brewer so desperately needed to win, he was not going to be able to craft the perfect argument nor shape his sentences into perfect prose. Whatever draft Brewer had by Sunday evening was going to have to be good enough to bring to court on Monday. Where there wasn't perfection, there was prayer.

Now that the scaffolding had been removed from the Bolivar County courthouse, Brewer could see where five giant slabs of limestone formed gleaming steps that sprawled nearly the entire front facade of the building. Recently renovated in polished granite and sandstone, Rosedale's courthouse was untouched by the grit of the town that was designed around it. At right angles to the limestone stairs were twin cement blocks. Each served as the base for a shining white column, which supported an ornate cornice that circled the roof.

Carrying five recently typed pages, Brewer entered through two large wooden doors and turned right. The fresh scent of pine stain drifted from pores in the timber and followed Brewer into a wide hallway that encircled a central courtroom. Brewer had argued cases in the old courthouse many times, but the fresh paint and sparkling floors of the new building appeared foreign to him. His heavy footsteps made a muffled echo against the tall wooden walls of the corridor.

Brewer walked down the hall to the second door on the right, the county clerk's office. Charles Jacobs, the county clerk, was a deeply religious man. He and his wife were founding members of the Bolivar County Calvary Episcopal Church, which had no actual church building, so they held services in a different public space every Sunday. Jacobs took the pages from the lawyer's hands. Peering over stacks of red-bound docket books scattered around the office, Brewer watched his words become legal record to the clatter of Jacobs's typewriter.

The clerk collected the papers in a folder and passed it to Brewer for his signature. Jacobs then took the file from Brewer and added his own seal. Brewer paid the clerk five dollars as an advance to the county sheriff, who would require payment for delivering summonses to school board members L. C. Brown, G. P. Rice, and Henry McGowen. With Brewer's deposit, Jacobs filed the petition and Brewer exited down the hallway and out the large wooden doors. Now all he could do was wait.

When Brewer's daughters were young, he used to tell them stories. Not one for fairy tales, he would regale the three girls with stories from his youth on the farm, and from the early days of his law practice in Water Valley, and the old jokes he used to share with his brother Claude. Every now and then, when the mood was right, Brewer would tell the story of his hero, a Scottish general from the great Wars of the Three Kingdoms, a man named James Graham, the Marquess of Montrose.

During the middle of the seventeenth century, a youthful James Graham was named lieutenant-governor of Scotland and captain-general of its military. His first mission was to build up the Scottish army, so he set out to gather men and supplies for the war against England. James Graham traveled far and wide, taking long trips across Europe to Denmark, Sweden, and Poland. But in the end his travels proved fruitless. The young general found two supporters, the King of Denmark and Queen Christina of Sweden, who offered him little more than encouragement.

Upon his return to Scotland, James Graham knew he did not have nearly enough men or supplies to sustain an army. Still, in April of 1650, against all reason, he mounted a battle against the British. Preparing his ranks for war, he ordered the words *Nil Medium* inscribed on his army's banners: "There is no middle way." As Graham's men marched onto the battlefield, their entire force was cut to pieces. General Graham was quickly captured by British forces, taken to Edinburgh, and condemned to death.

On May 21, 1650, James Graham, the Marquess of Montrose, took his last breaths in front of the rickety wooden gallows erected on High Street, on the east side of the Market Cross. As the executioner strapped the noose around the condemned man's head, he paused to string the general's biography across his chest. A minute later, Graham was hanged, his own life story dangling from his broken neck. The general's body was dragged from the gallows and torn to pieces by the crowd.

It was said that before entering that fateful April battle, James Graham wrote a poem to a distant lover. Centuries later, as if speaking for his own Scottish ancestors, Brewer recounted its lines: "He either fears his fate too much or his portion is but small, who dares to put it to the touch and win or lose it all."

CHAPTER VI

AUTUMN, 1924

EARL BREWER THUMBED THROUGH the stack of Saturday papers scattered across his dining room table. On weekends, after pulling himself from bed, Brewer spent his mornings riffling through the various editions of Delta newspapers. When his daughters were at home, they used to request he read the articles aloud. Now Brewer simply sat by himself, remarking on the assortment of local controversies to no one in particular.

About halfway through the *Bolivar County Democrat,* a blunt headline glared back from the page: CHINESE BARRED FROM ROSEDALE SCHOOLS. It had been less than a week since Brewer delivered the writ of mandamus to the Bolivar courthouse, and already the county was up in arms. News traveled quickly for such a slow-going town.

"A test case will be tried so as to settle the status of the Chinese as to school rights," the article read.

It is also stated, and we believe it true, that Ex-Governor Earl Brewer will espouse the cause of the Chinese in the controversy. This [is] fit and proper. A man who could not carry a single precinct in the State in his alleged race for Senator is surely the right man to try to force the white children of Mississippi to share their schools with the Chinese. And he will come as near to winning his case in court as he did being nominated for Senator at the primary election in August.

Fit and proper. A man who could not carry a single precinct in the State . . . The editor had nerve. To his credit, he was right. Brewer was precisely the "fit and proper" lawyer to take such a controversial case. The very fact that he lost the Senate race was motivation enough to bring such a fight against the county. If the *Democrat* thought that Brewer was going to recede into the shadows and wallow in his own defeat, they had the wrong man. Already a pariah, Brewer had not a shred of dignity left to destroy. He feared nothing because he had nothing—and in this way he was stronger than he had ever been.

On Monday, October 13, 1924, the rival *Clarksdale Register* published a response to the *Democrat*. Written by a young law student from Rosedale named Greek Rice Jr. and his classmate, I. J. Brocato, the editorial denounced the paper for its "malicious attack" on Brewer.

"You, as well as any other, and every citizen of the United States," they wrote, "have sworn, in every particular to uphold and sustain the constitution. This you have entirely and wholly failed to do, when you attempt to deprive and deny the Chinese, or any race or people under God's sun, the inherent right of equal and competent representation in any tribunal in the land."

They wrote that although they were also of the mind-set that Chinese should not attend white schools, every man had the right to a lawyer. If Brewer was going to be so bold as to file the suit, it was his professional prerogative.

There was an irony to the fact that Greek Rice Jr. was the man to defend Brewer from such an "unethical and unprincipled attack." Two days after Greek's article was published, the Bolivar County sheriff delivered summonses to his father, Greek Rice Sr., as well as L. C. Brown and Henry McGowen. They were charged with violating the constitutional rights of nine-year-old Martha Lum and ordered to appear at Rosedale's courthouse on November 5 for trial.

Setting the date for November was strategic. The judiciary would be in recess and would stay so until the end of the year. The Bolivar County judge was under no obligation to rule on the case until the court resumed session. Without a judge, the school board could delay the trial indefinitely. But on October 28, the Bolivar County court issued a notice that Judge William A. Alcorn of Coahoma County had agreed to take the case, despite the fact that court was not in session.

"The said cause shall be tried in vacation as in term time," read an announcement issued by Rosedale's first district court. "Judgments shall be entered therein in vacation as could be entered in term time."

While there is no record of any private conversation between Earl Brewer and the judge from his home district, it is likely Brewer had something to do with the fact that Alcorn decided to hear the case. Both men attended the same Presbyterian church in Clarksdale. They both began their public legal careers together in Mississippi's Eleventh District Court, and it was there they remained, aging into the twilight of their lives together.

Despite years of friendship, for Alcorn to assist Brewer by agreeing to hear the case, he was committing political suicide. Any other judge would have politely declined, using the excuse that the court was not in session. In doing so, he would avoid jeopardizing the support of the town's white electorate while still saving face with the local Chinese. There was no logical reason for why William Alcorn risked his entire career to hear a case he could have so easily ignored, but that is because Alcorn's reasoning had nothing to do with logic. It had all to do with history.

Born William Aristides Alcorn Jr. on October 20, 1868, the boy who would one day become a judge came into the world during the worst year of his father's short life. The first child of George and Mary Alcorn, young William, or Willie as he was called by his father, was burdened from birth as being the only glimmer of hope in a family devastated by war. The Alcorns of Friar's Point were once slaveholding planters, controlling great tracts of fertile cottonland in the Mississippi Delta. By the time William was born, the tables had turned and the Alcorns were vilified enemies of the Confederacy.

William's father, George Alcorn, and George's older brother, William Aristides, first moved to the Delta during the outbreak of the Civil War in April 1861. As Confederate troops opened fire on Fort Sumter, the two boys left Kentucky, the only home they had ever known, to live with their father, Randolph Alcorn, on his plantation at Friar's Point. Their uncle, James Alcorn, journeyed with them from the farmlands of Kentucky into the wilds of Mississippi.

"My uncle [brought us] to the Delta that day," William Aristides later wrote. "He led a horse with a side saddle on. My sister rode the horse . . . and I rode behind my uncle on his horse."

Uncle James had only one son, James Lusk, who also lived at a plantation on Friar's Point. In fact, it was James Lusk who was responsible for bringing the entire Alcorn family to the Delta—and it would be James Lusk who would come near to having the family exiled.

In 1844 Lusk, a swarthy, stock horse of a man, left the Kentucky legis-lature in search of fortune in the frontier country of the Yazoo Delta. He packed the family's household belongings, his wife, Mary Catherine, their children, and an elderly slave woman aboard a flatboat and set out on the Mississippi River.

After several days on the water, they arrived at a landing just south of Moon Lake in what had recently been christened Coahoma County. It was there Lusk decided to open a law practice and create the foundation for a cotton empire that would span generations. Within a decade, Lusk, his father, James, and his father's brother, Randolph, controlled nearly a dozen plantations, with hundreds of slaves working tens of thousands of acres of Delta farmland.

On the April day when young George and William Aristides Alcorn arrived at their father's plantation, their cousin, Lusk, was nowhere to be found. With the nation erupting into civil war, Lusk went to Louisiana in an effort to purchase slaves. He came home a few days later, the proud owner of "a slave girl named Molly of yellow color and about fourteen years of age." Molly would adopt the name Alcorn and spend the rest of her life at James Lusk's plantation. Of her six children, three were fair-skinned sons named James, Governor, and Judge, possibly after their father.

The two young brothers made a new home for themselves in the vast empire of their older cousin. They settled into the shade of wide porches and ate hog meat from polished silver. They rode horses along the edge of ripened cotton fields, careful not to lose their tracks. For just beyond the enchantment of their cousin's plantation was a fierce wilderness, a lawless frontier ruled only by nature.

Its thick woods of oak, gum, ash, and poplar were home to thousands of bears, panthers, wildcats, and wolves. In the still bayou waters, malaria festered and the brothers soon learned the taste of quinine and the metallic sweat of summer fevers. They grew to fear the Mississippi when spring rains caused the river stage to rise. They heard tales from nearby logging towns of a flood so strong it leveled the earth. Yet despite all the dangers of the wild, it was not the land that shaped the boys into hardened men. It was war.

"The soldiers began to drill at the schoolhouse where there was a nice playground," William Aristides recalled. "They started to form a company there, which I promised and did join." Both George and William became lieutenants in the Confederate Army. Their cousin, James Lusk, was appointed the brigadier general for the Mississippi state troops.

After Appomattox, George and his brother returned home to rebuild their plantations on the family land at Friar's Point. Four years of civil war had cost Mississippi fifty thousand lives and left much of the state a desolate forest of chimneys. For George and William Alcorn, to rebuild was to reckon with the devastation of a world they once ruled.

In 1868 George had a son. He named his firstborn child William Aristides Alcorn Jr., after his beloved older brother. The infant was born into a broken nation and a divided home. His father's cousin, once a brigadier general, returned to Mississippi to denounce the Confederacy and, bearing a signed presidential pardon, pledged his allegiance to the Republican Party. For reasons his cousins could not immediately comprehend, James Lusk revealed a fervid passion for black political equality.

The war had tested Lusk. It forced him to reckon with the cardinal sin of his people and his past. He had built an empire on the backs of enslaved men. He led children into battle to protect that empire. The longer he fought for the Confederacy, the less he believed in its cause. In private, Lusk discussed his admiration for the Union and for its president, Abraham Lincoln. Of all the hardship Lusk witnessed on the bloody battlefields of the Civil War, he expressed the most suffering following Lincoln's assassination.

"My heart is so sad from this news," Lusk wrote in his diary on April 20, 1865. "I see the future darkly, but oh the scenes of blood! When and where will this strife end?"

In the spring of 1865, the strife was far from ending. Lusk's eldest son, Milton, who had enlisted in the Confederacy at the onset of the war, was captured in Louisiana in 1863 and taken prisoner. Milton returned from the war a shadow of himself. He was nearly deaf and deeply disturbed. He drank to stave off fits of madness, and within a year of his homecoming committed suicide. Against his father's wishes, Lusk's youngest son, Henry, ran away in January 1865 to join his brother in the army. Less than a month after enlisting, Henry contracted typhoid fever and was dead by summer.

The war had taken two sons from James Lusk. It reshaped his morality and tested his faith. The great depths of depression and guilt that plagued Lusk transformed him. He became determined to make up for the sins of history. He declared himself a Republican and resolved to guide his state and its people out from slavery.

A politically ambitious man, Lusk also understood that if he wanted to hold office, he had to capitalize on the state's newly enfranchised freedmen. In the winter of 1867, the United States Congress passed a sweeping Reconstruction Act over the veto of President Andrew Johnson. For readmission into the Union, the act required Southern legislatures to ratify the Fourteenth Amendment and write new constitutions granting universal suffrage to black men. In Mississippi, the act created a new political majority almost overnight. More than eighty thousand black voters were registered by federal officials, as opposed to fewer than sixty thousand whites. These former slaves, liberated by Lincoln, joined the Republican Party.

James Lusk's reinvention as a Republican turned him from a war hero into a martyr. On December 8, 1868, Klansmen raided one of his plantations, inflicting an estimated $6,000 worth of damage. William Aristides Jr., living at a nearby plantation, was less than two months old.

George feared for the life of his infant son and spoke with his cousin. As Klan violence escalated, Lusk considered fleeing Friar's Point. On January 1, 1869, he wrote to Illinois representative Elihu Washburne: "I thought it best to guard the remainder of my plantations as well as I can until I see what Congress may do under Genl Grant's administration. Should there be no improvement, then I will make the best disposition of my estates, and leave the State."

But Lusk did not flee. Instead, he ran for governor on the Republican ticket, campaigning on the pledge that "society should no longer be governed by the pistol and the Bowie knife." His cousins stood firmly beside him. George Alcorn began publishing a newspaper, titled the *Weekly Delta*, which fully endorsed Lusk and consistently defended the Republican Party. His brother, William Aristides, ran for sheriff as a Republican.

Despite threats on their lives and their property, the Alcorn men held firmly to their positions. In the wake of the announcement of Lusk's candidacy, full-scale riots erupted in several Delta counties. Lusk's wife, Amelia, tried to persuade her husband to drop out of the race, believing that he "would fall at martyr under a cloud that would cover [his] grave."

James Lusk won the election by an overwhelming majority and was inaugurated governor of Mississippi on March 10, 1870. For the first time in the state's history, a black electorate had chosen its leader. "Secession," Lusk remarked in his inaugural address, "I have ever denounced as a fatal fallacy."

Throughout his time in office, Lusk remained true to his base. The centerpiece of his administration became a radical education platform, which would establish a system of public schools for both races. Free to all students, the governor's new education program consumed more public money in 1870 than all other government programs combined. The program proved to be remarkably successful, establishing the state's first university for blacks, Alcorn State University, and enrolling half of all Mississippi's children in elementary classes by 1875.

In developing the state's most successful model for public education, Lusk unwittingly brought about his own political demise. He built a school system that ran like a trip wire from the Piney Woods to the Yazoo Delta. All across Mississippi, clapboard classrooms fell victim to the aftershocks of war. In the words of Lusk's biographer, "Public education brought to the foreground the delicate and unresolved problem of race relations."

The Alcorn system of education, as it came to be known, proposed no integrated schooling, but the fear of such an idea sparked riots across the state. The *Jackson Clarion* warned that "a fund will be raised by taxing the property of people to build up a gigantic system of 'Public Education,' under the control of the imported amalgamationists."

Before the end of 1870, the Mississippi Klan surpassed all others in the South at purging public school teachers from the state. On November 30, 1871, Governor Alcorn resigned to accept an appointment to the US Senate. His dreams of ushering in a new era of racial equality ended in failure. After serving six years in the Senate, Lusk returned home to Friar's Point, where he endured yet another tragedy.

In 1878 a devastating epidemic of yellow fever swept through the Delta, killing thousands. In the river town of Greenville, more than a fifth of its twenty-three hundred residents died from the virus. "Criers went through the streets, shouting 'bring out your dead,'" wrote one historian, describing alleyways packed with burial wagons. The fever was a gruesome killer that "struck without warning," one Deltan recalled. "First, the flushed yellow face, the drunken look, the chills . . . then the delirium, black vomit, hemorrhage—and miraculous recovery or merciful death." For George Alcorn, who caught the virus in the fall of 1878, the illness brought "merciful death." His son, William Aristides Jr., was ten years old.

With no father in his life, the bright, impressionable boy was raised by his uncle and his second cousin, James Lusk. William spent his youth in the wide halls and high-ceilinged rooms of his cousin's Victorian mansion. His bare feet touched walnut floors, his bare hands Italian marble. Above him sparkled ornate crystal chandeliers, imported from Europe.

His life was a world away from the tenant cabins, clustered around his family's cotton fields. But there was something about the way Lusk spoke about his past that changed the way William saw his future. There was a great legacy left to be filled by the Alcorn family. It began with Governor James Lusk and would end with Judge William Aristides Jr.

Just four days before Judge Alcorn was to hear arguments in Brewer's case, the trustees of the Rosedale school board filed a demurrer. Their hope was that the case would be thrown out before even going to trial. The justification for excluding Martha Lum, the demurrer stated, was rooted in Mississippi's own constitution, specifically Section 207, which called for "separate schools for the white and colored races." The trustees argued that because Martha was colored, she was subject to the same laws that applied to colored children. The race of the child was reason enough to prove there was no legal basis for the suit.

"The bill shows on its face that complainant is a member of the Mongolian, or yellow race," the demurrer read. "Therefore, [she is] not entitled to attend the schools provided by law in the State of Mississippi for children of the white, or Caucasian race."

Had any other judge been assigned the case, the demurrer would likely have been granted and the suit discarded. The school board clearly had Mississippi law on its side. But Judge Alcorn was once Willie Alcorn, a fatherless boy of ten, who fell into the care of a cousin who believed that all children deserved to be educated as equals. Judge Alcorn's ruling on November 5, 1924, reflected that past. He ordered the board of trustees to admit Martha Lum into Rosedale's segregated white school.

"It is by the court ordered that the demurrer . . . is hereby overruled," Alcorn wrote in his decision. "The Clerk of the Circuit Court of the First Judicial District of Bolivar County, Mississippi, is hereby ordered and instructed to issue a writ of mandamus as prayed for in the petition . . . to admit petitioner, Martha Lum, as a pupil in the Rosedale Consolidated High School."

Judge Alcorn gave Brewer the victory he so greatly needed. Martha would be able to return to Rosedale Consolidated. Brewer told his clients they could send their daughter back to school, but he counseled them to wait for a short while, until tensions quieted down. Brewer didn't want to risk Martha's safety by sending her into the classroom while emotions ran high. He also had a sinking feeling that the school board would file an appeal to the state supreme court.

The board understood that the longer the litigation continued, the longer Martha would be forced to stay out of school. Without a verdict, she would be trapped in the indeterminate middle between black and white. Martha, and every other Chinese child in Mississippi, would have to wait for a judge to decide their social status, their race, their identity. As long as the case remained in court, Martha was neither black nor white. In a society with room for only two races, Martha belonged nowhere.

On December 5, just as Brewer feared, Rosedale's school board filed an appeal. The defendants, "feeling aggrieved at said judgment," demanded the case be heard again in Jackson, before the Mississippi Supreme Court. The appeal was signed by a new lawyer, a man by the name of Rush Knox, the state's attorney general. With the board's motion granted, Brewer's fight was far from over. In fact, it had only just begun.

The doors of the birdcage elevator whined to a close. An impeccably dressed colored man stood at the controls, cast in the tinted light streaming through the stained glass windows lining the elevator shaft. The controlman waited for Brewer to request a floor. For four years of his life, Brewer had given the same destination, the third floor, Office of the Executive. Now, on April 6, 1925, nearly a decade since leaving office, Brewer gave a different answer. He requested the second floor, the Mississippi Supreme Court.

The operator pulled a lever and the steel carriage shot upwards, past white tiled walls and a blur of colored glass. When the elevator came to a stop, its doors opened onto an alcove. Brewer stepped out, turned to his left, and entered a broad corridor. A line of gleaming Italian columns extended like sentries along the walls. Brewer followed the hallway to its eastern end, where four pillars of marble marked the entrance to the state supreme court chamber.

The small courtroom had already begun to fill with spectators. The majority of visitors were more voyeuristic than concerned with the outcome of the case. The trial was seen as a novelty, the first of its kind. "This is the first case of this nature ever to be brought to the courts of Mississippi," wrote a local reporter. "It is believed there has been no case similar to this one ever brought in the courts of the United States."

The swarm of onlookers milled about between the columned entryway and a gate of varnished wood. Running across the center of the room, the gate divided the audience from the bench of judges, an imposing semicircular row at the far side of the chamber. Brewer crossed through the crowd toward his seat beside the bench.

It was only when looking back on the public that the edges of the room became visible. There, standing quietly in the corners, dressed in the nicest linens poverty could afford, were members of the Chinese community. They came to see what would become of their children. Mothers held hands of daughters. Fathers held shoulders of sons. They waited.

Inside the marbled depths of an elegant statehouse, the fate of a young girl would now determine the fate of thousands. A future would be decided that day, and with it the future of a generation. Brewer took his place at the counsel's table as, with the crack of a gavel, the trial began.

Unlike most cases to reach the Mississippi Supreme Court, the verdict of *Rice v. Gong Lum* would be decided en banc. This meant that every judge would be present, a distinction reserved only for cases of significant importance. The full bench was composed of six judges: Chief Justice Sidney McCain Smith, John Burt Holden, William Henry Cook, William Dozier Anderson, James McGowen, and George Hamilton Ethridge.

Of the six men seated before Brewer, there was only one judge whose opinion would likely determine the outcome of the case. Judge Ethridge, unlike the other five justices, had experience in the field of education. He was a former teacher, who entered into politics to serve as the state's assistant attorney general during Brewer's administration. During the end of Brewer's term, as Theodore Bilbo ruthlessly forced Brewer out of office, Ethridge rode Bilbo's rising tide of popularity into a seat on the state supreme court. He had been there ever since. Brewer was keenly aware of the pull Ethridge would have in the court's decision, so much so that he planned to call the man out by name.

A cold and serious personality, Ethridge believed that a strong democracy was forged in the classroom. The role of education served only to shape and control the nation's electorate. "We must educate those who are to have the right of selecting the agents who are to exercise power and discharge its functions," he once wrote. He believed that public schools should be employed strictly to foster a dominant white political class that would determine the future of Mississippi.

Ethridge, like most statesmen of his day, was a steadfast segregationist. His father, Mark Ethridge, fought in the Civil War as a member of the Confederate Cavalry Corps under General Nathan Bedford Forrest, who'd risen to the highest ranks of the Ku Klux Klan. Ethridge saw segregation as the only means of maintaining a civil society, the best defense against another deadly war.

"The races are doomed to live side by side," Ethridge once wrote, "but must have separate associations and education. . . . No racial mixture has ever been satisfactory or produced good results for society. We are now living in harmony in the same land but in separate social spheres and this must continue for all time."

The chief justice selected the state's assistant attorney general, Elmer Clinton Sharp, to begin the trial by reading his oral argument in defense of Rosedale's school board. Sharp was a tired-looking man with gray eyes, a gray complexion, and thick, graying hair. It was evident from his build that he had not always been so frail. The years had merely caught up with him. Back in college, Sharp played right guard on the varsity football team. The team's captain was a young law student named William Henry Cook, who was now staring at Sharp from his position behind the supreme court bench.

Sharp began his argument by reciting both Section 207 of the Mississippi Constitution ("Separate schools shall be maintained for children of the white and colored races") and Section 1 of the Fourteenth Amendment ("No state shall make or enforce any law which shall abridge the privileges or immunities of citizens of the United States"). By juxtaposing the two sections, Sharp was able to demonstrate that the state and federal constitutions were fundamentally at odds when it came to the education of Martha Lum.

He calculated that Brewer would have to rely almost exclusively on the Fourteenth Amendment, while Sharp could build his argument around Section 207 of the Mississippi Constitution. To grant or deny Martha Lum entry into a white high school would require enforcing the laws of one body while violating the laws of another. In a few short sentences, Sharp had resurrected an age-old conflict, that between nation and state. He wagered everything on the belief that sons of the Confederacy would always side with Mississippi. The only way Sharp figured he would lose would be if Martha could somehow be classified as white.

"We come back to the question, and really the only question, involved in this case," he said. "Are Chinese children of the white race and entitled as such to attend the schools of the white race?"

Segregation, Sharp argued, was for the purpose of protecting the white race from all other races. This included the Chinese.

"It has been at all times the policy of the lawmakers of Mississippi to preserve the white schools for members of the Caucasian race alone," he continued. "Our lawmakers . . . were desirous of prohibiting an intermingling of any race with the Caucasian or white children of our state."

If the Caucasian race was considered white, then all other races were to be categorized as colored. Therefore, Sharp argued, Martha and all children of Chinese descent should be classed as Negroes. He stressed that there was no need for the judges to refer to the federal constitution in their deliberations. Mississippi had created segregation to the exclusive benefit of the white race.

"We do not have to look to the cases of other states," he said, "to determine the legislative classification of the Chinese or Mongolian race in Mississippi. The *status* or classification of this race has been declared and fixed by our own legislature. It has in unmistakable terms placed the Chinese or Mongolian race in the same category with the negro."

"We, therefore, submit that the demurrer should be sustained," Sharp concluded. "And that the judgment of the lower court should be reversed."

Sharp returned to his seat. His address had lasted only a few minutes. It may have been even shorter. Everything he could have said was already written into the state's constitution: "Separate schools shall be maintained for children of the white and colored races." In the eyes of the state, Martha was a colored child. Even while in the eyes of the nation, she was simply a child.

Brewer rose from his chair, his hulking figure towering over Sharp. He loped to the front of the court, his hands empty. He had no notes. He never needed any. At the back of the room, the Chinese were gathered together, a silent and powerful presence. Brewer leveled his gaze, took a breath, and began.

"The demurrer admits that Martha Lum is a citizen of the United States and of the state of Mississippi and a resident of Rosedale consolidated school district," Brewer stated. "She is denied admission to the school at which she presented herself solely on the ground that she is a Chinese child."

Before launching into the main argument of his defense and invoking the federal protections guaranteed by the Fourteenth Amendment, Brewer drew back. He was theatrical by nature and relished these waning moments of his fading career. Instead of talking about Martha, Brewer segued into a history lesson.

He recalled the passage of Mississippi's 1890 Constitution, a document that outlined the means by which segregation would be upheld in the state. It was a story and a document with which every judge—and every member of every single Mississippi court—was familiar. Brewer was simply biding his time. After the long-winded lecture, he returned to Martha.

"It is conceded that she is not of the race whose presence in the south occasioned the Constitutional and statutory provisions for separate schools," said Brewer. "The requirement in the Constitution of 1890 that separate schools must be maintained for the races dealt with only two races. The purpose was to make it certain that negro children should not attend the same school with white children."

There was no need to explain segregation to the court. They understood as well as he did that the races would always be separated in the South. Yet, in order for Brewer to win over the judges, he had to convince the men to see Martha as the federal government saw her. He had to shift the focus away from the color of her skin, to the strength of her character. He had to somehow convince the judges that a person should not be defined by their race, but by their ambition. Such words were so dangerous, they could have splintered stone.

"The state collects from all for the benefit of all," Brewer declared. "Martha Lum is one of the state's children and is entitled to the enjoyment of the privilege of the public school system without regard to her race."

There it was, the Fourteenth Amendment, the guardian of privileges for all citizens of all races. By speaking its lines, Brewer was demanding that the state see Martha not as a Mongolian, a Chinaman, a colored girl, or a yellow child, but as a citizen of the United States. He begged the State of Mississippi to do something it had never done before, to treat a student as a citizen "without regard to her race."

If there was silence, it was never recorded. If there were cheers, they too went unmarked. For as soon as Brewer uttered the words, he recoiled back on them. Maybe the notion was too revolutionary for the very man who devised it, or maybe he saw on the judges' faces the resolute prejudice against any threat to social order. He tempered his rhetoric into words they would understand. And in doing so, he committed a fatal flaw. He forced Martha back into her skin and let it dictate her future.

"It is merely suggested by opposing counsel that the Chinese children should attend the negro schools," said Brewer.

But it is clearly shown by the authorities cited herein that the Chinaman is not a "colored person" within the meaning of our laws. He would therefore not go to the negro school as a negro. The court will take judicial notice of the fact that members of the Mongolian race under our Jim Crow statute are treated as not belonging to the negro race. The Japanese are classified with the Chinese. These two races furnish some of the most intelligent and enterprising people. They certainly stand nearer to the white race than they do to the negro race. If the Caucasian is not ready to admit that the representative Mongolian is his equal, he is willing to concede that the Mongolian is on the hither side of the half-way line between the Caucasian and African.

In a feeble attempt to return to the equality that he was so quick to cast aside, Brewer closed out his speech with a reiteration of the Fourteenth Amendment. He recalled its lines from memory.

"We wish to be understood," he concluded, "that to exclude a Chinese citizen child from the public schools . . . is to do a thing prohibited by the last clause of the Fourteenth Amendment."

Brewer walked back to the counsel's table and eased himself into his chair beside the bench. The judges told the lawyers that they would confer and announce their ruling within the coming weeks. With a parting thud of the gavel, the session was over.

Brewer walked back through the crowd of spectators, under the marble pillars of the court's entryway and into a wide corridor. Its low ceiling seemed to bear down on the hallway.

At the end of the hall, the low beams opened into a soaring white plaster dome, the main rotunda of the state capitol building. Brewer could see senators, secretaries, and porters milling about in the balconies overhead. Their activity echoed off the dome's yellowing, smoke-stained walls.

At the upper reaches of the vault, carved into the rotunda, was a bust of Lady Justice. Her eyes were tied with a blindfold. In her hair were two magnolia blossoms, one above each ear. Her jaw was set in deliberation. Brewer passed beneath her as he made his way to the exit.

Four weeks after the trial, the Mississippi Supreme Court issued a verdict. The unanimous decision, written by Judge George Ethridge, was in favor of excluding Martha Lum from Rosedale's white school. In the ruling, Ethridge cited a decision that he himself had written eight years earlier.

He relied almost entirely on the precedent of *Moreau v. Grandich*, a case in which the white children of Antonio Grandich of Hancock County, Mississippi, were expelled from public school due to a rumor that the children's great-grandmother bore "negro blood." The rumor came about in part due to a revelation that two of Grandich's great-aunts may have married outside their race.

When it was brought to the court's attention that the children's great-grandparents were fully white and that the children could not possibly have descended from the great-aunts, Judge Ethridge still ruled in favor of expulsion—despite the undisputed fact that the children were genetically white. He sided with the school's board of trustees, giving them full power to determine the race of a student, regardless of the child's genetic history.

"In *Moreau v. Grandich*," Ethridge wrote in the *Rice v. Gong Lum* decision,

> we held that . . . the word "colored" included, not only negroes, but persons of mixed blood. In the argument in the present case it is insisted that this definition of "colored" limited and restricted the term "colored" entirely to persons of the negro race or who were of negro descent. We

think a careful reading of the opinion in the *Moreau v. Grandich* case, supra, in the light of the statement of the facts, shows that the court did not intend to restrict the term "colored" to persons having negro blood in their veins or who were descendants of negroes or of the negro race.

"It is the policy of this state to have and maintain separate schools and other places of association for the races so as to prevent race amalgamation," Ethridge continued. "Race amalgamation has been frowned on by Southern civilization always, and our people have always been of the opinion that it was better for all races to preserve their purity. However, the segregation laws have been so shaped as to show by their terms that it was the white race that was intended to be separated from the other races."

The court's ruling had serious consequences for ethnic enclaves throughout the state. Suddenly, to be anything other than white was to be defined as black. Thousands of first- and second-generation immigrants, who once navigated a permeable line between the races, now found themselves forced onto the Negro side of the Jim Crow South.

Upon conclusion of his decision, Ethridge dictated the terms by which Martha Lum, and all Chinese children in the state of Mississippi, could receive an education.

"If the plaintiff desires," Ethridge wrote, "she may attend the colored public schools of her district, or, if she does not so desire, she may go to a private school. . . . A parent under the decisions of the supreme court of the United States has a right to educate his child in a private school if he so desires. But the plaintiff is not entitled to attend a white public school."

CHAPTER VII

SPRING, 1925

THE NEWS CAME TO Martha by way of her mother. There was an anger in her voice that Martha had never heard before, like the sound of a snake writhing under its own skin. Katherine ordered her children to pack their bags. She said the courts had rendered a decision to exclude all Chinese students from Rosedale's high school. If Katherine's children could not return to classes, they would have to leave Mississippi.

It was early May and the rain swells had finally given way to summer. Just ten months earlier, Martha was preparing for exams, unfolding her books onto milk crates and Royal Crown Cola boxes. Now, in the spring of 1925, there was no reason to study. Martha and her sister had been out of school for nearly a year and there was little hope of ever returning.

Katherine decided to send the children north to Jackson, Michigan, where Jeu Gong's brother operated a laundry in the center of the city. Meanwhile, Katherine and Jeu Gong would sell the store in Mississippi. Katherine would find a new home, where the children could attend school. When the time was right, she would send for them.

The only land Martha had ever known were the river towns of the Mississippi Delta. What she knew of the North she learned mostly from Negros, a story about a cousin who went up to Detroit and returned with his own Cadillac, a sister who left for Chicago and never looked back. Then there were her own family's stories, recounted to Martha by her big sister Berda, the vague childhood memories of their uncle, Ah Bok, and his son Lee, who came south when the war in Europe was over.

They talked about the chop suey shops and teahouses, streets of people speaking their native Cantonese. Berda was suddenly an expert in this foreign land of their distant family. There was something deep within her that had always wanted to leave Mississippi, to travel, to know more of the world outside Rosedale.

Unable to discern exactly what she would need in the North, Martha packed what she could. She selected several hand-sewn dresses, each one not quite fashionable enough for metropolitan life, with their faded fabric and uneven collars. Martha's mother urged her daughter to wear the dresses with pride. Miss Sales was a good seamstress. She worked hard.

Miss Sales didn't have a sewing machine of her own, so she came to the Lum house to do her sewing. Martha watched Miss Sales work, her brown fingers binding the thread, feet moving steadily over the pedal. She built a business out of that machine, hemming and sewing dresses for all the colored folk.

In return, Miss Sales cared for the children. On Saturdays, when Katherine was busy at the grocery, Miss Sales prepared supper. On weekdays, when the children returned home from school, Miss Sales made sure they completed their studies. Martha grew accustomed to the meter of her machine, the taste of her cooking, the comfort of her conversation.

Then one day Miss Sales was gone, the sewing machine frozen in place, untouched. When Martha asked her mother where Miss Sales had gone, Katherine responded that she moved to Chicago. There was no more of an explanation. Katherine didn't tell her daughter that Miss Sales left in a hurry, that she begged Katherine to come with her, that the souls strung from branches, hung from bridges, drowned in rivers were too much a burden to bear. Folding Miss Sales's dresses, Martha packed all that was left of her nanny into a suitcase and prepared to follow her north.

The children arrived at the Rosedale depot shortly before the midday train from Vicksburg. Across the tracks, the bright letters of the Lum grocery flashed along the red brick of their house at the far end of Bruce Street. Katherine placed into Berda's palm a tiny purse, bursting with rolled bills. She was told to guard it carefully, for the money would provide a safe passage north.

Martha, Berda, and Biscoe, who was just barely six, stood on the platform as the Illinois Central eased into the station, passing the old hay warehouse, the ice plant, and the vacant outpost of the Coca-Cola Bottling

Company. This was the same train Martha used to chase, watching the faces pass by in the windows, traveling to cities she could only imagine. Now it was Martha's turn to become one of those faces, staring out from a boxcar as it hurtled through small country towns, where barefooted children chased the pound of an engine, waving at strangers headed to those far-off, imaginary places.

Martha picked up her suitcase and walked to the entrance of the train, taking her place in line. A railing divided the stairs on the platform, one side for white passengers, the other for colored. Shifting on her feet, Martha moved to the left side of the stairs, where the white passengers waited to board the back of the train. The colored car was always the front car of the train, closest to the engine and the danger and soot that went along with it. The children trailed each other through the open door of the train and down its narrow aisles. Coming to an empty row, they folded themselves onto the frame of their seats and waited for departure.

Once, in third grade, when Martha was studying American literature, she read a story about a colored girl named Olive who was raised to believe she was white. The girl's mother, Madame Delphine, tried to give her daughter a better life. She promised Olive to a charitable banker named Monsieur Vignevielle, but in order to make this promise, Madame Delphine had to disown her only child.

"Oh, my darling little one, you are not my daughter!" Madame Delphine said to Olive.

On a warm summer day, at a noon wedding inside a little church, Madame Delphine quietly watched her daughter marry the wealthy white banker and become a proper Southern lady. After the service, Madame Delphine entered the confessional, where she told the priest the sin of her deception. There kneeling, with her forehead resting in her hands, Madame Delphine died.

"It makes little difference whether it is all true to life or not," read a passage in Martha's textbook. "In literature one looks for the spirit of a time and place, not for historical accuracy." What was important about the story, the textbook said, was the lesson of a mother "who for the sake of her beautiful daughter, sacrifices herself."

With a shudder of steel, the train pulled away from the station. Martha watched as the wide platform of the depot slowly drifted from view. Behind her was a childhood, races over the levee walls, hymnals, revivals and churchyard picnics, the slow pop of salted fatback sputtering in her mother's skillet, the shine of cotton pickers, cleaned up sharp on a Saturday night after harvest. The train gathered speed and with it Martha's old life moved into the past. She prepared herself for a future in a distant city.

Biscoe was restless. He complained about needing to relieve himself. As the eldest, and the one in charge of the money, Berda acted the parent. As Biscoe's complaints continued to escalate, Berda promised to escort him to the restroom. She nudged Martha out of her seat and pushed her two siblings up the aisle. Together, they tottered along the train cars until Biscoe finally found the toilet.

The calm that followed Biscoe's crisis quickly dissipated. In her rush to soothe her brother, Berda had forgotten the coin purse on the seat. The children worked their way back to the rear of the train. When they arrived at their bench, it was empty. All of the money was gone.

A sense of dread passed over the children. Without money, there would be no food, no way to send a telegram home. There was nothing with which to purchase a return voyage if Ah Bok was not waiting for them in Michigan. Without any hope of recovering the coin purse, the children resigned themselves to their fate. After several hours, the train reached Cairo, where the track crossed over a wide river and turned northward, toward Chicago.

It was long past nightfall when the lights of the city began to shimmer along the shoreline of Lake Michigan. As the engine slowed to approach the station, a ripple of excitement ran through the train car. The children stirred themselves awake and looked out at the magnificent spectacle of Chicago's Illinois Central Station.

Overhead, a thirteen-story clock tower glimmered above a giant pavilion. Its wide shadow darkened a string of wooden pilings that wandered into the surf, following one another to the end of the line, where the railroad's lakeshore tracks met Michigan Avenue. For thousands of Southern blacks, the depot was far more than a destination, it was a beacon, the threshold to a promised land. The Illinois Central Station connected Chicago to the South and served as the city's primary site of arrival for what came to be known as the Great Migration.

Arriving at the station, passengers from the colored car exited in one steady torrent, filling the platform in a matter of minutes. Like Martha and her siblings, they carried with them all they owned for their new life in the North. They came wearing headscarves, holding rucksacks, and speaking in slow Delta drawls. Hundreds came every day. They arrived in swells, flooding the station by the carload, from every southern branch of the Illinois Central.

Just three years earlier, a twenty-one-year-old trumpeter arriving from New Orleans stepped off the very same train onto the very same platform. His name was Louis Armstrong. "When the conductor came through the train hollering, 'Chicago, next stop,'" the musician recalled years later, "a funny feeling started running up and down my spine."

The excitement that crawled down the spine of Louis Armstrong now found its way into Martha Lum. The children exited the car and crossed through the station. They boarded another train near the switching yards. Its engine jerked into motion and soon the lights of the city were behind them as they journeyed east along the southern shores of Lake Michigan.

The train arrived at Jackson Station in the early-morning hours. At the west end of the depot, a gatekeeper swung open a fence that stretched across the tracks. He flagged the train toward the platform. Hungry and exhausted, the children exited the train car. A long, overhanging eave blanketed the depot, blocking the thin rays of morning light that were starting to move west along the rails and onto the city beyond. Martha and her siblings crossed out of the station and turned onto Main Street.

The roadway was crowded with the chaotic choreography of an industrialized city at daybreak. Enginemen tromped to the track yards, coal shovels slung over their shoulders. Negro train porters hurried inside the station, their chests lined with polished brass buttons. Metalworkers gathered in packs outside iron and steel mills, as sparks flared onto the sidewalk from foundry furnaces along East Michigan Avenue. Paperboys shouted from street corners, hocking the labor party's *Square Deal* newspaper to hundreds of factory workers, all flocking to build rims, wheels, nuts, bolts, lugs, and wrenches for Detroit's automobiles.

The children passed under awnings of fruit vendors, where old Italian men scolded their grandsons and unloaded crates of produce. A streetcar barreled past, making its way down the winding row of storefronts.

Michigan was like no place Martha had ever seen. Even the air was different. Coal smoke burned like a scorched rag in her throat. Somewhere off in
the distance shone the hazy gray peak of the power company.

At the corner of Mechanic and Main, the children turned right. Just a
few paces brought them to the doorstep of their uncle's laundry, their new
home. Mechanic Street teemed with life. At one end was City Hall and at
the other a prison. Gow Lum's laundry was somewhere in between. The
small business was sandwiched between two boarding houses, a butcher,
a coffee roaster, a fish market, a drugstore, the Union Restaurant, and the
Grand Union Tea Company.

Standing at the door to the laundry, waiting to enter, Martha was not
so different from the young Jeu Gong, who had also arrived on the shores
of Lake Michigan, holding in his memory all that remained of a life in a
distant land. Yet Martha's homeland was not the old country of her father.
He spoke a language of *nam fong* and *bok bok*. He knew of ancient villages,
of great dynasties, of deep family tradition. Martha spoke a language of
"ain'ts" and "reckons." She knew the taste of sweet tea and grits, the smell
of pole beans boiled in salt pork. Arriving in the North, Martha became a
migrant among immigrants, still a child, already twice removed from the
ancestry she was taught to call her own.

The laundry was a crowded place. Rows of flames flickered behind dark
curtains of drying cloth. A machine called "the mangle" towered over the
room, its two round pressing wheels crushing pile after pile of steaming
white cloth. The children wended their way between great vats of boiling
linens and strange men shouting strange words over the spit of irons. Their
uncle spoke to his wife in Cantonese; neither was eager to greet the children. To Gow Lum and his wife, Martha and her brother and sister were
simply three more mouths to feed. It did not matter that they were family
or that Jeu Gong had cared for his brother after the war. Gow Lum would
make it known to the children that they were a burden on him.

Berda took her uncle's rejection harder than Martha. Living in a home
where she knew she was not welcome, Berda became spiteful. She learned
Cantonese so she could curse at her aunt and uncle in their native tongue.
She studied all the terrible words first and let them fall from her lips with
practiced precision.

Once Berda began to understand full sentences, her aunt, *Ah Mo*, re-taliated with language far more hurtful than curse words. She told Berda that the children's mother was not really a Wong, but a *mui tsai*, a slave. Katherine was bought from poverty, from a nothing family somewhere near the coast. She was traded for a red packet of money, sold like a beast. Jeu Gong's wife was a stain on the face of the family and now the stain had made its way into *Ah Mo's* home. Out of anger, Berda hid their mother's secret. She kept it from her sister for another sixty years.

Martha made no effort to learn Cantonese, and she complained about her aunt's traditional Chinese cooking. Instead, Martha focused her en-ergies on schoolwork and the labor of the laundry. As summer turned to fall and fall to winter, Martha studied with the other immigrant children, walking down Mechanic, through the snow to the schoolhouse. There were twenty public schools within the city limits, and Martha was not excluded from any of them. In Rosedale there was only one school and it was for the white children. In Jackson, there were schools for all kinds of children, most of them immigrants, Irish, Polish, German, Italian, Russian, and Chinese.

Even with her immigrant roots, Martha had more in common with the colored children who lived in crowded city blocks on the other side of town. To keep Martha from being classed as colored, from being forced into col-ored schools and colored society, the Lum family joined an exodus as large as any wave of immigration, the exodus of millions of Negroes from the American South.

It followed a current that traced the central spine of the continent, from the cotton fields of Mississippi, Alabama, Tennessee, and Arkansas to the industrial cities of Cleveland, Detroit, Chicago, Milwaukee, and Pitts-burgh. In leaving Rosedale, the children became part of a protest that was taking place in homes all across the South.

"Oftentimes, just to go away," wrote John Dollard, a Yale scholar study-ing Negro migration in the 1930s, "is one of the most aggressive things that another person can do, and if the means of expressing discontent are lim-ited, as in this case, it is one of the few ways in which pressure can be put."

Martha did not see herself as part of a greater movement. She was a ten-year-old girl, with worries far more immediate and personal. She did not know when she would see her mother again. She longed for the famil-iar things she used to taste, smell, and touch. She could not write in the language of her father and he could not write to his daughter in words that she could read. So Martha lived in isolation, a stranger in a cold world.

One day in early spring, Martha's mother arrived on a train from Chicago. When Katherine entered the laundry, she was alarmed at the changes her children had undergone. Their bodies were thin and fragile, their skin streaked with soot. Their clothing was torn, their shoes full of holes. For decades, Martha would remember the sting of ice against her feet. After one year in the North, Katherine's children appeared to her as beggars. She packed their belongings and led them to the depot. She bought four tickets back to the South.

CHAPTER VIII

AUTUMN, 1925

RAIN HAMMERED AGAINST THE roof of the Clarksdale courthouse. Along Delta Avenue, a trail of hooded figures lumbered through the storm toward the bright electric lights of the court. The meeting was called for eight o'clock, which was well past nightfall on this particular Saturday in late October. A row of ushers lined either side of the lobby, each dressed in matching white robes, their faces cloaked in ghostly triangular hoods. Greeting and shaking hands, local members of the Ku Klux Klan welcomed visitors to the evening's lecture. The guest of honor was Dr. Sam Campbell of Atlanta. His topic, "The Making of a Klansman."

Pastor Macon Vick of the First Baptist Church began the evening with a sermon, his voice modulating with the deliberate reverence of a Sunday service. When he finished his invocation, Vick led the congregation in song. "My country 'tis of thee," the pastor began softly. "Sweet land of liberty."

A chorus of cheers erupted from within the crowded hall as the audience joined in the singing. "Land where my fathers died, land of the pilgrims' pride. From ev'ry mountainside, let freedom ring!"

As applause filled the courthouse, Dr. Campbell made his way to the stage. He was a tall, forceful-looking middle-aged man with a high forehead, a pale, narrow face, and a stern mouth that seemed to tether one taut cheek to the other. He carried none of the markings of the stone-broke field hand he had once been. Sometime in his twenties, Dr. Campbell left behind his mule and plow in the high Georgia hills to be reborn a minister. He traveled the country preaching the doctrine of white supremacy and the teachings of the Holy Book.

Campbell began his speech with a discussion of Congress and its recent ratification of the Johnson-Reed Immigration Act. He mentioned that while they never received credit, the Knights of the Ku Klux Klan were directly responsible for the passage of the bill. It was the Klan that "put it over," he explained, and the Knights were well overdue for their public recognition.

He warned the people of Clarksdale that America was under threat from the many different races living within its borders. "There is no melting pot, and never can be," he declared emphatically. "It is impossible for the negro, Mexican, Jap, Chinaman, Turk and what-not to mix with true-blooded Americans.

"We cannot allow foreign peoples to trample Christ under foot," he continued, "and tear down our Christian institutions and ideals for which our forefathers have always stood, ever since our nation was founded. The Klan at the close of the Civil War came to the rescue and in this instance our ideals were preserved. The very soul of our country is at stake, and it is our sacred duty to protect the soul of our beloved America, just as much today as it was then."

As Campbell came to the end of his lecture, the audience grew silent, hanging on every word.

"It requires three things to make a Klansman," he concluded:

purpose, material and time. The purpose of the Klansman is to promote and sustain a love of God and country, to protect the Christian ideals and institutions of our country, to uphold white supremacy, to aid in the enforcement of the laws of our nation. What sort of material is required for the qualification of a Klansman? "Not for self, but for others," is a Klansman's motto and if he fails in this, he has failed in his trust. When will the Klan die? Never! Not until victory is won and each Klansman and Klanswoman has done their bit.

The audience leaped from their seats, clapping their hands with wild enthusiasm. They shouted and pounded their boots against the floor. The walls rattled inside Clarksdale's courthouse.

In a small, dimly lit jail one block away, a black prisoner stirred in his cell. The air was cold, near freezing, and John Fisher struggled to keep warm. He had been there for over a week and was starting to lose track of time. On the night of October 16, he'd awakened to torchlights and the howl of bloodhounds outside his cabin beside Traynham Plantation. Someone pounded on Fisher's front door until it snapped on its hinges and swung open. A pack of dogs surged through the entryway and tore at Fisher's clothes and body.

Then the men came. More than a dozen of them, white and rabid in the eyes, lawmen and townsmen, shouting all the ways they would kill Fisher that night in the woods. The men held in their hands the instruments with which to carry out the attack; they had known before leaving their homes that morning there would be a lynching come nightfall. Such an assembly, so common to Mississippi, was described in chilling detail by James Howell Street, a journalist born and raised in Jones County. Street witnessed his first lynching at fourteen. He wrote:

> They called the neighbors. They pulled pistols from oiled rags in bu-
> reaus, lifted shotguns from pegs over the mantels. They needed dogs.
> Bob Gant's were the best in the state. Three men piled into an auto-
> mobile and thundered into the night—ninety miles over rough roads to
> Bob's house.

The Clarksdale men arrived at Traynham Plantation before midnight. They followed Gant's hounds to the backwoods shanty that belonged to John Fisher. Had it not been for four of the sheriff's deputies, who safely spirited Fisher to jail, he would have been dead by sunrise.

The following morning, Fisher was charged with the murder of Grover C. Nicholas, the adopted son of a prominent Delta planter named James Traynham. Nicholas's body had been found inside the plantation's commis-sary, bludgeoned to death with the blunt end of an ax. Fisher denied any part in the crime, telling the officers he'd spent the previous day repairing an old car with his neighbor.

By the end of October, the officers jailed four other Negroes for the same crime: Raeford Leonard, who worked on the Traynham plantation; Lindsey Coleman, a young tenant farmer who lived with Leonard; Smith Bunns, a local teenager; and Albert Hobbs, a former preacher.

Throughout the course of several days, the sheriff's deputies, led by a man named Hicks Ellis, employed what they called a "rope and water cure" to extract confessions from the five prisoners. Fisher recalled the group of men forcing him to the floor and binding his arms and legs with rope. Then Hick Ellis lifted Fisher's chin and allowed water to pour over his face and into his nostrils. The last thing Fisher remembered before falling unconscious was the fear that he was drowning.

After a week of this torture, Fisher finally cracked. He gave a confession on November 4. Leonard and Hobbs confessed shortly thereafter. Bunns died in jail. He was found dead in his cell with a broken neck; the authorities said he'd suffered an epileptic seizure. Lindsey Coleman was the only man who continued to proclaim his innocence.

When it came time for trial, Hobbs turned on the other prisoners. Newspapers reported that he "made a splendid witness for the prosecution," telling jurors, "how he fasted and prayed to God for guidance and help and finally decided that God would not help or hear him with a lie upon his lips." For his service, Hobbs was released. With the help of his testimony, John Fisher was sentenced to death and Raeford Leonard was sentenced to life in prison.

It was Coleman, the only man not to break under torture, who was the last to face trial. On December 19, 1925, he stood before a jury and affirmed his innocence, just as he had when jailers poured water into his lungs, bent his fingers until they nearly broke, and called him "nigger" as they tied a noose around his neck. After eight hours of deliberation, Judge Alcorn read the jury's verdict, his voice breaking in disbelief: "The jury finds the defendant not guilty."

Earl Brewer was not present for the trial. He, like everyone else in Clarksdale, assumed the Negro would hang. Instead, Coleman exited the courthouse on that cold December night a free and innocent man. Brewer was not there to see the way Coleman walked down the courthouse steps, dressed in the same jacket he wore as a soldier in the Great War, the finest suit he ever owned. Brewer was not there to see Coleman taken by a group of white men and forced into a waiting car. He was not there to see the men speed off down Yazoo Avenue.

Instead, Brewer was there to read the coroner's report, to learn that Coleman's body, still dressed in his army uniform, was found riddled with twenty-six bullet holes and tossed onto the street just three blocks from the courthouse. He learned that the sheriff and his men refused to intervene to save the Negro's life. He was told there were witnesses, including the sheriff himself, but that no one was willing to testify. A murder had been committed outside the town's very hall of justice, and the city did not have the courage to prosecute the killers.

Brewer could not know how the lynching of Lindsey Coleman would alter the course of his life, and therein alter the course of history. He had no idea that the seeds of an entire revolution were sitting in stacks of half-written briefs inside his law office. He did not know that in seeking retribution for Coleman, he would neglect another fight. He would forsake a case that could have brought one of the greatest civil rights victories in American history. He would lose sight of Martha Lum and, in doing so, abandon the first United States Supreme Court case to challenge segregation in public schools.

The telephone in the parlor room rang without pause. Minnie Marion Brewer held the mouthpiece in her hand, directing calls in the same manner a captain might steer a ship. She answered questions from the governor, from United States senators, from newspapers throughout the country.

"It was high-handed murder," Marion shouted through the telephone at a reporter from the Associated Press. "The women of Coahoma County are outraged at this mob violence in the heart of our city."

Brewer had never seen this side of his wife's character. When he was governor, Marion received accolades for her success as a dutiful homemaker. "She has made an especially gracious mistress of the Mansion," a biographer wrote after visiting the Brewer family in Jackson. "Mrs. Brewer is a considerate helpmeet to her husband . . . and has kept his home life serene and sweet, and afar from the bitter turmoil of public life."

It was not like Marion to take up causes. She was faithful and loving, but never political, never outspoken. This was a changed woman sitting on the small wooden chair beside the telephone. He loved her now more than ever.

On the Tuesday following the murder, Mrs. Brewer held a meeting at City Hall, inviting over one hundred women from across the county. She stood before a packed house and appointed a committee of women to investigate the lynching of Lindsey Coleman. She dictated a resolution that was printed in papers throughout the state. "Be it resolved that we unqualifiedly condemn all acts of lawlessness," she announced. "That we pledge ourselves and call upon every other citizen to uphold the law and aid in every way possible the officers of the court in its enforcement and in the punishment of those responsible for the murder."

Meanwhile, Brewer tried to determine the means by which he could conduct a trial. Such a case had never been tried in the county. It would be the first time a white man had gone on trial for his life in the murder of a Negro. If Brewer wanted Coleman's killers to face a jury, he had to first find a credible witness to testify against them. He knew there were dozens of men who were present when Coleman was taken, but no man in Coahoma County would risk his social standing, and possibly his life, to testify against the lynchers. Determining that it would be impossible to turn a citizen into a witness, Brewer came up with another idea. He would make a witness out of the sheriff.

The day following the lynching, Brewer spoke with Judge Alcorn and arranged to have the county sheriff indicted on two counts of "failing to perform his duty." One count was for failing to protect Coleman as he was leaving the courthouse and the other was for failing to intervene when John Fisher was tortured in jail. For both indictments, Brewer invoked Section 1024 of Mississippi's Hemingway's Code, which stated, "If any judge, justice of the peace, constable, member of the board of supervisors, sheriff, coroner or other peace officer, shall willfully neglect or refuse to return any person committing any offense against the laws committed in his view or knowledge . . . he shall upon conviction be fined not less than $100 nor more than $500 and may in the discretion of the court be removed from office."

In reality, Brewer didn't want the sheriff's case to go to trial. It would have likely resulted in a hung jury and an elaborate string of appeals that would have gone on for months. Of course, this was not what he told Sheriff S. W. Glass. Brewer and Alcorn explained to Glass that if the jury found him guilty, he would be removed from office, destroying any chance he had for reelection. For a man whose only pride was in his occupation, the threat was a death sentence. Glass quickly struck a deal with the judge that he would plead guilty, pay a fine of $500, and quietly vacate his post until the trial was over, at which point he would resume his position as the county's chief law officer. In return, Glass had to serve as a witness for the state.

As Mrs. Brewer was forming her coalition of women at City Hall, Brewer was at the courthouse, where nearly a hundred men had gathered before Judge Alcorn for the selection of a grand jury. Alcorn calmed the crowd. Then he ordered the assembly to "find out the parties that did this, use the power of the state and bring to justice anyone that has had a part in this crime." Alcorn selected the twelve men who would compose the jury and render a verdict in the murder of Lindsey Coleman. Now all Brewer needed were the defendants to charge with the crime.

The next day, Brewer called for a meeting of the Coahoma County Bar Association. Twenty-five lawyers from across the county met at the courthouse to discuss the lynching. When they arrived, Sheriff Glass was sitting near the front of the courtroom. He came at the request of Brewer, who had asked the sheriff to submit to questioning before the panel of lawyers.

Brewer jumped right into the interrogation. He directed Glass, in a stern voice, to name the men responsible for the lynching. Glass grew visibly uncomfortable. He moved his eyes over the room. He responded that he "wasn't sure if it was proper" to answer such a question. Brewer changed his tone. He grew forceful and impatient. They made a deal. He wanted names.

"You are the sheriff and chief law officer in the county," Brewer snapped. "The bar here assembled in mass wants to know from you, the sheriff, who these parties were."

In response, the sheriff listed four names: James Traynham, the Delta planter and adoptive father of Grover Nicholas; Thomas Nicholas, the brother of Grover Nicholas; Gold Cane, a manager at Traynham Plantation; and H. S. Blockley, a photographer from Clarksdale who was married to Grover Nicholas's niece.

On Christmas Eve, the grand jury returned indictments of murder against all four men. It was decided that Gold Cane would be the first to face trial. He had the least social standing of the four, but was likely to have the strongest defense, as he had already hired a team of six attorneys. On the day the trial was announced, Brewer volunteered his services for the prosecution. In doing so, the ex-governor became the first lawyer in Coahoma County to try a white man for the murder of a Negro.

James Flowers sat at his law office in Jackson, Mississippi. His desk was flooded with letters, most of them congratulatory, with a spare few offering a barrage of insults. As president of the Mississippi Bar Association, he had recently taken the first political stance of his life and published a pamphlet condemning lynching. It was a bold move for a man who, until this point, had been a corporate lawyer for the Gulf, Mobile and Ohio Railroad.

Flowers was now in the process of preparing a second edition of the pamphlet, just two weeks after he issued the first. There had been a lynching in Clarksdale just before Christmas, so he felt compelled to update the report to include the events of December 19, 1925. "Sinking to depths of ignominy with the lynching of the acquitted negro Lindsey Coleman at Clarksdale," Flowers inserted in italics, "Mississippi closed the year with six of the nation's total of 16 lynchings."

Flowers relied heavily on statistics. His hope was that the sheer number of lynchings would be "enough to stagger and to shame." He was a practical man, who believed in motivating the public through fact over emotion, and his antilynching pamphlet showcased this trait. "During the last forty years, mobs murdered 4,144 men and women," he wrote, adding that "1,036 of the victims were white and 3,162 were colored. . . . Mississippi has 530 lynchings to her discredit."

For a man who did not champion political causes, the lawyer's report provided precise documentation of the nation's legacy of lynching. His research was meticulous and demonstrated a commitment to accuracy rarely seen in political propaganda. He closed out his passage on statistics with a heartbreaking clause explaining his margin of error.

These figures patiently and persistently gathered over four decades do not tell the full story of bloodshed and lawlessness. They do not take into account the hundreds killed in the bloody race riots at East St. Louis, Tulsa, Washington, and Chicago, or the isolated individuals done to death in the dead of night by craven cowards, with no feature story in the newspapers and little or no investigation in the grand jury room.

Jokingly nicknamed General Flowers due to a demeanor that was quite the opposite of a general, at age fifty-five, James Nathaniel Flowers had finally taken a stand. Some of his greatest praise came from the former governor Earl Brewer. Brewer, like Flowers, had been born in Carroll County. Both men had received degrees from the University of Mississippi, and both were the favorite sons of Confederate veterans. Yet when it came to law, the two men could not have been more different. Brewer began his career as a labor lawyer, taking cases for injured railroad workers and their families. Flowers was currently chief counsel for one of the largest rail lines in the state.

So it came as both a compliment and a surprise to Flowers when Brewer asked him to take over as lead attorney on a Fourteenth Amendment case that was on its way to the US Supreme Court. It was an appeal out of Rosedale by a Chinese family who wanted to send their daughter to the white public high school. Flowers had very little experience with these kinds of cases, but Brewer asked a favor of him, and out of respect for the ex-governor, Flowers obliged.

Brewer, for his part, would offer Flowers some support, but also made it clear that he was going to lead the prosecution against four men responsible for the Clarksdale lynching. This would mean that Flowers would be shouldered with most of the responsibility in the school case. Through one simple arrangement, the case of *Gong Lum v. Rice*, and the fate of Martha Lum, was handed off to a novice.

Court convened at 9:30 a.m. on January 7 for the murder trial of Gold Cane. In total, forty-one witnesses had been subpoenaed to testify in the case, so everyone in town knew someone involved in the trial. By midday, the courtroom was overflowing with spectators. They stood in clusters behind rows of chairs spread out across the courtroom.

A reporter for the *Clarksdale Register* noted that a significant number of Negroes had come to witness the deliberations. This seemed unusual to him, as he rarely saw colored spectators in court, and he made a point of adding an additional paragraph at the end of his article to highlight the abnormality.

Rumor was that Sheriff Glass was going to testify against Cane. As the afternoon wore on, the crowd grew restless with anticipation. Glass took the stand shortly after 4 p.m. His face was pale and he tapped his fingers nervously on the wooden banister by his waist. The jury sat directly to his right, all twelve of them, elevated above the court in two rows of six. They were an imposing sight, wealthy planters and bankers, dressed in expensive suits, leaning their heads on their hands, waiting.

Glass collected his nerves and, in a somber tone, began to describe what he saw on the night of December 19. Two men grabbed Coleman as he was leaving the courthouse. Glass recognized one of them as Gold Cane. The two men took Coleman out onto Yazoo Avenue, on the east side of the courthouse.

"They brought him to the car," Glass explained. "There were twelve or fifteen men around them. . . . I grabbed Coleman but was pushed back onto the street."

When Glass stood up, the men and the car were gone. The next thing he heard was that a body had been found on Desoto Avenue, bleeding onto the street from twenty-six bullet wounds.

Although visibly uncomfortable, Glass gave a strong performance, and Brewer left the court with a sense of relief. When a journalist from Memphis tried to stop the lawyer on his way out the door, shouting questions over the noise of the crowd, Brewer merely responded with a smile. The reporter noted that Brewer's wide grin was all his readers needed to know about the direction of the case.

Five days later, on January 12, the jury reported to the court for closing arguments. They had heard dozens of testimonies and sat through hours of cross-examination. Following a rather short speech by the defense, Brewer gave the final word for the state. He made it clear to the men of the jury that he already served his time as the county's district attorney, that he had no expectation of ever trying another murder case. But this heinous crime drew him back into the courtroom, not as a hired lawyer, but as a citizen of Clarksdale.

"I am before you today as a representative of the people of Coahoma County," he said. "I am here because an effort has been made to run over the law and trample it beneath the feet of those who disregard lawful society and set up mob law in this peace."

Brewer's wife watched from the audience. Facing the judge and jury, he could not meet her eyes. It was only when he turned around to address the crowd that he saw her. She was surrounded by other women, her own coalition, a body politic of wives, mothers, and daughters, seeking retribution for the murder of a colored man they did not know.

"Some folks enjoy killing," Brewer continued. "I know some men who would drive halfway across the state to assist in the hanging of a negro, even when they didn't know a thing about the crime he is supposed to have committed. That's the vicious element. Let folks once understand that [if] lawlessness will be permitted, a state of anarchy will exist."

Following the death of his father, Brewer had organized a club called the Wildcat Society in a little country schoolhouse near his farm in Carroll County. The club met on Saturday nights to hold mock debates between local farmboys. One night, two older men came to the meeting. They talked about another society called the Ku Klux Klan. They made a proposal: the boys would do the work of the Klan and gain the privilege of binding themselves to a respectable society. The men said there were some worthless Negroes in the neighborhood who needed to be whipped, and that it was the duty of the Wildcats to attend to it.

The boys then unanimously passed a resolution to devote themselves to the cause of the Klan, to go out on Saturday nights and "take these negroes out and whip them and run them out of the country." Brewer, the youngest boy in the room, was the only member to voice concern that whipping Negroes was against the law.

"He got a rabbit in him," one boy chided. "He's gettin weak in the melt," said another.

As the boys laughed, Brewer silently returned to his seat, afraid to be called a coward. He agreed to meet back at the clubhouse the following week and bring with him a white mask that he sewed at his mother's kitchen table. The next week, as Brewer left to attend the Saturday meeting, his mother stopped him at the door. She told Brewer that a society that hides its face is not a society worthy of her son. "You don't owe them any duty to assist them or encourage them in the commission of crime," she warned.

Brewer stayed home with his mother that night and never returned to a meeting of the Wildcats. During the following weeks and months, he heard of Negroes being whipped on Saturday nights. Then, one Sunday morning, the body of a Negro turned up with a fatal bullet wound. A group of white men were arrested and jailed on the charge of murder.

When the case went to trial, Brewer snuck into the back of the courtroom to watch the proceedings. He recognized the defendants as members of his old society. He watched as one of the most distinguished lawyers in Mississippi defended each boy and listened as the jury entered the verdict of "not guilty." It was the first time Brewer was confronted with evil and saw it go unpunished. Now, standing before a grand jury, Brewer had the chance to punish men for the crimes he did not have the courage to condemn as a child.

As Brewer came to the end of his closing argument, he paced from one side of the floor to the other. Gold Cane showed no expression. Under the table, his hands moved restlessly.

"Coahoma County is being weighed in the balance," Brewer concluded. "Men dissatisfied with law and order have taken civilization into their own hands. They have said, 'Let civilization be damned!' This county has met every exigency, it must not fail in this case. Give the lawless an inch and they will take a mile. There is no reason to doubt this man's guilt."

Judge Alcorn called for an adjournment while the jury made their deliberations. The fate to be decided was not just that of Cane, but of all four indicted men. "It is generally believed that if an acquittal comes in the Cane case," wrote one reporter, "it will be useless to prosecute the other three men." Filing out of the box, the jurymen followed one another into a room behind the judge's bank. They did not reach a verdict for twenty-six hours.

When it was announced that the jury had rendered a decision, Alcorn called the court back into session. As the back door swung open, the only sound was the footfalls of jurymen making their way back to the box. One jury member handed the verdict to a clerk, who read its words aloud to the court: "We, the jury, find the defendant 'not guilty.'" Cane jumped to his feet, grasping the hands of the jurors as he murmured his thanks. Upon Cane's acquittal, indictments against the other three men were dismissed.

Immediately following Gold Cane's release, Brewer filed another lawsuit, this time on behalf of a Negro prisoner named Marshall Jones, who was also charged with murder and was held at the Coahoma County jail with John Fisher when he was tortured. In the case, *Jones v. State*, Brewer again invoked Hemingway's Code to protest misconduct within law enforcement. This time, he was able to win Jones another trial and stay his execution. In pairing Hemingway's Code with the Fourteenth Amendment, Brewer found a renewed sense of purpose in his work. He joined the national fight against coerced confessions.

For more than a decade, Brewer continued to take cases similar to *Jones v. State*. In 1936, serving as lead defense counsel in a case financed by the National Association for the Advancement of Colored People, Brewer finally earned the victory that he'd dedicated his life to win. In *Brown v. Mississippi*, the US Supreme Court, for the first time in its history, reversed a state criminal conviction on the grounds that the conviction was based upon a coerced confession. The landmark decision affirmed that the Constitution must be applied in all police interrogations, regardless of color.

Legal scholars later noted that Brewer's keen understanding of the Fourteenth Amendment played a key role in the victory. He claimed the protections of the amendment belonged to every American, even prisoners. Yet in the vast sweep of history, the victory was bittersweet. For as Brewer devoted his career to securing the rights of prisoners, he overlooked another landmark case. *Gong Lum v. Rice*, the first Fourteenth Amendment case to challenge the constitutionality of segregated schools in the Jim Crow South, was neglected by the very man who could have been its greatest champion.

CHAPTER IX

SPRING, 1927

JAMES FLOWERS STARED AT the blank leaf of paper rolled into his typewriter. Lawyers of much greater stature called this affliction "pen paralysis." For Flowers, it was not so much a deficiency of words as a deficiency of character. He was a humble man and would have been the first to admit that he was out of his depth when tasked with writing the Supreme Court brief for *Gong Lum v. Rice.*

Immediately upon graduating from law school at the University of Mississippi in 1896, Flowers went to work as counsel for the railroads, a role he would maintain for most of his life. His colleagues praised the manner in which he practiced law, "with little drama and less sensationalism," "quietly, effectively, practically and sincerely." Flowers conducted his personal life in exactly the same manner. "Gentle and tender to the point of sensitiveness," he was the polar opposite of the lawyer who had handed him the brief. Try as he might, Flowers could not conjure up the style of Earl Brewer, because when it came down to it, he was an entirely different type of man.

Flowers's greatest obstacle was the central statute in the case, the equal protection clause of the Fourteenth Amendment. Flowers had never filed a Fourteenth Amendment suit before, and his understanding of the article was limited at best. Regardless, he decided to begin his brief by invoking the amendment about which he knew the least.

"The single question," he wrote, "is whether the State of Mississippi has denied to plaintiffs in error the equal protection of the laws in excluding Martha Lum from a public school. We say it has."

The next logical step would have been to answer *how* such equal protection was denied to the plaintiff, but Flowers skipped that step entirely and jumped instead to Section 207 of the Mississippi Constitution.

In writing the decision for the Mississippi Supreme Court, the judges had relied on Section 207, which stated: "Separate schools shall be maintained for children of the white and colored races." They based their decision exclusively on that section, without referencing the Fourteenth Amendment or its equal protection clause. Flowers, on the other hand, addressed Section 207 by pointing out its hypocrisy.

> Of course it is the white, or Caucasian race, that makes the laws and construes and enforces them. It thinks that in order to protect itself against the infusion of the blood of other races its children must be kept in schools from which other races are excluded. The classification is made for the exclusive benefit for the lawmaking race. . . . It levies the taxes on all alike to support a public school system but in the organization of the system it creates its own exclusive schools for its children and other schools for the children of all other races to attend together.

Flowers followed his condemnation of Section 207 with an argument in its favor. He suggested that the privilege denied to Martha, the privilege bestowed to her by the United States Constitution, was the privilege of segregation, the right to be schooled away from blacks. "If there is a danger in the association," he wrote, "it is a danger from which one race is entitled to protection just the same as another. . . . The White race creates for itself a privilege that it denies to other races; exposes the children of other races to risks and dangers to which it would not expose its own children. This is discrimination."

After claiming segregation as a privilege, Flowers went on to argue its merits. He advanced a theory that had festered in the depths of Southern culture since long before he was born.

> That negroes were once slaves and, as a race, had to begin as children is judicially known, even adjudicated. Laws are upheld that recognize this well-known fact. Because of their racial peculiarities, physical as well as moral, the white race avoids social relations wth [*sic*] members of that race. Such intercourse is objectionable; in many instances would

be repulsive and impossible. The White race protects itself against conditions that would require social contact—this, as the Mississippi court says, to preserve the integrity of the Caucasian race. But has not the Chinese citizen the same right to protection that the Caucasian citiizen [*sic*] has? Are they not equal before the law? ... The White race has made its laws with a view to preventing such social contact as would have a tendency to foster social relations and social equality. But this same precaution, taken with respect to its own children, is omitted when it comes to dealing with the children of the other races.

Flowers brought his argument to a close by quoting a single Supreme Court decision, *Plessy v. Ferguson*, the case that established the legal precedent for segregation itself: "Thrusting the company of one race upon the other, with no adequate motive, is calculated ... to foster and intensify the repulsion between them, rather than towards extinguishing it."

Flowers wanted to make it clear to the justices that he stood before them a strong defender of segregation. He came not to topple its walls, but to make them stronger, to make the "privilege" of segregation available to every American child. In citing *Plessy v. Ferguson*, Flowers took from judicial history the very words that had first legitimized state-sponsored segregation. "The above is repeated here," he wrote, "to show that the courts take notice of the undesirability of association with the Negro race. ... The state [of Mississippi] gives to the Caucasian race the exclusive privilege of a school that none but the children of that race may attend and denies the same privilege to the children of other races including the Chinese race."

As the brief strayed so far from its original purpose that it appeared as though Flowers sided with the defense, the lawyer typed one final paragraph with one radical suggestion: that segregated schools are, by their very nature, unequal.

Clearly the authorities agree that if separate public schools are provided for different classes of children, the children in one class do not enjoy equal protection of the laws unless the accommodations and facilities afforded them in their separate institutions are equal to those furnished other classes. ... Turning [Martha Lum] away from the Rosedale Consolidated High School can in no way be justified except by proof that there was another school furnishing equal accommodations available to her. Can a court assume that there was such a school? Can the placing of one class in one school and another class in another school be justified, when questioned, except by the showing that the two schools furnish substantially the same accommodations?

As Flowers typed those last biting words, he tore the final page from his typewriter. Gathering the brief into a pile, he carried it through the busy streets of Jackson and placed it into the hands of a printer, who copied and bound the brief. Then, in a matter of days, Flowers carefully sealed his brief into an envelope and mailed it to the United States Supreme Court.

For a successful man, Justice Louis D. Brandeis kept a simple home. He saw no need for decoration or such amenities as a telephone. He disliked typewriters, preferring to compose his opinions for the Supreme Court in longhand. Only recently, at the urging of his wife and friends, had he begun to entertain the notion of owning an automobile. He considered himself a public servant, a man the press branded "the people's lawyer," and a person of such caliber had no need for opulence.

Brandeis had served as an associate justice of the US Supreme Court for over a decade. Throughout that time, he preferred his own office to that provided him by the court. The offices of the Supreme Court were located in an old Senate chamber that had been in a constant state of disrepair since 1801. Only recently, with the arrival of a new chief justice, William Howard Taft, was there any discussion of relocating the court. For the time being, the justices would each have to continue to work from their own private residences. While his colleagues complained about the court's accommodations, Brandeis rarely, if ever, criticized the dilapidated hall over which he presided. His nature was to overcome obstacles.

The son of Jewish immigrants, Louis Dembitz Brandeis was born in Louisville, Kentucky, where his father was a successful grain merchant. At the age of eighteen, without a college diploma, Brandeis enrolled in Harvard Law School and graduated in the top of his class. Less than a year after graduating, he opened a law practice in Boston with his classmate Samuel Warren. It was through the establishment of his own firm that Brandeis took up the cause of the Progressive movement and fought to reform labor laws. In 1916 he was rewarded for his efforts and appointed to the United States Supreme Court by President Woodrow Wilson. The appointment made history, as Brandeis became the first justice of Jewish ancestry to serve on the nation's highest court.

After more than a decade on the Supreme Court, Brandeis was even less of a conventional figure than he had been in his youth. His gray hair grew long and bushy and he moved with a perpetual slouch. Friends and critics alike compared his appearance to that of a biblical prophet. While Brandeis's body had begun to deteriorate, his mind was still sharp, sharper perhaps than several of his colleagues. This worried him. He had admired Justice Oliver Wendell Holmes since his early days as a young attorney in Boston. Now, at the age of eighty-six, Holmes seemed weak. "His aim is no longer sure," Brandeis told a friend in confidence.

The case at hand, *Gong Lum v. Rice*, was unlike any the court had seen before and would require all justices to be at their sharpest. The appeal, sent up from the Mississippi Supreme Court, came from the father of a nine-year-old Chinese girl. The father, Gong Lum, challenged a ruling that classified his daughter as "colored" and therefore made her ineligible to attend the state's segregated white schools. From inside the sparsity of his home, Brandeis pored over the brief.

The entirety of its twenty-three pages was a disaster. The lawyer, a Mr. J. N. Flowers, made two arguments at once, and both were equally confusing. One advocated for the admission of the child, Martha Lum, to a superior white school in her town of Rosedale, and the other advocated for the expansion of school segregation, to create separate public educational facilities for every race known to man. Upon close inspection, it would seem as if the lawyer was defending the very decision he was assigned to appeal. Worst of all, for Brandeis, was the brief's excessive use of the Fourteenth Amendment.

Brandeis hated the Fourteenth. He wanted it repealed from the US Constitution. "Much ado about nothing," was how he once described the amendment to a fellow lawyer. Brandeis believed its clauses were far too intrusive on states' rights. As Brandeis's biographer noted, the justice "was loath to use it even to strike down segregation." This could have been due to the fact that Brandeis was raised in the South or maybe his fear of federal overreach extended even into defending Jim Crow legislation. Regardless of how Brandeis developed his contempt for the Fourteenth Amendment, he took out his anger by voting with the conservative majority in every race-discrimination case that reached the Supreme Court.

The case of *Gong Lum v. Rice* was similar in some ways to another case from 1922. In *Ng Fung Ho v. White*, Brandeis wrote the majority opinion in favor of the plaintiffs, five Chinese residents of California who were taken into custody by the commissioner of immigration for the Port of San Francisco and threatened with deportation. The Chinese residents, in turn, filed a writ of habeas corpus against the commissioner for holding them against their will. The writ was denied by the state court and was appealed to the federal court. Brandeis, invoking the Fifth Amendment, agreed that the Chinese men and women were held unlawfully, writing, "The Fifth Amendment affords protection in its guarantee of due process of law."

In the brief for *Gong Lum v. Rice*, the Fifth Amendment was never mentioned. It could have been argued that Martha Lum was deprived of her education without "due process," a claim to which Brandeis was sympathetic. In September 1924, when the initial writ of mandamus on behalf of Martha Lum was filed with the lower courts, Earl Brewer invoked the Fifth in his argument that "the right to attend said Rosedale Consolidated High School is a valuable opportunity to her, and [one] that she is being deprived thereof without the process of law." But Flowers, in his Supreme Court brief, did not reference the language of the writ, nor any other amendment aside from the Fourteenth. He did not cite *Ng Fung Ho v. White* or any other case related to people of Asian descent.

With an effective lawyer to argue before the court, the case of *Gong Lum v. Rice* might stand a chance. Brandeis wrote to Felix Frankfurter, founder of the American Civil Liberties Union, to see if the Chinese plaintiffs could obtain better representation. "Some steps should be taken," he wrote, "through Chinese minister, consuls or otherwise, to help Chinese to better counsel."

The news came in a telegram from the United States Capitol Building, signed by the head clerk of the Supreme Court. Reading the message, Flowers tried to keep himself from panicking.

NOW THINK GONG LUM AGAINST RICE, NUMBER TWO FORTY, ON
CALL AND PROBABLY REACHED FOR ARGUMENT ABOUT WEDNESDAY

It had been less than a week since Flowers filed the brief, and the case was already going before the justices. Brewer was impossible to reach and Flowers was in no way prepared to argue the case alone. He immediately wired the clerk a response.

WE DESIRE THAT GONG LUM VS RICE . . . SHALL NOT BE HEARD BEFORE THIRTY DAYS STOP PLEASE WIRE IF THIS CAN BE ACCOMPLISHED

While many lawyers wait their entire careers for the chance to argue a case before the Supreme Court, Flowers was not like most lawyers. He avoided public speaking at all costs. Unlike Brewer, the courtroom only made Flowers anxious. Brewer's gift for oratory was known throughout the state. He captivated a courtroom audience like a pastor at the pulpit. Without Brewer, the appeal didn't stand a chance.

A few days later, the clerk at the Supreme Court wired Flowers his response.

CASE CANNOT BE CONTINUED EXCEPT BY STIPULATION OF COUNSEL OR BY MOTION MADE IN OPEN COURT AND SUFFICIENT REASONS GIVEN

Flowers now risked forfeiting the case. He sent the clerk an application to remove *Gong Lum v. Rice* from the docket and reschedule the hearing for a later date. He wired the clerk and waited.

STIPULATION OF COUNSEL TO PASS CASE GONG LUM VERSUS RICE NUMBER EIGHT HUNDRED ELEVEN MAILED YOU YESTER-DAY STOP IS IT ESSENTIAL THAT ONE OF US BE PRESENT TO PRESENT APPLICATION

"If stipulation, properly signed by counsel," the clerk wired back, "to continue Gong Lum against Rice, is received Monday, I will present it to court and counsel need not appear."

The response was exactly what Flowers wanted. He had successfully stalled the case. The delay would buy him a few more weeks, maybe even months, to convince Brewer to travel to Washington and argue the case. Flowers could now get back to the lucrative work of representing the railroads. To delay *Gong Lum v. Rice* was to finally rid himself of its nuisance. Flowers discarded the case and returned to the corporate law in which he specialized.

In the absence of legal counsel, the Lum family, and the rest of the Mississippi Chinese, took matters into their own hands. They appointed J.K. Young, Jeu Gong's old friend from Tunica, to be their representative. The two men had not kept in close contact over the years, but Young was deeply interested in the case and reached out to the Lum family to offer his support. With Katherine and Jeu Gong's blessing, Young posed as their lawyer and sent letters to the US Supreme Court. He asked for copies of the other lawyers' briefs and requested notification for when the case would be argued before the court. He planned to attend the hearing in person.

During the first week of October 1927, Young received word that oral arguments were to be held within a few days. Writing on his own stationery, Young sent letters to every conceivable person involved in the case. He wanted them to know how important the outcome would be for all Chinese Americans. Hundreds of futures hung in the balance, and he was currently their only representative.

On October 5, 1927, Young mailed a letter to the US Supreme Court. In broken English, he voiced a desperate fear that his people would be forgotten: "I has been wrote to Mr. J. N. Flowers of Jackson, Mississippi in told him at once coming on your city pay attention this business, and trust that he notify you for same. Thanking you for above favors. J. K. Young, Esq."

The day before *Gong Lum v. Rice* was to be argued in court, the clerk received a telegram from Brewer and Flowers.

WE DO NOT WISH TO ARGUE THE CASE OF GONG LUM ET AL VS
RICE NUMBER TWENTY NINE AND WE REQUEST AND AUTHO-
RIZE YOU TO HAVE THE CASE SUBMITTED ON BRIEF

The lawyers ceded their right to argue to case before the justices. A verdict would be rendered in secret, behind closed doors, with only the brief written by J. N. Flowers to serve as the defense for Martha Lum. J. K. Young would never stand in the courtroom. He would not be present for a decision that would determine the fate of his friends and family. The consequence of Brewer's inaction would shape history, and a verdict would be rendered with the power to oppress millions of Americans for generations to come.

. . .

On November 21, 1927, the nine justices of the United States Supreme Court, notorious for rendering 5–4 decisions, delivered a unanimous verdict in the case of *Gong Lum v. Rice*. Chief Justice William Howard Taft assigned the task of writing the court's opinion to himself.

"The question here is whether a Chinese citizen of the United States is denied equal protection of the laws when he is classed among the colored races," he wrote. "Were this a new question, it would call for very full argument and consideration; but we think that it is the same question which has been many times decided to be within the constitutional power of the state Legislature to settle, without intervention of the federal courts under the federal Constitution."

Taft went on to cite *Plessy v. Ferguson*, the very case that Flowers cited in his brief.

In Plessy v. Ferguson, in upholding the validity under the Fourteenth Amendment of a statute of Louisiana requiring the separation of the white and colored races in railway coaches, a more difficult question than this, this court, speaking of permitted race separation, said: "The most common instance of this is connected with the establishment of separate schools for white and colored children, which has been held to be a valid exercise of the legislative power even by courts of states where the political rights of the colored race have been longest and most earnestly enforced."

Taft ended his opinion with an added clause, a statement so bold that it would rattle even his strongest supporters. The chief justice of the Supreme Court and former president of the United States gave individual states full constitutional power to segregate public schools and assign students to any race they saw fit: "The decision is within the discretion of the state in regulating its public schools, and does not conflict with the Fourteenth Amendment. The judgment of the Supreme Court of Mississippi is affirmed."

Without the participation of any person of the Negro race, the Supreme Court rendered a decision that sanctioned racial segregation within all public schools. The Court's unanimous ruling provided Mississippi with one of its strongest weapons to uphold segregation. A case that could have dismantled the "separate but equal" doctrine of *Plessy v. Ferguson* now became a pillar for its defense.

"*Gong Lum* is an ugly, unfortunate case," legal scholar Jamal Greene later wrote. "Part of the ugliness stems from the fact that this was not a test case; the stakes of the litigation were clear to the Court. . . . Racial division was neither an unintended nor an instrumental consequence of the policy, but was in fact its goal."

On the morning of November 22, 1927, thousands of Americans opened their newspapers to see Taft's decision quoted by the Associated Press. "Race segregation of children in public schools was sustained yesterday by the Supreme Court," the article pronounced. "Chief Justice Taft, in delivering the opinion said it was 'within the constitutional power of the State legislature to settle without intervention of the Federal courts.'"

It would be four days before the residents of Bolivar County, Mississippi, read an abridged version of the same article, in the back of the paper, between advertisements for estate sales and Standard Motor Oil. The editor removed the article's last few paragraphs, ending instead with one unyielding sentence: "Material harm would be done by the intermingling of children of all races."

As the verdict received little coverage at home, the rest of the country was galvanized into debate over its implications. Editorials appeared in both the white and the black press. Liberal and conservative papers were equally fascinated with the significance of the ruling.

Just two days after the verdict was announced, the *Los Angeles Times* ran an editorial at the front of its paper defending the decision. "In deciding the case the court referred to the 'Jim Crow' law which it has heretofore upheld, and thus apparently broadened the basis of the decision so that it seems to cover any sort of reasonable segregation that may be made." The author went on to praise the court for giving white America a legal precedent to uphold segregation at every level of society.

That the race problem has not been even more acute is due to the fact that segregation, extralegal but fairly effective, already exists. The Supreme Court's opinion points the way to making it still more effective.

So far segregation depends largely upon private agreement, and private agreements sometimes break down when they are submitted to severe strain. It will be better all around when they can be given legal backing.

In black America, the agony was palpable. The Court's ruling only reaffirmed the reality that constitutional rights afforded to whites did not apply to colored citizens. All men were not created equal before the law. Segregation served as the mores of a society that was inherently unjust.

"Why can [Americans] not educate their children without restriction as to color," asked the *Pittsburgh Courier*. "And why can they not occupy any seat in a train for which they are able to pay? If citizens of Chinese descent can be forced to attend jim-crow schools, then it is only logical to suppose that they can be segregated on trains, in hotels, in restaurants, in parks and at theaters, as are the Negroes."

For many blacks, the true bigotry lay not in the language of the ruling, but in the court's failure to recognize the indignities created by segregation itself.

"It is the opinion of the Chief Justice William Howard Taft that these opportunities are equal," read the front page of the *Chicago Defender*.

The little shacks you attend, in which a large coal stove in the center of the single room furnishes both heat and smoke—the ramshackle, tumble-down contraption, situated far down among the cotton stalks— is equal of the beautiful brick and stone structure attended by whites. You see, the three months you are allowed to attend this institution, between the sowing, chopping and picking of cotton, are equal to the nine months white children go to school. Your teachers, barely out of the primary school themselves, possessing no special training for teachers, are the equals of white teachers all especially trained and prepared for the work they undertake.

No longer was the case about Martha Lum, about Rosedale High School, even about Mississippi. The court's ruling established a precedent more powerful than the Lum family could have imagined. By fighting, they only made the enemy stronger. Every state in the nation now had legal grounds to exclude students of any race or nationality from its white schools.

CHAPTER X

WINTER, 1927

JEU GONG LUM LOADED a heavy stack of logs into an iron stove. Each piece of timber kicked up a cascade of soot, sending flutters of ash into the kitchen. Katherine stood on a stool beside the table, her sleeves rolled up above her elbows, pounding her fists into a dozen loaves of dough.

It was barely dawn and Katherine's body was already streaked with flour and sweat. Ever since the family left Rosedale for Wabash, work started earlier. The days were longer and the pay scarcer. "You work like a darn fool to get a dollar," Katherine recalled of her days in Wabash, "a darn fool."

The town was nothing more than a station stop along the Missouri Pacific Railroad, a small patch of cotton land in the northern reaches of the Arkansas Delta. The Lums ran the only grocery in town, an old plantation commissary at the end of a dusty road. There was no running water, no electricity, no indoor plumbing. The days began with the lighting of the woodstove and the hauling of water from the well. They ended with the deafening cry of cicadas and a silence that settled wearily over the empty fields.

The riches of Rosedale did not follow the Lum family over the river into Arkansas. They lived in isolation, thrown back into the poverty that Jeu Gong so longed to escape. Forces far from his control had taken everything he once made for himself, for his family. In the stillness of the early-morning hours, he gathered wood to heat a home he did not build and leaven bread he would not eat.

This was not the life that Jeu Gong had envisioned so many years before, on the night he willed his body to cross a frozen river. This *Gam Saan* was made of rules that were written in skin. They could not be broken. They could not be won. Jeu Gong's children inherited his blood, his skin, and no matter what he gave them, it would never be whiteness.

When the judgment came from the Mississippi Supreme Court, Katherine was devastated. She hid her heartbreak in her temper. She wouldn't speak to the *lo fan*. She stopped going to church. In order to keep the children in school, Jeu Gong sent them north to live with his brother in Michigan. While they studied, Katherine made the decision to leave Rosedale. She no longer wanted to live in a town that had been so cruel to her family.

Throughout the Delta, dozens of Chinese families made similar decisions, leaving in exodus from Mississippi. They moved to more tolerant cities with greater Chinese populations, like Memphis or Houston. Many left the South entirely or sent their children elsewhere to be educated. By the late 1920s, the largest demographic to leave the Delta became the children themselves, forced to live in other states with distant relatives.

Some parents made a greater sacrifice and sent their children back to China as the country erupted into war with Japan. In 1933 Katherine's sister-in-law traveled from Rosedale to China with her three children, the youngest only two years old. She left them in the care of an uncle in Nanking. "It still pains me to recall the agony of our parting," she later wrote of the four years spent separated from her children.

"Since the Chinese have been excluded from the white schools, the pain and anguish born by their parents can hardly be described in words," she confided in her native Cantonese. "Living in this unjust society, to what avail is it to complain or worry. Our solution was to send our children back to our home to be educated."

For a period of twenty years, from the 1925 *Gong Lum* decision until the end of World War II, the majority of Delta Chinese received little formal schooling of any kind. Those families with younger children who could not travel hired private tutors. Such was the case with the Dongs, the Jees, and the Gees of Ruleville, the Gongs and Lings in Duncan, and the Jues in Indianola. For the older children, there was the option of moving out of state or to towns on the fringes of the Delta, such as Marks, Crenshaw, and Senatobia, which continued to allow Chinese students to attend white schools.

It was not until the 1930s that Chinese families in the Delta began creating their own private schools. In 1930 a one-room schoolhouse in Greenville was reassigned to Chinese students. Residents of Rosedale created a separate Chinese school in 1933. In 1937 a similar school was erected in nearby Cleveland. Due to limited enrollment, the schools remained open only a few years. Greenville became the last school to shutter its doors, in 1947.

As for the Lum family, Katherine eventually found a white high school in Elaine, Arkansas, that agreed to accept the children. Its facilities were not new, nor was its program accredited like that of Rosedale, but the conditions were far better than the rundown, clapboard shacks reserved for colored students. In the spring, Katherine traveled north to Michigan while Jeu Gong bought a grocery six miles from Elaine in Wabash.

Just as the Lums prepared to leave what little remained of their old life, the rains came. The downpours lasted for months. April saw record rainfall, with more than seven inches falling on Arkansas's capital city in just a few hours. As surrounding lakes, rivers, and streambeds began to fill, the Mississippi continued to swell. Riverbanks struggled to contain the water, causing currents to flow upstream, toward the source of the river itself.

With such pressure, the levees could not hold. One by one, the man-made mounds of earth began to crumble. In Arkansas, every levee between Fort Smith and Little Rock failed under one enormous surge of water. A reporter in Arkansas City wrote that "mules were drowning on Main Street faster than people could unhitch them from wagons."

By May, nearly 13 percent of the state lay under water, with more than sixty-five hundred square miles of land completely inundated. Almost twice as much farmland was flooded in Arkansas as in Mississippi and Louisiana combined. In Wabash, the planted cotton fields were engulfed in more than five feet of water. Rows of whitewashed sharecropper cabins carried watermarks high above their doorways.

In total, an estimated forty thousand Arkansans were driven from their homes during the flood of 1927. Ninety percent were tenant farmers. In the Lums' new home of Phillips County, the number of refugees exceeded seventeen thousand. For many farmers, the prospect of rebuilding their plantation seemed futile. The crop had been washed away in the flood. For the sharecroppers, a year's earnings disappeared under the water. They took what they could carry and abandoned the fields. By summer, the Delta was a mud-swept desert, without any cotton or labor remaining at harvest.

·   ·   ·

Most of Jeu Gong's customers left with the waters. Their preachers told them the Lord had leveled the land on account of man's sin. Under steeples in Harlem, Saint Louis, and Chicago, they sang gospels of redemption and recited the Book of Genesis.

The words God once spoke to Noah, they now took for themselves. *I am going to put an end to all people, for the earth is filled with violence because of them.* He told Noah to build an ark of cypress, for within him was all that remained of man's righteousness. *I am going to bring floodwaters on the earth to destroy all life under the heavens, every creature that has the breath of life in it.*

They carried north their Bibles, clutched against breasts when the levees caved, when the river boiled under the fields, when they lifted their children to the ginnery roof and prayed to the raining heavens for strength. When, at last, the land was dry, they boarded boxcars, a thousand arks made of steel, and fled the South.

As the waters receded, Jeu Gong awaited a decision from the US Supreme Court. He left the Rosedale store in the care of his nephew, Lee, with the hopes that maybe one day his family could return to the brick house he built for them on the east end of Bruce Street. When the verdict came in early November, Jeu Gong learned his family would never return.

The decision that tore his children from him, forced them north to Michigan, the decision that left his family without a business, without a home, was now upheld by the highest court in America. The fight was over. The Lums had lost.

Still, Jeu Gong gave his children the best life he could make for them in Arkansas. He enrolled them all in school and promised Martha she would one day go to college. He taught his son to hunt waterfowl and rabbits in the sloughs between river and levee. He and Katherine bought a boat and taught Berda how to fish for turtles. As the Lum family moved on with their lives, the verdict became a tragedy relegated to the past, a story they did not tell, a memory they refused to keep.

Decades later, when Martha had children of her own, the war she'd waged in childhood returned to grip the nation. In June of 1953, the justices of the US Supreme Court ordered a rehearing for five school-desegregation cases, known collectively as *Brown v. Board of Education of Topeka*. The justices wanted to rehear each case in order to determine the original intent of the framers of the Fourteenth Amendment. The question that Earl Brewer first asked inside the Rosedale courthouse in 1924 was now posed, twenty-nine years later, to the lawyers of *Brown*.

"What evidence is there," the justices wanted to know, "that the Congress which submitted and the State legislatures and conventions which ratified the Fourteenth Amendment contemplated or did not contemplate, understood or did not understand, that it would abolish segregation in public schools?"

The question could not be answered easily. The team responsible for the five cases, the NAACP's Legal Defense and Educational Fund, knew they would need help. To strengthen their argument, the organization's chief counsel, Thurgood Marshall, enlisted more than two hundred lawyers and historians to research the framers' intent.

It was in this context that John Hope Franklin, then a visiting professor of history at Cornell University, received a frantic phone call late in the summer of 1953. The man on the line was a lawyer Franklin had known for years, from when he first taught history at Howard University. The two had worked together back in 1947 to bring a lawsuit against the University of Kentucky for denying admission to a black graduate student named Lyman Johnson. Although Franklin did not end up taking the stand as an expert witness, Johnson's lawyer, Thurgood Marshall, won the case, and the student was admitted into graduate school at the University of Kentucky.

"What are you going to be doing in the fall?" came Marshall's voice on the other end of the telephone.

"There's nothing else I'm going to do in the fall," Franklin replied. "Except go back to Howard University and teach."

"You know what else you're going to be doing?" Marshall asked.

"Oh, no." He suspected what was coming next.

"You're going to be working for me," Marshall announced.

"Doing what?"

"Doing what you've done before. You've got to work and help to shape the argument in a case."

Marshall explained that his team had to provide answers to questions that were raised by the United States Supreme Court. Rather than render a decision on a series of school desegregation cases, the court instead asked Marshall's team to answer a number of additional questions. Only historians or people trained as historians could answer such questions, Marshall told the professor impatiently. This was not an offer he was extending to Franklin. It was an order.

"He threatened me in a way that I knew that I was going to be in danger if I didn't accept his invitation or his command," Franklin recalled years later. "So . . . I decided to join forces with him."

By late August, Franklin was spending between four and five days a week at Marshall's office in New York. For months, Marshall's team of historians, social scientists, psychologists, and lawyers worked and reworked the *Brown v. Board of Education* brief. Finally, in November of 1953, less than a month before the case was to be reheard in December, the team produced a 235-page manifesto. Its language, depth, and persuasiveness exceeded all expectations, said Franklin.

Hours before dawn on December 7, 1953, scores of black Americans were already lining up outside the Supreme Court with hopes of witnessing history. Franklin, as a member of the team's research staff, was not ranked high enough to earn one of the courtroom's coveted seats. He never heard the arguments. Instead, Franklin was issued copies of the team's brief. In reading his research on the page, Franklin felt a strong sense of pride. His work was present in court that day, despite his absence.

After making their arguments, the lawyers told Franklin that all he could do was wait. They were under the assumption that the Supreme Court would not hand down a decision until the end of its term in June.

On the afternoon of May 17, 1954, Franklin received a call to his office at Howard. His wife, Aurelia, a librarian at a local public high school, was on the line.

"Have you heard what the decision is?" she asked.

"No," Franklin replied.

"Well, the Supreme Court handed down its decision today."

"What was the decision?"

"Linda Brown can go to an integrated school in Topeka, Kansas."

Franklin froze. Hearing the words of Chief Justice Earl Warren, he was overcome with disbelief. "We conclude," read the Supreme Court's unanimous decision, "that in the field of public education, the doctrine of 'separate but equal' has no place. Separate educational facilities are inherently unequal. Therefore, we hold that the plaintiffs and others similarly situated for whom the actions have been brought are, by reason of the segregation complained of, deprived of the equal protection of the laws guaranteed by the Fourteenth Amendment."

The professor hung up the telephone and stood at his desk. Then, as if moved by a higher power, he walked out of the university and into the street. Along the crowded blocks of row houses, the students, the people, were dancing. For a lifetime, Franklin would hold on to that moment.

"We felt," Franklin said, recalling the memory, "that maybe the long and hard work in which we had been engaged was worthwhile."

AFTERWORD

EARL BREWER WOULD NOT live to see his words cited in the briefs for
Brown v. Board of Education. He never witnessed Thurgood Marshall use
the equal protection clause, as he once had, to win a verdict that would call
for the end of state-sponsored segregation. On March 10, 1942, Brewer died
at a hospital in Jackson. His wife and youngest daughter were by his side.
The next day, his body was laid in state under the dome of the Mississippi
Capitol. Citizens throughout the South came to pay their respects to the
former governor. Brewer is buried beside his mother at Oakridge Cemetery
in Clarksdale, the town in which he drafted his greatest case.

Martha and Berda Lum graduated from high school during the height
of the Great Depression in 1933. Following graduation, Martha enrolled
in a teacher's program at Arkansas State University. By 1934 she could no
longer afford her tuition and dropped out of college to help her parents at
the grocery in Wabash. When the United States entered World War II,
Berda and Martha moved west. The sisters joined a growing number of
women who secured manufacturing jobs during the war. Berda and Martha found work building bombers for the Douglas Aircraft Company in
Long Beach, California.

After graduating high school, Biscoe found a job at a grocery in Mar-
ianna, Arkansas. On October 16, 1940, he registered with the local draft
board and entered the service after the attack on Pearl Harbor in December
1941. Biscoe served overseas as an army medic throughout the course of the
war. In the fall of 1943, he was transferred to China, where he worked at a
field hospital in western Yunnan Province. He wrote nearly every day to his
father and mother from their native country.

At the end of the war, Katherine drove from Arkansas to Houston,
Texas, to stay with her daughter Berda, whose husband had recently earned
a degree in architecture from the city's Rice Institute. Jeu Gong soon sold

the store in Wabash and followed his wife to Houston. There they opened a grocery and purchased a home at 508 Milwaukee Street. Martha moved into the house and married Henry Gee, who worked as a butcher at the family store. Together they had two children and spent the rest of their lives in Houston. Berda and her husband, Charles Chan, raised two daughters and a son in Houston. Biscoe returned from war and joined the postal service in Houston. He married and had three daughters. Jeu Gong died of cancer in the summer of 1965. Katherine followed him in 1988. They lived long enough to send their grandchildren to the nation's first generation of integrated schools.

ACKNOWLEDGMENTS

THIS BOOK WOULD NOT have been possible without the support of a staggering number of people. I will begin by thanking the Lum family for their gracious support throughout the entire process. They opened up their homes, dinner tables, and churches to me. This work is a testament to their kindness. I also wish to thank Minnie and Claudia Brewer. While neither woman lived to see her father represented in this light, their words and images are deeply present throughout the narrative. My research and writing was supported by multiple grants from the J. Anthony Lukas Work-in-Progress Award, the Lynton Fellowship in Book Writing, the Mississippi Delta Chinese Heritage Museum, the Mississippi Humanities Council, and the King's Daughters and Sons Circle Number 2 of Greenville, Mississippi.

A stalwart supporter from day one, Emily Jones, the archivist at Delta State University, allowed me to live in her guest room, dig mercilessly through her archives, and write from a makeshift den on the top floor of her office. She is a saint, as is her husband, Matt, for putting up with a journalist in the house. Other supporters from Delta State are Frieda Quon, Sally Paulson, Janet Horne, Laura Orsborn, Conor Bell, Whitney Carter, and Matthew Hancock. The Delta Chinese community was exceedingly helpful to me throughout my work on this project. I owe my gratitude to Dorothy Chow, Paul Wong, John Jung, and Bobby Joe Moon for their interest and help with the research.

Sam Freedman has been in my corner since the book was only a seed of an idea. Without his guidance, it would not exist in this form today. My agent, Anna Ghosh, and editor, Gayatri Patnaik, patiently steered me through the writing of my first book. My mother and her parents shared with me their world of the Mississippi Delta. I have come to know and love them more than I could ever convey in print. There were dozens of librarians who guided me through the research. They are the unsung heroes of this profession. One in particular stands out, because I am lucky enough to spend my life with him. To Jesse Kelley I owe a world of gratitude.

NOTES

INTRODUCTION

(1) "Of all the kinds of people . . ." Chan and Gee, 1992; Morganti, "Recollections of Rosedale," 11.

(1) "Word had filtered back . . ." Minute Book H, Board of Supervisors, Bolivar County, June 1, 1924, p. 367, located at Bolivar County First District Courthouse; Walter Sillers Jr. to Mr. E. H. Green, Election Commissioner, Cleveland, MS, June 5, 1924, Walter Sillers Jr. Collection, Box 47, Folder 37A, Delta State University Archives, Cleveland, MS.

(1) "The cotton market crash . . ." Lamar, *History of Rosedale*, 22.

(2) "If the rumors were true . . ." Description based on photographs of Martha Lum, courtesy of Alvin Gee.

(2) "Mornings had their own rhythm . . ." Lamar, *History of Rosedale*, 30; Morganti, "Recollections of Rosedale."

(2) "Next came the whistle for . . ." Sillers and Williams, *History of Bolivar County*, 203–9; Lamar, *History of Rosedale*, 33.

(2) "Classes began at eight thirty . . ." "Notice," *Bolivar County Democrat*, Rosedale, MS, September 6, 1924; "Schools Open Sept. 15th," *Cleveland Enterprise*, Cleveland, MS, July 17, 1924; Walter Sillers Jr. to Walter Sillers Sr., Chicago, August 22, 1924, Walter Sillers Jr. Collection, Box 34, Folder 101, Delta State University Archives, Cleveland, MS.

(2) "The more interesting route . . ." Sanborn Map Co., Rosedale, MS, 1918 and 1924.

(3) "After crossing Bruce Street . . ." Sillers and Williams, *History of Bolivar County*, 343–45.

(3) "At the end of Court Street . . ." Lamar, *History of Rosedale*, 98–100.

(3) "The most famous . . ." Ibid., 106–12.

(3) "Continuing north along . . ." "The Demise of an Old Movie Theater," *Bolivar Commercial*, Cleveland, MS, October 9, 1975; Lamar, *History of Rosedale*, 38.

(3) "Just past the Talisman . . ." Lamar, *History of Rosedale*, 34–35.

(4) "A block and a half north . . ." US Dept. of the Interior, National Register of Historic Places Inventory, Grace Episcopal Church, Rosedale, MS; Sillers and Williams, *History of Bolivar County*, 505–6.

(4) "The new brick schoolhouse . . ." Sillers and Williams, *History of Bolivar County*, 353; Lamar, *History of Rosedale*, 51–53.

(4) "At the beginning of every year . . ." Morganti, "Recollections of Rosedale," 24.

(4) "Martha's name was always . . ." Chan and Gee, 1992; Eng and Eng, 2014; Eng et al., 2014.

(5) "Before taking the position . . ." Lamar, *History of Rosedale*, 52.

(5) "Out of the relatively diverse . . ." Chan and Gee, 1992; Transcript of Record with Supporting Pleadings, Gong Lum v. Rice, US Supreme Court, 275 US 78, *The Making of Modern Law*.

(6) "Once safely inside the walls . . ." Chan and Gee, 1992.

PART ONE

(9) "Dear Sir . . ." H. E. Tippett, Chinese Inspector in Charge for Port of Detroit, to L. T. Plummer, Chinese Inspector in Charge for City of Chicago, March 31, 1904, Folder 1/81, General Records of the Immigration and Naturalization Service, Record Group 85, National Archives and Records Administration for Great Lakes Region, Chicago.

CHAPTER I

(11) "A thin ray . . ." Anderson, "Detroit River"; Eng et al., 2014.

(11) "A furious wind . . ." Chan and Gee, 1992; H. E. Tippett to L. T. Plummer, March 31, 1904; *Vancouver Daily World*, "Chinese Smuggled into the States," August 19, 1907. Note: This article depicts what many immigrants experienced: "The four Chinamen had been landed in Vancouver two weeks ago and smuggled across the Detroit river, where they had remained in the bushes just below Detroit for twelve hours."

(11) "Jeu Gong waited for a signal . . ." Mann, *Local Merchants*, 127–33; Smith, *Empress of China*.

(11) "The wait was with him . . ." A. E. Blake, "Trip Across Canada and the American Rockies," Box 42, Folder 1, Chung Collection, University of British Columbia. Note: This is a handwritten travel diary of a journey taken in 1900 by Blake and H. A. Jamieson across Canada and to the United States, via the Canadian Pacific Railway. The diary includes 104 black-and-white photographs of their journey. Canadian Pacific Railway Company, *The Highway to the Orient: Across the Prairies, Mountains and Rivers of Canada to Japan, China, Australasia, and the Sunny Isles of the Pacific*, Montreal Litho Co. Ltd., 1906, Box 195, Folder

17–2, Chung Collection, University of British Columbia, Vancouver. Note: Pamphlet advertising destinations and Canadian Pacific Railway Co. services in Canada; includes a map of the Canadian Pacific Railway.

(12) "Just over the water . . ." Tippett to Plummer, March 31, 1904; Hsu, *Dreaming of Gold*, 110–12; Siu, *Agents and Victims*, 67–68, 81, 243.

(12) "The waters Jeu Gong . . ." Siu, *Agents and Victims*, 20.

(13) "Streams and tributaries . . ." Hsu, *Dreaming of Gold*, 105; Siu, *Agents and Victims*, 16, 28, 35; Thomas, *A Trip on the West River*, 26.

(13) "The rivers carried flower . . ." Thomas, *A Trip on the West River*, 2, 4.

(13) "There were the large junks . . ." Ibid., 5; Hsu, "Trading with Gold Mountain," 24.

(13) "Beside the large boats . . ." Thomas, *A Trip on the West River*, 28.

(13) "There were the duck farmers . . ." Ibid., 12.

(13) "On the riverbeds grew . . ." Ibid., 43, 60; Siu, *Agents and Victims*, 18.

(14) "These were the waters . . ." Hsu, *Dreaming of Gold*, 108; Lee, "Defying Exclusion," 5.

(14) "Between 1882 and 1920 . . ." Hsu, *Dreaming of Gold*, 72, 93; Lee, "Enforcing the Borders," 55–56.

(14) "While less expensive . . ." "How Orientals Are Smuggled," *Vancouver Daily World*.

(14) "When Jeu Gong took his first step . . ." Siener, "Through the Back Door," 45.

(15) "Low-skilled laborers were not the only . . ." Ibid., 46.

(15) "According to newspapers . . ." Ibid.

(15) "Immigration inspectors were more likely . . ." Ibid., 50.

(15) "Edward Baltz was a smuggler and inspector . . ." Ibid., 45; "Customs Official Caught Smuggling," *Manitoba Morning Free Press*; "Smuggle Chinks into the States," *Fort Wayne Daily News*; "Smuggle Chinese in Cold Storage," *Hawaiian Star*.

(16) "Such widespread corruption . . ." Siener, "Through the Back Door," 38.

(16) "In many cases, corrupt agents . . ." "Smuggle Chinese in Cold Storage," *Hawaiian Star*.

(16) "Crossing into the United States . . ." Lee, "Enforcing the Borders," 59.

(16) "Every act of legislation aimed . . ." Siener, "Through the Back Door," 50.

(17) "At the frontier along the shores . . ." Ibid., 43.

(17) "A 1912 report . . ." Unnamed Chinese Inspector in Detroit to Unnamed Chinese Inspector in Montreal, February 29, 1912, Folder 19/11, General Records of the Immigration and Naturalization Service, Record Group 85, National Archives and Records Administration for Great Lakes Region, Chicago.

(17) "Hundreds of Chinese immigrants . . ." Siener, "Through the Back Door," 44; "Smuggle Chinese in Cold Storage," *Hawaiian Star*.

(17) "Despite the risks . . ." Hsu, *Dreaming of Gold*, 33.

(18) "The influx of Chinese immigrants . . ." Siener, "Through the Back Door," 34; Ngai, *The Lucky Ones*, 136.

(18) "That same year . . ." Lee, "Enforcing the Borders," 66; Ritchie, *American Journalists*, 125.

(18) "The prairie, the plains . . ." Ralph, "The Chinese Leak."

(18) "While exaggerated . . ." Lee, "Enforcing the Borders," 74; Beaver, *US International Borders*.

(18) "Policing the border . . ." Lee, "Enforcing the Borders," 84–86.

(19) "For the majority of Chinese immigrants . . ." "An Act to Execute Certain Treaty Stipulations Relating to the Chinese," May 6, 1882, *Enrolled Acts and Resolutions of Congress, 1789–1996*, General Records of the US Government, Record Group 11, National Archives, Washington, DC.

(19) "The act effectively halted . . ." Siener, "Through the Back Door," 37; Hsu, *Dreaming of Gold*, 65.

(19) "The sole voice in opposition . . ." Gold, *Forbidden Citizens*, 63–66, 95–111, 124–27, 202, 386; Daniels, *Coming to America*, 271.

(19) "Hoar's remarks fell . . ." Lee, "Enforcing the Borders."

(20) "Jeu Gong was crossing . . ." Daniels, *Not Like Us*, 48.

(20) "In the year following . . ." Daniels, *Coming to America*, 274.

(20) "In 1891 eleven Italian immigrants . . ." Jaret, "Troubled by Newcomers," 15.

(21) "As Jeu Gong set out for *Gam Saan* . . ." National Park Service, "The Immigrant's Statue."

(21) "Some thirty miles east . . ." Cold Spring Harbor Laboratory, "CIW Station"; Cold Spring Harbor Laboratory, "Eugenics Record Office"; Jacobson, *Whiteness of a Different Color*, 78.

(21) "In the forested fringes . . ." Yee, Poon, and Chan, 2013.

(21) "Once in Chicago . . ." Bing, "To Stand Alone"; Eng et al., 2014; Chan and Gee, 1992; Yee, 2012; Poon, 2012.

(22) "A city was too risky . . ." Chan and Gee, 1992.

(23) "An alluvial plain . . ." Cobb, *The Most Southern Place on Earth*, 4.

(23) "With slightly over 50 percent . . ." Ibid., 5; Percy, *Lanterns on the Levee*, 3–4.

(23) "The Delta was settled . . ." Cobb, *The Most Southern Place on Earth*, 8.

(24) "At the dawn of the nineteenth century . . ." Daniels, *Coming to America*, 240.

(24) "The so-called 'coolie' market . . ." Pfaelzer, *Driven Out*, 26.

(24) "'It was a brutal . . .'" Ibid., 26; Daniels, *Coming to America*, 240.

(24) "Following the Civil War . . ." Krebs, "The Memphis Chinese Labor Convention"; Commons, *A Documentary History*, 80–88.

(24) "On June 22, 1869 . . ." Krebs, "The Memphis Chinese Labor Convention"; Cohen, *Chinese in the Post–Civil War South*, 67.

(24) "Isham Green Harris, a lawyer . . ." Cohen, *Chinese in the Post–Civil War South*, 67; Gyory, *Closing the Gate*, 33.

(25) "'A number of Chinamen . . .'" "Minor Topica," *New York Times*, July 13, 1869.

(25) "The notion of introducing . . ." Gyory, *Closing the Gate*, 36; "National Labor Conference: First Day's Proceedings," *New-York Tribune*, August 17, 1869.

(25) "Despite such concerns . . ." Cohen, *Chinese in the Post–Civil War South*, 68, 82; Gyory, *Closing the Gate*, 33.

(25) "As increasing numbers of Chinese . . ." Cohen, *Chinese in the Post–Civil War South*, 100; Loewen, *The Mississippi Chinese*, 2–4, 26

(25) "Fleeing the plantation . . ." Ibid., 83.

(26) "'When the paroxysm of humanitarianism . . .'" "Chinese Immigration," *Washington Post*, November 14, 1905.

(26) "With the help of his relative . . ." Chan and Gee, 1992; Eng et al., 2014.

(26) "In his new life . . ." Hsu, *Dreaming of Gold*, 154.

(26) "J.K. Young ran a Chinese grocery . . ." Paul Wong to Adrienne Berard, October 29, 2013, e-mail describing old friend J. K. Young, photographs included. US Bureau of the Census, Census for 1910.

(27) "A self-taught scholar . . ." Wong to Berard, October 29, 2013; Shepherd, *The Chinese of Greenville*, 4–5.

(27) "It was the language . . ." Headlines pulled from Associated Press, "Disloyal Troops Murder Hundreds in Cities of China," October 12, 1911.

(27) "Even as the old country . . ." Loewen, *The Mississippi Chinese*, 74–81.

(27) "Like every other immigrant group . . ." Jacobson, *Whiteness of a Different Color*, 8–10.

(28) "There was talk of a servant . . ." Chan and Gee, 1992; Yee, Poon, and Chan, 2013; Certificate of Birth for Berda Beadel Lum, October 22, 1913, Records of the State of Mississippi, State Board of Health, Bureau of Vital Statistics; Application for Status as Permanent Resident for Katherine Toy Lum, September 3, 1972, Records of the Immigration and Naturalization Service, US Department of Justice; Deposition of Wong Hang Toy, Case Number 2244, Chinese Exclusion Acts Case Files, 1895–1943, Records of the Immigration and Naturalization Service, Record Group 85, National Archives, Seattle; Passenger Arrival Record for Hang Toy Wong, September 22, 1906, in Portal, ND, on Canadian Pacific Railway to Gunnison, MS, Record of Chinese Passenger Arrivals, 1903–44, Immigration and Naturalization Service, Seattle District, Chinese Passenger Arrival and Disposition Volumes, 1903–44, ARC: 646080, vol. 41, Records of the Immigration and Naturalization Service, Record Group 85, National Archives, Seattle.

(28) "Jeu Gong and Katherine married . . ." Certificate of Marriage for Lum Dock Gong and Wong Hang Toy, Marriage Licenses for 1912–1914, First District Court of Bolivar County, Mississippi, p. 414.

(28) "Although it was June . . ." "Two Hundred Drown in River Flood," *Bismarck (ND) Tribune*, April 20, 1912; "Flood at Its Worst," *Manning (SC) Times*, May 8, 1912; "Water Covers Branch of Yazoo & Mississippi Railroad," *Courier-Journal* (Louisville, KY), February 1, 1913; "River Crest Is Near," *Waco (TX) Morning News*, January 29, 1913; "No Breaks Reported in Levees Along Mississippi River," *Courier-Journal* (Louisville, KY), January 30, 1913; "Levees Break in Mississippi Damage Great," *Fairbanks (AK) Daily Times*, January 26, 1913; "Traitors, He Calls Beulah Levee Men," *Monroe (LA) News-Star*, January 30, 1913; "Beulah Crevasse the Worst Spot in Flood Situation," *Tennessean* (Nashville), January 29, 1913; Sillers and Williams, *History of Bolivar County*, 201–3.

(29) "Still, Katherine and Jeu Gong . . ." Eng et al., 2014; Chan and Gee, 1992; Yee, Poon, and Chan, 2013.

(29) "After the floodwaters . . ." Eng and Eng, 2014.

CHAPTER II

(30) "Berda was born . . ." Certificate of Birth for Berda Beadel Lum; "Benoit, Mississippi," 1913, Sanborn Fire Insurance Co. Maps.

(30) "The construction of her defenses . . ." Sillers and Williams, *History of Bolivar County*, 274. Description per photograph of Lum and Wong family circa 1918, courtesy of Marilyn Joe.

(30) "Merely a child . . ." Certificate of Birth for Berda Beadel Lum, courtesy of Candy Yee; Application for Status as Permanent Resident for Katherine Toy Lum.

(30) "They named her Berda . . ." Chan and Gee, 1992; Sillers and Williams, *History of Bolivar County*, 275.

(31) "On Sundays . . ." Sillers and Williams, *History of Bolivar County*, 273; Sanborn Fire Insurance Co. maps.

(31) "Katherine understood . . ." Eng and Eng, 2014.

(31) "When it came time . . ." Chan and Gee, 1992.

(31) "They would learn English . . ." For more on the second-generation immigrant experience, see Delta State University's collections of Italian Oral Histories, Chinese Oral Histories, and Jewish Oral Histories, http://www.deltastate.edu /academics/libraries/university-archives-museum/guides-to-the-collections /oral-histories/.

(31) "The change began . . ." Cobb, *The Most Southern Place on Earth*, 111.

(31) "In 1905 as many as . . ." Ibid., 111.

(32) "Many immigrants unwittingly . . ." Woodruff, *American Congo*, 34–36.

(32) "The story of Joseph Callas . . ." Ibid., 35; Callas, "The Meaning of Peonage."

(32) "In 1914 twelve . . ." Woodruff, *American Congo*, 34–36.

(32 "Although they spoke . . ." Cobb, *The Most Southern Place on Earth*, 110.

(32) "Some immigrants . . ." Ibid., 110.

(33) "In 1907 a plantation . . ." Ibid.

(33) "It was this failed effort . . ." Ibid., 173.

(33) "Their enterprise . . ." Ibid.

(33) "In an act of defiance . . ." Loewen, *The Mississippi Chinese*, 39.

(33) "While groceries . . ." Ibid., 51.

(34) "Saturdays were the busiest . . ." Chan and Gee, 1992.

(34) "As soon as Martha . . ." Ibid.

(34) "Always, there were the smells . . ." Interviews with Fay and Juanita Dong [OH 228], Kit Gong, Bobbie Gore, Joy Gore, Amy Gore, and Billie Gore [Unnumbered], Penney Cheung Gong [OH 247], Bobby and Laura Jue [OH 231], Dr. Audrey Sidney [OH 238], Delta State University Chinese Oral History Collection, http://www.deltastate.edu/academics/libraries/university-archives-museum/guides-to-the-collections/oral-histories/chinese-oral-histories/; Dickard, *Cantonese Recipes*.

(34) "As evening set in . . ." Chan and Gee, 1992; Yee, Poon, and Chan, 2013; Quan, *Lotus Among the Magnolias*, 29; Loewen, *The Mississippi Chinese*, 60.

(34) "Both the grocery . . ." Sanborn Fire Insurance Co. maps, Benoit, 1915.

(34) "In autumn . . ." Whitaker, *On the Laps of Gods*, 6.

(35) "The cotton . . ." Ibid.; Sanborn Fire Insurance Co. maps.

(35) "Even with its cutting-edge . . ." Sanborn Fire Insurance Co. maps.

(35) "Benoit began life . . ." Sillers and Williams, *History of Bolivar County*, 272.

(35) "James was the . . ." Woodruff, *American Congo*, 35–37; US Census Bureau, 1850 Federal Census.

(35) "Edmund Richardson was not always . . ." Woodruff, *American Congo*, 35–37.

(35) "The contract struck . . ." Ibid.

(36) "Through this new system . . ." Ibid.

(36) "An inveterate gambler . . ." Ibid.; Sillers and Williams, *History of Bolivar County*, 272; Subject File, Benoit, Record Number 35988, Mississippi Department of Archives and History (hereafter MDAH).

(36) "With hundreds of miles . . ." Cash, *The Mind of the South*, 32.

(36) "Until the final decade . . ." Ibid.

(37) "After the railroads . . ." Ibid., 179–80.

(37) "With laborers no longer . . ." Ibid.

(37) "With their hegemony . . ." Ibid., 190.

(37) "The new mills . . ." Ibid., 198.

(37) "Still, from Mississippi's . . ." Ibid., 198–202, 216.

(37) "They rose before dawn . . ." Ibid., 216.

(37) "'I have known . . .'" Edgar Gardner Murphy, *Problems of the Present South: A Discussion of Certain of the Educational, Industrial, and Political Issues in the Southern States* (New York: Young Reader's Missionary Movement of the United States and Canada, 1909).

(38) "Yet with the factories . . ." Ibid., 218.

(38) "Benoit's two-room schoolhouse . . ." Subject File, Benoit, Record Number 35988, MDAH; Sillers and Williams, *History of Bolivar County*, 273; Chan and Gee, 1992; Sanborn Fire Insurance Co. maps.

(38) "Mr. Bonds, twenty years . . ." US Bureau of the Census, 1920 Federal Census; Subject File: "Private Collections, Art Libraries, Antiques," Benoit, Record Number 35988, MDAH.

(38) "Until Martha was old . . ." Chan and Gee, 1992.

(39) "At last, March . . ." Whitaker, *On the Laps of the Gods*, 5.

(39) "By early May . . ." Ibid.

(39) "At the end of spring . . ." Ibid.

(39) "Again, the men . . ." Ibid., 6.

(40) "The school was located . . ." Sanborn Fire Insurance Co. maps; Sillers and Williams, *History of Bolivar County*, 273.

(40) "Adams, lined with . . ." Sanborn Fire Insurance Co. maps; Cobb, *The Most Southern Place on Earth*, 120; US Bureau of the Census, 1920 Federal Census, Benoit, Bolivar, MS; Whitaker, *On the Laps of the Gods*, 4.

(40) "Richardson ran on a . . ." Sanborn Fire Insurance Co. maps.

(40) "The children in these houses . . ." Quotes taken from: Annie Clark Jacobs, "Glimpses of Life on a Cotton Plantation Before the War Between the States," and Mary Carson Warfield, "The Antebellum Woman," in Sillers and Williams, *History of Bolivar County*, 110–26.

(41) "Martha and Berda passed . . ." Sanborn Fire Insurance Co. maps.

(41) "In the cramped room . . ." Chan and Gee, 1992; Eng et al., 2014; Yee, 2012; Yee, Poon, and Chan, 2013.

CHAPTER III

(42) "Moonlight leaked through the gaps . . ." Chan and Gee, 1992; Yee, Poon, and Chan, 2013; Biscoe birth date learned from "Hamilton Biscoe Lum," WWII Registration Draft Cards, Records of the Selective Service System, 1926–1975, RG 147, National Archives, Atlanta.

(42) "Katherine was growing sicker every day . . ." Chan and Gee, 1992.

(42) "Even if Jeu Gong . . ." Ibid.; Ferguson, "The Elaine Race Riot," 17.

(43) "January was 'movin'" month . . ." Cobb, *The Most Southern Place on Earth*, 108–9.

(43) "A report by the US Department of Labor . . ." Ibid., 118; Dillard, "Negro Migration."

(43) "As immigration plunged . . ." Wilkerson, *The Warmth of Other Suns*, 161–63; Cash, *The Mind of the South*, 254.

(43) "To fill the jobs left vacant . . ." Cobb, *The Most Southern Place on Earth*, 118; Wilkerson, *The Warmth of Other Suns*, 161–63; Cash, *The Mind of the South*, 254.

(43) "Such accounts passed . . ." Cobb, *The Most Southern Place on Earth*, 283; Grossman, "Blowing the Trumpet," 90; Hicks, "The Coverage of World War I," 60.

(43) "Local white leaders . . ." Woodruff, *American Congo*, 93.

(44) "Measures were quickly taken . . ." Ibid., 107.

(44) "Despite the risk . . ." Ibid., 118.

(44) "The most famous . . ." Evans, "High Water Everywhere," 59. Note: Evans has a slightly different interpretation of Patton's "Pea Vine Blues," which he sees as "merely a precursor" to Patton's classic "High Water Everywhere."

(44) "The railroads, which first fueled . . ." Cobb, *The Most Southern Place on Earth*, 115.

(44) "They vowed to stem . . ." Ibid., 117.

(45) "After the United States . . ." Ibid., 104; Woodruff, *American Congo*, 59–60.

(45) "When the black men . . ." Shaw and Rosengarten, *All God's Dangers*, 161.

(45) "In the spring of 1919 . . ." Wilkerson, *The Warmth of Other Suns*, 145.

(45) "In the Mississippi Delta . . ." Cobb, *The Most Southern Place on Earth*, 121; Woodruff, *American Congo*, 127.

(46) "The social and economic forces . . ." Woodruff, *American Congo*, 44–45.

(46) "The Lums and other merchant families . . ." Eng et al., 2014; description based on photographs of Lum family, circa 1920, courtesy of Alvin Gee.

(46) "As their customer base dwindled . . ." US Bureau of the Census, 1920 Census, Benoit, Bolivar, MS.

(46) "At the time he made . . ." Ibid.; US Bureau of the Census, 1910 Census, Roll: T624_733; Page: 36A; US Bureau of the Census, 1900 Census; US Bureau of the Census, 1880 Census, Roll: 658; Family History Film: 1254658; Page: 380A; Wallace, "I Remember Normal."

(47) "In the winter . . ." Chan and Gee, 1992.

(47) "On January 21, 1919 . . ." Deed records courtesy of Michael and Cathy Gee.

(47) "Jake's relationship with . . ." Deposition of Don Chuck Tai Wong, Case Number 2244, Chinese Exclusion Acts Case Files, 1895–1943, Records of the Immigration and Naturalization Service, Record Group 85, National Archives, Seattle.

(47) "When all of the details . . ." Deed records courtesy of Michael and Cathy Gee; Sperry, "Walter Sillers and His Fifty Years Inside Mississippi Politics"; MDAH, *The Official and Statistical Register of the State of Mississippi*, 833–35.

(48) "Sillers had been . . ." Sillers and Williams, *History of Bolivar County*, 391–93.

(48) "As a ten-year-old . . ." Ibid., 148–53.

(48) "In March 1919 . . ." Ibid., 273.

(48) "In keeping with tradition . . ." Oral history with Dr. John Paul Quon, F341.5.M57, vol. 748, pt. 2, Center for Oral History and Cultural Heritage, University of Southern Mississippi; Dong and Dong, 2000; Gong et al., 2000; Quan, *Lotus Among the Magnolias*, 41.

(49) "The relatives . . ." Chan and Gee, 1992.

(49) "While many of Katherine's . . ." US Bureau of the Census, 1920 Census, Benoit, Bolivar, MS; Wong family tree and history courtesy of Dorothy Chow.

(49) "Gow brought a son . . ." US Bureau of the Census, 1920 Census, Benoit, Bolivar, MS; Yee, 2012; Eng and Eng, 2014; C. L. "Lee" Kow to Martha Lum, July 13, 1933, courtesy of Alvin Gee.

(49) "The girls called . . ." Chan and Gee, 1992; Eng and Eng, 2014; Quan, *Lotus Among the Magnolias*, 20.

(50) "For Berda . . ." Yee, Poon, and Chan, 2013.

(50) "With a little money . . ." Coaching papers for Jeu Gong Lum, courtesy of Alvin Gee, trans. Paul Wong.

(51) "Over time . . ." Chan and Gee, 1992.

(52) "Whenever Jeu Gong . . ." Ibid.; Lee, 2015.

(52) "The first floor . . ." Yee, Poon, and Chan, 2013; Lee, 2015; description from photograph of Jeu Gong Lum in his garden, courtesy of Candy Yee.

(52) "Katherine designed . . ." Lee, 2015; Chan and Gee, 1992.

CHAPTER IV

(53) "Bruce Street was so alive . . ." Sanborn Map Co. maps for Rosedale, MS, 1918 and 1924; US Bureau of the Census, 1910 Census, Beat 3, Bolivar, MS; Roll: T624_733; Page: 1A; Enumeration District: 0009; FHL microfilm: 1374746, Record Group 29; US Bureau of the Census, 1920 Census, Rosedale City, Bolivar, MS; Roll: T625_871; Page: 1A; Enumeration District: 6; Image: 6, Record Group 29.

(53) "The street's loudest . . ." Lamar, *History of Rosedale*, 36–38.

(53) "Whether it was the vibrancy . . ." Chan and Gee, 1992.

(53) "Throughout most of the year . . ." Woodruff, *American Congo*, 23, 26, 149.

(54) "By September . . ." Description from photograph of third- and fourth-grade class at Rosedale School in Bolivar County, MS, in 1924, courtesy of

the Delta State University Archives, Cleveland, MS, Boyd-Walters-Bobo Collection, M100, Box 33, Folder 91; Chan and Gee, 1992.

(54) "The consolidated school . . ." Woodruff, *American Congo*, 144–46.

(54) "Mrs. Walter Sillers Sr. . . ." Ibid.; Mrs. Walter Sillers Sr., "Community Farms for Americans Proposed," *Bolivar County Daughters of the American Revolution*, c. 1920s, Walter Sillers Sr. Papers, Box 3, Sillers Family Papers, Delta State University Archives, Cleveland, MS.

(54) "Immediately following the school's . . ." *Biennial Report and Recommendations of the State Superintendent of Public Education to the Legislature of Mississippi, 1921–1923*, Call Number: Miss L 166.B1, Special Collections, McCain Library and Archives, University of Southern Mississippi, pp. 14–16.

(55) "Seeing as the school . . ." Walter Sillers Jr. Collection, Box 34, Folder 115, Sillers Family Papers, Delta State University Archives, Cleveland, MS.

(55) "On April 16, 1924 . . ." Description from photograph of third- and fourth-grade class at Rosedale School in Bolivar County, MS, in 1924.

(56) "The two men wanted . . ." Jacobson, *Whiteness of a Different Color*, 79–90.

(56) "Congressman Johnson . . ." US Congress, *The Eugenical Aspects of Deportation: Hearings Before the Committee on Immigration and Naturalization House of Representatives*, Seventieth Congress, First Session February 21, 1928, statement of Dr. Harry H. Laughlin, Committee on Immigration and Naturalization (Washington, DC: US Government Printing Office, 1928), Government Documents Collection Y 4.Im 6/1:D 44/10, Ellis Library, University of Missouri; Harry Hamilton Laughlin, *A Report of the Special Committee on Immigration and Alien Insane Submitting a Study on Immigration Control* (New York: Chamber of Commerce of the State of New York, 1934), Depository 325.73 L368r, University of Missouri; Jacobson, *Whiteness of a Different Color*, 79–90.

(57) "At noon on Wednesday . . ." US Congress, *Congressional Record*, 6449.

(57) "'Mr. President,' Senator . . ." Ibid., 6465–66.

(57) "Described by those . . ." Meriwether, *Jim Reed*, 38, 51, 143.

(58) "James was the only . . ." US Congress, *Congressional Record*, 6467–71.

(58) "Before the end of the session . . ." US Congress, *Congressional Record*, Sess. 1, ch. 190, 43 Stat. 153.

(59) "The act proved . . ." Koven and Götzke, *American Immigration Policy*, 133.

(59) "The three women . . ." Chan and Gee, 1992.

(59) "For the past several weeks . . ." Ibid.; Minute Book, Board of Supervisors, Bolivar County, June 1, 1924, Book H, pp. 367–72, First District Court of Bolivar County, Rosedale, MS.

(59) "She knew all too well . . ." Woodruff, *American Congo*, 131–32; Walter Sillers Jr. Collection, Box 34, Folder 65, Sillers Family Papers, Delta State University Archives, Cleveland, MS.

(60) "Still, if Katherine . . ." Yee, Poon, and Chan, 2013; Eng et al., 2014.

(60) "Jeu Gong was uneasy . . ." Chao, *In Search of Your Asian Roots*, 116–17; Bi Gan Trust, "The Origins of the Lin Family Name." Note: For the names, I used Chao's Cantonese versions because that is how Jeu Gong would have known them. The Mandarin names are Bi Gan [Pi-Kan], who was the son of Wen Ding [T'ai Ting] and the uncle of the cruel king Chou-hsin [Zhou Xin]. The Cantonese-speaking community uses "Lam" or "Lum" for the Mandarin word *lin* or *lim*, meaning trees or forest.

(61) "The two girls returned . . ." Chan and Gee, 1992.

(61) "As to whether or not . . ." September 13, 1924, response from query from W. F. Bond, Superintendent of Education of Mississippi, to Attorney General Rush Knox, from Attorney General's Biennial Report, 1923–1925, MDAH, 246–47. Note: The same conclusion was made in regard to Chinese children in Greenville, Mississippi, in 1920: "The conclusion seems to be inescapable," said Frank Roberson, Mississippi attorney general, February 13, 1920. "The Chinese child should be excluded by the trustees from attending a white school because such child is not a member of the white or Caucasian race but is a member of the yellow, or Mongolian race." Frank Roberson, Mississippi attorney general, February 13, 1920, queried by the assistant Superintendent of Education, J. W. Broom, cited in the Biennial Report of the Attorney General 1919–1921, Archival Reading Room, MDAH, pp. 57–58.

(61) "The girls were confused . . ." Chan and Gee, 1992.

(62) "In a desperate attempt . . ." Bing, "To Stand Alone," 12.

(62) "For Katherine to send . . ." Chan and Gee, 1992; Eng et al., 2014; Eng and Eng, 2014.

(62) "Jeu Gong slid . . ." Information from photograph of Jeu Gong Lum, circa 1920s, courtesy of Carol Hong Chan.

(62) "With the engine . . ." Eng and Eng, 2014; Eng et al., 2014.

(63) "The drone of. . . ." Sanborn Map Co., Clarksdale, MS, 1923.

(63) "Jeu Gong had no way . . ." Chan and Gee, 1992.

(63) "So on a September . . ." Ibid.

CHAPTER V

(67) "A wave of fresh cigar smoke . . ." Strite, *Biography of Earl LeRoy Brewer*, 11.

(67) "Brewer was a giant . . ." Ibid.

(67) "Every aspect of Brewer's . . ." Ibid.

(67) "He could no longer keep . . ." Williford and Strite, "Unfinished Manuscript for Biography of Earl Brewer."

(67) "Due to a steady . . ." Ibid.; Strite, *Biography of Earl LeRoy Brewer*, 21.

(68) "If the woman felt . . ." Yee, Poon, and Chan, 2013; Eng and Eng, 2014; descriptions based on photographs of Katherine Lum, circa 1920, courtesy of Alvin Gee.

(68) "She introduced herself . . ." Yee, Poon, and Chan, 2013; Eng et al., 2014; descriptions based on photographs of Jeu Gong Lum, circa 1920, courtesy of Alvin Gee.

(69) "'Nobody in Washington . . .'" "Battle for 33 Senate Seats Opens Tuesday," *New York Times*, March 23, 1924.

(69) "'It is very unbecoming . . .'" "Harrison and Brewer," *Cleveland (MS) Enterprise*, July 10, 1924.

(69) "Even before the final votes . . ." "Harrison's Victory Conceded by Opponent," *Baltimore Sun*, August 20, 1924.

(70) "Dusk was thickening . . ." Strite, *Biography of Earl LeRoy Brewer*, 20; author's multiple site visits to Cassidy Bayou between August 2014 and March 2015.

(70) "Sundown was quitting time . . ." Whitten, *To Beulah and Back*, 21–22.

(70) "Its furrowed fields . . ." Williford and Strite, "Unfinished Manuscript for Biography of Earl Brewer."

(70) "Brewer was born . . ." Strite, *Biography of Earl LeRoy Brewer*, 1.

(71) "As the eldest son . . ." Ibid., 2–3; Williford and Strite, "Unfinished Manuscript for Biography of Earl Brewer."

(71) "In the fall . . ." Strite, *Biography of Earl LeRoy Brewer*, 2; Williford and Strite, "Unfinished Manuscript for Biography of Earl Brewer."

(71) "By 1884 . . ." Strite, *Biography of Earl LeRoy Brewer*, 3; Williford and Strite, "Unfinished Manuscript for Biography of Earl Brewer."

(71) "Two years earlier . . ." US Bureau of the Census, *Foreign Commerce and Navigation of the United States*, 245–48; Williams, "The One They Had in 1882."

(72) "The brutality of levee work . . ." Williford and Strite, "Unfinished Manuscript for Biography of Earl Brewer"; Komara, *Encyclopedia of the Blues*, 596.

(72) "Aderholdt offered Brewer . . ." Williford and Strite, "Unfinished Manuscript for Biography of Earl Brewer."

(72) "When spring came . . ." Ibid.; Strite, *Biography of Earl LeRoy Brewer*, 3.

(72) "In 1893 Brewer opened . . ." Williford and Strite, "Unfinished Manuscript for Biography of Earl Brewer"; Strite, *Biography of Earl LeRoy Brewer*, 5

(73) "Realizing the limits . . ." Hamilton, *Progressive Mississippi*, 30.

(73) "Brewer's bold campaign . . ." Williford and Strite, "Unfinished Manuscript for Biography of Earl Brewer"; Strite, *Biography of Earl LeRoy Brewer*, 5.

(73) "In 1911 Brewer decided . . ." Hamilton, *Progressive Mississippi*, 30; Williford and Strite, "Unfinished Manuscript for Biography of Earl Brewer"; Strite, *Biography of Earl LeRoy Brewer*, 11–13; "Earl Brewer Announces Has a Ringing Platform Will Run as a Candidate of the Masses," *Memphis Commercial Appeal*, May 28, 1911.

(73) "During his inaugural address . . ." Hamilton, *Progressive Mississippi*, 30; Strite, *Biography of Earl LeRoy Brewer*, 11–13.

(73) "By the time Brewer took office . . ." Oshinsky, *Worse Than Slavery*, 20–21.

(74) "At the heart of the codes . . ." Ibid., 20–21, 31–32.

(74) "'In slavery times . . .'" Ibid., 34; Irvin, "Autobiography of Squire Irvin," 1082.

(74) "Mississippi's first Negro convicts . . ." Oshinsky, *Worse Than Slavery*, 45.

(74) "It was this state-sponsored . . ." Ibid., 45; Williford and Strite, "Unfinished Manuscript for Biography of Earl Brewer."

(74) "'It is not the shame . . .'" W. G. Orr, Okolona, MS, to Governor Robert Lowry, about the evils of convict leasing, 1884, cited in Oshinsky, *Worse Than Slavery*, 31.

(74) "In 1904, shortly after . . ." Ibid., 109–10, 139, 143.

(75) "Vardaman's farm . . ." Flemming, "Governor Earl Brewer." Note: According to the *Houston Post*, "Claims State Lost on Cotton," January 10, 1914, during the five years between 1909 and 1914, the state lost more than $300,000 worth of cotton profits. At the time, one bale went for about $1,000.

(75) "Once rumors began . . ." Williford and Strite, "Unfinished Manuscript for Biography of Earl Brewer." Note: Brewer took out loans from his own bank to fund the Legislative Investigative Committee. This information was found in a letter from Earl Brewer to A. C. Anderson, chair of LIC, October 15, 1913, Series 874, Box 1261, MDAH.

(75) "In August 1912 . . ." Strite, *Biography of Earl LeRoy Brewer*, 14.

(75) "In times of great struggle . . ." Ibid., 31.

(75) "Smith's eventual conviction . . ." Williford and Strite, "Unfinished Manuscript for Biography of Earl Brewer"; Earl Brewer to M. A. McKinnon of Coldwater, MS, May 28, 1913, Series 874, Box 1260, MDAH.

(76) "Brewer questioned the legality . . ." Ross A. Collins, Attorney General, to Earl Brewer, April 1, 1913, Biennial Report of the Attorney General of the State of Mississippi, 1913.

(76) "By the summer of 1913 . . ." Williford and Strite, "Unfinished Manuscript for Biography of Earl Brewer."

(76) "'It is freely predicted . . .'" "8 Prison Officials Convicted in Mississippi," *North Wilkesboro (NC) Hustler*, August 12, 1913.

(77) "On February 12, 1914 . . ." Penitentiary Investigation Transcripts, Vol. 4, Series 1563/Box 7738, RG 49, Department of Corrections Penitentiary Records, MDAH, Jackson, MS, entire volume; Strite, *Biography of Earl LeRoy Brewer*, 17.

(77) "The Parchman interviews . . ." Ibid., 55.

(77) "At 3:25 in the afternoon . . ." Ibid., 23; Williford and Strite, "Unfinished Manuscript for Biography of Earl Brewer."

(77) "Brewer needed to uncover . . ." Penitentiary Investigation Transcripts, 65; Williford and Strite, "Unfinished Manuscript for Biography of Earl Brewer."

(77) "As Brewer closed out . . ." Isaiah 1:27.

(78) "During one of his last . . ." Earl Brewer to Mr. Phillip Seigel of Vicksburg, MS, May 14, 1915, Series 874, Box 1264, MDAH; US Bureau of the Census, 1920 Census, Record for "Phillip Segel [*sic*]," Vicksburg Ward 3, Warren, MS; Roll: T625_897; Page: 3A; Enumeration District: 70; Image: 744, NARA microfilm publication T625, 2076 rolls.

(79) "As Brewer's horse slowed . . ." Williford and Strite, "Unfinished Manuscript for Biography of Earl Brewer"; Strite, *Biography of Earl LeRoy Brewer*, 20.

(79) "The collapse of Brewer's estate . . ." "He Made a Good Fight," *Clarksdale (MS) Register*, reprinted in *Woman Voter*, February 29, 1924.

(80) "Brewer entered his mansion . . ." Description based on photographs of interior of 41 John Street, circa 1920, courtesy of Carnegie Public Library, Clarksdale, MS.

(80) "A wide chiffonier . . ." Ibid.; Strite, *Biography of Earl LeRoy Brewer*, 20.

(81) "After decades, Brewer still . . ." Strite, *Biography of Earl LeRoy Brewer*, 9; Sanborn Map Company, Clarksdale, MS, 1925; Clarksdale, MS, City Directory, 1927, Ancestry.com; US City Directories, 1822–1995, database online, Provo, UT, Ancestry.com; postcard of Planters Bank Building, Clarksdale, MS, Cooper Forrest Lamar Postcard collection, PI/1992.0001, MDAH, Jackson, MS.

(81) "The office was located . . ." "The Alcazar Hotel," Historic Resource Inventory, 027-CLK-0588, Offices of the Historic Preservation Division, MDAH, Jackson, MS; Williford and Strite, "Unfinished Manuscript for Biography of Earl Brewer"; Weeks, *Clarksdale and Coahoma County*; Strite, *Biography of Earl LeRoy Brewer*.

(81) "The hotel's marble-clad . . ." "The Alcazar Hotel," Historic Resource Inventory.

(81) "Stationed at his desk . . ." Strite, *Biography of Earl LeRoy Brewer*.

(81) "Brewer's first order . . ." Transcript of Record with Supporting Pleadings, Gong Lum v. Rice, U.S. Supreme Court, 275 US 78, *The Making of Modern Law*; Hamilton, *Progressive Mississippi*, 47, 152; Bond, *I Had a Friend*, 86.

(82) "Willard Faroe Bond . . ." Bond, *I Had a Friend*, 78–79, 86.

(82) "Before Bilbo . . ." Hobbs, *Bilbo, Brewer, and Bribery*; Tindall, *The Emergence of the New South*, 23–25; Hamilton, *Progressive Mississippi*, 87–88, 222–23, 304–5.

(82) "Bond was born . . ." *The Talon*, Southern Mississippi Alumni Association publication (Fall 2004): 12–13; SF/Bond, Willard Faroe, record no. 44035, MDAH, Jackson, MS.

(82) "One year into the job . . ." Hamilton, *Progressive Mississippi*, 152–53.

(83) "Bond, on the other . . ." Bond, *I Had a Friend*, 78–79, 86.

(83) "Bilbo was facing . . ." Hamilton, *Progressive Mississippi*, 152–53, 301.

(83) "Brewer was not . . ." Transcript of Record with Supporting Pleadings, Gong Lum v. Rice, U.S. Supreme Court, 275 US 78, *The Making of Modern Law*.

(83) "Once a writ is filed . . ." Ibid.

(84) "At the opening of the Thirty-Ninth . . ." *Congressional Globe*, 39th Congress, 1st Session; Domestic Intelligence, *Harper's Weekly*, March 3, 1866, p. 131, c. 3; Domestic Intelligence, *Harper's Weekly*, March 10, 1866, p. 147, c. 4.

(84) "Congressman John Bingham . . ." Gerard N. Magliocca, "The Father of the 14th Amendment," *New York Times*, September 17, 2013.

(85) "In the end . . ." *Congressional Globe*, 39th Congress, 1st Session; Domestic Intelligence, *Harper's Weekly*, March 3, 1866, p. 131, c. 3; Domestic Intelligence, *Harper's Weekly*, March 10, 1866, p. 147, c. 4.

(85) "On May 10 . . ." Domestic Intelligence, *Harper's Weekly*, May 26, 1866, p. 323, c. 4; Domestic Intelligence, *Harper's Weekly*, June 23, 1866, p. 387, c. 3; Domestic Intelligence, *Harper's Weekly*, June 30, 1866, p. 403, c. 4; Domestic Intelligence, *Harper's Weekly*, July 7, 1866, p. 419, c. 4, and p. 418, c. 4, to p. 419, c. 1, "The President and the Amendment."

(85) "Scarcely had Howard . . ." B. F. Pershing, "Senator Edgar Cowan," read before the Historical Society of Western Pennsylvania, May 31, 1921; *Congressional Globe*, 39th Congress 1st Session, No. 182, Vol. 36, p. 2890; Boucher, *Edgar Cowan*.

(85) "According to one of . . ." Pershing, "Senator Edgar Cowan."

(86) "Despite widespread . . ." Ibid.

(86) "'The honorable . . .'" *Congressional Globe*, 39th Congress 1st Session.

(86) "Cowan's quandary . . ." Domestic Intelligence, *Harper's Weekly*, May 26, 1866, p. 323, c. 4; Domestic Intelligence, *Harper's Weekly*, June 16, 1866, p. 371, c. 4; Domestic Intelligence, *Harper's Weekly*, June 23, 1866, p. 387, c. 3; Domestic Intelligence, *Harper's Weekly*, June 30, 1866, p. 403, c. 4; Domestic Intelligence, *Harper's Weekly*, July 7, 1866, p. 419, c. 4; Domestic Intelligence, *Harper's Weekly*, July 7, 1866, p. 418, c. 4, to p. 419, c. 1, "The President and the Amendment"; Congress, *Harper's Weekly*, June 16, 1866.

(87) "Earl Brewer poured . . ." Strite, *Biography of Earl LeRoy Brewer*, 31.

(87) "Sometimes when Brewer . . ." Ibid.

(87) "The case, he decided, should begin . . ." Transcript of Record with Supporting Pleadings, Gong Lum v. Rice, US Supreme Court, 275 US 78, *The Making of Modern Law*.

(87) "Brewer's long stride . . ." Strite, *Biography of Earl LeRoy Brewer*, 32–33; author's multiple site visits to cemetery.

(88) "A lifetime had passed . . ." Dumenil, *The Modern Temper*, 7–9, 23, 135, 235–36. Note: For a full account of the lives of Brewer's daughters, see the

uncatalogued Dorothy Shawhan Collection at Delta State University Archives and the entire archive of the *Woman Voter*, a newspaper edited and published by Minnie Elizabeth Brewer, Carnegie Public Library, Clarksdale, MS.

(88) "In the fall of 1924 . . ." Ibid., 244–48.

(88) "She is advised . . ." Transcript of Record with Supporting Pleadings, Gong Lum v. Rice, US Supreme Court, 275 US 78, *The Making of Modern Law*.

(88) "This case, unlike . . ." Westlaw database search, cases of "Earl Brewer," http://campus.westlaw.com; White, "The Lost Episode," 197.

(89) "Said consolidated high . . ." Transcript of Record with Supporting Pleadings, Gong Lum v. Rice, US Supreme Court, 275 US 78, *The Making of Modern Law*.

(89) "Now that the scaffolding . . ." Sillers and Williams, *History of Bolivar County*, 343–45.

(89) "Carrying five . . ." Author's multiple visits to fully restored Rosedale courthouse.

(90) "Brewer walked down . . ." Sillers and Williams, *History of Bolivar County*, 274.

(90) "The clerk collected . . ." Author's multiple site visits to Rosedale courthouse, held original docket book.

(90) "When Brewer's daughters . . ." "Dad's Prayers" and "Governor Brewer's Stories," Earl Brewer Manuscript Collection, Z348.005 Box 1, MDAH.

(90) "During the middle of the . . ." Paul, *The Scots Peerage*, 205–52.

(91) "It was said . . ." James Graham, Marquess of Montrose, "My Dear and Only Love," in *English Poetry I: From Chaucer to Gray*, vol. 40, The Harvard Classics (New York: P. F. Collier & Son, 1909–14), also Bartleby.com, 2001, www.bartleby.com/40/.

CHAPTER VI

(92) "Earl Brewer thumbed . . ." Strite, *Biography of Earl LeRoy Brewer*.

(92) "About halfway through . . ." "Chinese Barred from Rosedale Schools," *Bolivar Democrat*, Rosedale, MS, October 4, 1924.

(93) "On Monday . . ." G. P. Rice and I. J. Brocato, "Chinese Barred From Rosedale School: Governor Brewer Attacked and Defended for Taking Up Case," *Clarksdale (MS) Register*, October 13, 1924.

(93) "There was an irony . . ." General Docket, Civil Cases for 1924, First District Court, Bolivar County, MS, Case 6122, p. 73.

(93) "Setting the date . . ." Transcript of Record with Supporting Pleadings, Gong Lum v. Rice, US Supreme Court, 275 US 78, *The Making of Modern Law*. Minutes of the Circuit Court, 1924, Bolivar County, MS, Case 6122, pp. 35 and 46.

(94) "Born Williams Aristides Alcorn Jr. . . ." US Bureau of the Census, 1870 Census, Friars Point, Coahoma, MS, population schedules, NARA microfilm publication M593, Roll 1761.

(94) "William's father . . ." Weeks, *Clarksdale and Coahoma County*, 112–16.

(95) "In 1844 Lusk . . ." Pereyra, *James Lusk Alcorn*, 183.

(95) "On the April day . . ." Act of Sale, "Mollie," April 12, 1861, accessed on Ancestry.com, http://mv.ancestry.com/viewer/6d468b76–8018–4652-a5c8-fcf33d 60b755/48593762/12909786885; US Bureau of the Census, 1880 Federal Census, Beat 3, Coahoma, MS; Roll: 645; Family History Film: 1254645; Page: 419B; Enumeration District: 099; Image: 0261; United States Bureau of the Census, 1900 Federal Census, Beat 3, Coahoma, MS; Roll: 805; Page: 5B; Enumeration District: 0024; FHL microfilm: 1240805; US Bureau of the Census, 1870 Federal census, population schedules, Coahoma, MS; Roll: M593_727; Page: 39B; Image: 82; Family History Library Film: 552226, NARA microfilm publication T132, 13 rolls.

(95) "The two young . . ." Hamilton, *Trials of the Earth*, 47.

(95) "Its thick woods . . ." Ibid., 47; Weeks, *Clarksdale and Coahoma County*, 112.

(96) "'The soldiers . . .'" Pereyra, *James Lusk Alcorn*, 69.

(96) "After Appomattox . . ." Newton, *The Ku Klux Klan in Mississippi*, 24.

(96) "The war had tested . . ." Pereyra, *James Lusk Alcorn*, 70; James Lusk Alcorn 1865 diary from private collection of Mrs. V. A. Hain, entry on "Memoranda" page.

(96) "In the spring of . . ." Pereyra, *James Lusk Alcorn*, 70–71.

(97) "A politically ambitious . . ." Oshinsky, *Worse Than Slavery*, 22.

(97) "James Lusk's reinvention . . ." Newton, *The Ku Klux Klan in Mississippi*, 24.

(97) "George feared . . ." Ibid., 24; Trelease, *White Terror*, 124.

(97) "But Lusk did not . . ." Pereyra, *James Lusk Alcorn*, 101.

(97) "Despite threats . . ." Ibid.; Montgomery, *Reminiscences of a Mississippian*, 283.

(98) "James Lusk won . . ." Newton, *The Ku Klux Klan in Mississippi*, 25; Pereyra, *James Lusk Alcorn*, 102.

(98) "Throughout his time . . ." Pereyra, *James Lusk Alcorn*, 120; Newton, *The Ku Klux Klan in Mississippi*, 31. Note: Before the Civil War, Mississippi had no public education system, and the only funds set aside strictly for education came from a small budget to build schools for Native Americans.

(98) "In developing the state's . . ." Pereyra, *James Lusk Alcorn*, 123

(98) "The Alcorn system . . ." Newton, *The Ku Klux Klan in Mississippi*, 31, 37; Horn, *Invisible Empire*, 149.

(98) "Before the end of 1870 . . ." Newton, *The Ku Klux Klan in Mississippi*, 31, 37.

(98) "In 1878 a devastating . . ." Oshinsky, *Worse Than Slavery*, 112.

(99) "With no father in his life . . ." Pereyra, *James Lusk Alcorn*, 183–85; Miriam Dabbs, "The Sage of Eagle's Nest," *This Is Clarksdale*, City of Clarksdale, 1972, 6–12.

(99) "Just four days . . ." Transcript of Record with Supporting Pleadings, Gong Lum v. Rice, US Supreme Court, 275 US 78, *The Making of Modern Law.*

(99) "Had any other judge . . ." Ibid.

(100) "Judge Alcorn gave . . ." Chan and Gee, 1992.

(100) "On December 5 . . ." Transcript of Record with Supporting Pleadings, Gong Lum v. Rice, US Supreme Court, 275 US 78, *The Making of Modern Law.*

(100) "The doors of the birdcage . . ." Author's multiple site visits to restored Capitol building in Jackson, MS; Minute book of the Mississippi Supreme Court, April 6, 1925, Archival Reading Room, State Government Records, Series 2467/ Box 26250 1924–1926: Book A-A, MDAH; History Resources Inventory, Record Number 049-JAC-0002-NHL-ML, Historic Preservation Division, MDAH.

(101) "The small courtroom . . ." "Noted Chinese Question Up in Supreme Court of State on Public School Question," *Daily Clarion Ledger* (Jackson, MS), April 8, 1925.

(101) "The swarm of onlookers . . ." Author's multiple site visits to restored Mississippi Supreme Court chamber, Jackson.

(101) "It was only when . . ." *Daily Clarion Ledger*, April 8, 1925.

(101) "Unlike most cases . . ." Rice v. Gong Lum 139 MS 760 (Miss. 1925).

(101) "Of the six men . . ." Skates, *A History of the Mississippi Supreme Court*, 75, 80, 95.

(102) "A cold and serious . . ." Subject File, George Ethridge, MDAH, Jackson, MS; George Ethridge, "Educating Democracy," Series Z1245, Box 5, Folder 21, MDAH, Jackson, MS.

(102) "Ethridge, like most statesmen . . ." Subject File, George Ethridge.

(102) "'The races are doomed . . .'" Ethridge, "Educating Democracy."

(102) "The chief justice . . ." Skates, *A History of the Mississippi Supreme Court*, 70; University of Mississippi yearbook, 1898, Oxford.

(102) "Sharp began his . . ." *Rice v. Gong Lum*; physical description of Elmer Clinton Sharp: World War I Draft Registration Cards, 1917–1918, Registration State: Mississippi; Registration County: Prentiss; Roll: 1683980, Ancestry.com; Subject File, Elmer Clinton Sharp, Record 58547, MDAH.

(104) "Brewer rose . . ." Strite, *Biography of Earl LeRoy Brewer*; *Rice v. Gong Lum.*

(105) "Brewer walked back through . . ." Guided walking tour of fully restored Capitol building in Jackson, MS, July 6, 2015.

(106) "Four weeks after . . ." *Rice v. Gong Lum.*

(106) "He relied almost . . ." Moreau v. Grandich, 114 Miss. 560 75 South 434.

CHAPTER VII

(108) "The news came to Martha . . ." Eng et al., 2014; Chan and Gee, 1992.

(108) "It was early May . . ." Interviews with Fay and Juanita Dong [OH 228], Kit Gong, Bobbie Gore, Joy Gore, Amy Gore and Billie Gore [Unnumbered], Penney Cheung Gong [OH 247], Bobby and Laura Jue [OH 231], Dr. Audrey Sidney [OH 238], Chinese Oral History Collection, Delta State University, Cleveland, MS; author's multiple site visits to re-created Chinese grocery store, Mississippi Delta Chinese Heritage Museum, Delta State University, Cleveland, MS.

(108) "Katherine decided . . ." Yee, Poon, and Chan, 2013.

(108) "They talked about . . ." Ibid.

(109) "Unable to discern . . ." Ibid.; Lum, c. 1990; Eng and Eng, 2014.

(109) "Miss Sales didn't . . ." Lum, c. 1990.

(109) "The children arrived . . ." Yee, Poon, and Chan, 2013; Sanborn Co. Maps, Rosedale, MS, 1924; Lamar, *History of Rosedale*, 30.

(109) "Martha, Berda, and Biscoe . . ." Sanborn Co. Maps, Rosedale, MS, 1918, 1924.

(110) "Martha picked up her suitcase . . ." Wilkerson, *The Warmth of Other Suns*, 5; Kornweibel, *Railroads in the African American Experience*, 299.

(110) "Once, in third grade . . ." Cable, *Madame Delphine*; Metcalf, *American Literature*, 320; textbook from third-grade list of Mississippi textbooks was found in *Biennial Report and Recommendations of the State Superintendent of Public Education to the Legislature of Mississippi; 1921–1923*, pp. 68–71, Special Collections, McCain Library and Archives, University of Southern Mississippi. Note: Rosedale would have had to comply with these suggestions for its accreditation.

(110) "With a shudder of steel . . ." Yee, Poon, and Chan, 2013.

(111) "Biscoe was restless . . ." Yee, 2012; Poon, 2012.

(111) "It was long past . . ." Records of Illinois Central Railroad Company for 1924, Illinois Central Gulf Railroad Miscellany, Collection Number 5197, Box 5, Folder 1, Kheel Center for Labor-Management Documentation and Archives, Cornell University Library, Ithaca, NY.

(111) "Overhead, a thirteen-story . . ." Description from photo of Illinois Central Station, 1894, South Loop Historical Society, Chicago.

(112) "Arriving at the station . . ." Wilkerson, *The Warmth of Other Suns*, 218.

(112) "Just three years earlier . . ." Armstrong, "Louis Armstrong," 17–26.

(112) "The excitement . . ." Records of Illinois Central Railroad Company for 1924.

(112) "The train arrived . . ." Santer, *A Historical Geography of Jackson, Michigan*; Berry, "Railroad History Story."

(112) "The roadway was . . ." Jackson, MI, City Directory, 1924, Ancestry. com; US City Directories, 1822–1995, Provo, UT, Ancestry.com; Jackson District Library Historical Image Collection, Jackson District Library, Jackson, MI.

(113) "At the corner . . ." Gow Lum in Jackson, MI, City Directory, 1924; US City Directories, Provo, UT.

(113) "The laundry was . . ." Lee, 2014; Chan and Gee, 1992; Yee, Poon, and Chan, 2013.

(113) "Once Berda began . . ." Chin, "Implementing Government Policy," 126. Note: The Chin article describes the dress of a *mui tsai*, which fits exactly with how Katherine is dressed in early photographs with the Wong family. Chin writes, "A mui tsai was easily distinguished from the members of the family owning her. She was usually dressed in cast-off clothes or in a garment of the coarsest material, with a round neck and button-up front, worn over loose trousers, and she was often barefooted. Her hair would either be plaited behind or be cut short like a skull cap." Yee, Poon, and Chan, 2013; Chan and Gee, 1992.

(114) "Martha made no effort . . ." Yee, Poon, and Chan, 2013; Chan and Gee, 1992.

(114) "It followed a current . . ." Wilkerson, *The Warmth of Other Suns*, 178.

(114) "'Oftentimes, just to go away . . .'" Dollard, *Caste and Class*, 307.

(115) "One day in early spring . . ." Eng et al., 2014.

CHAPTER VIII

(116) "Rain hammered . . ." "Ku Klux Klan Has Lecturer," *Clarksdale (MS) Register,* October 24, 1925; "Dr. S. Campbell Speaks on Klan," *Clarksdale Register,* October 26, 1925.

(116) "Pastor Macon Vick . . ." "Rev. Macon C. Vick," Clarksdale, MS, City Directory, 1927, Ancestry.com; US City Directories, 1822–1995, Provo, UT, Ancestry.com.

(116) "A chorus of cheers . . ." "Dr. S. Campbell Speaks on Klan."

(116) "As applause . . ." Ibid.; Samuel H. Campbell to Thomas E. Watson, September 16, 1922, Thomas E. Watson Papers, #755, Southern Historical Collection, Wilson Library, University of North Carolina at Chapel Hill; US Bureau of the Census, 1880 Federal Census, "Samuel Campbell," field hand, age twelve, District 538, Clayton, GA; Roll: 140; Family History Film: 1254140; Page: 534B; Enumeration District: 036; description from grave marker for Samuel Campbell, Restland Memorial Park, Dallas; physical description for Samuel Campbell from US Passport Applications, 1795–1925, National Archives and Records Administration (NARA) Series: Passport Applications, January 2, 1906—March 31, 1925; Roll #: 101; Volume #: Roll

0101—Certificates: 19975–20874, 05 Feb 1910–25 Feb 1910, NARA, Washington, DC; "Sam H Campbell," Texas Death Certificates, 1903–1982, Ancestry. com; Texas, Death Certificates, 1903–1982 [database online]. Provo, UT, USA: Ancestry.com Operations, Inc., 2013.

(117) "Campbell began his . . ." "Dr. S. Campbell Speaks on Klan."

(117) "In a small, dimly lit . . ." Testimony from Jones v. State, 141 Miss. 894, 107 So. 8; Newton, *The Ku Klux Klan in Mississippi*, 91–95; "Bloodhounds Lead to Arrest of Negroes," *Clarksdale (MS) Register*, October 17, 1925.

(118) "'They called the neighbors . . .'" Oshinsky, *Worse Than Slavery*, 103; Street, *Look Away!*, 11–38.

(118) "The Clarksdale men . . ." Newton, *The Ku Klux Klan in Mississippi*, 91–95.

(118) "Throughout the course . . ." "Based on Third Degree, State Charges Torture," *Memphis Commercial Appeal*, January 1, 1926; Fisher v. State, 145 Miss. 116, 110 So. 361; Fisher v. State, 150 Miss. 206, 116 So. 746.

(119) "After a week . . ." Newton, *The Ku Klux Klan in Mississippi*, 91–95.

(119) "When it came time . . ." Ibid.; "Women Condemn Mob Violence at Meeting," *Clarksdale (MS) Register*, December 22, 1925.

(119) "Earl Brewer was not present . . ." "G. O. Cane Goes on Trial for Life Today," *Clarksdale Register*, January 7, 1926. Note: Cited is a second coroner's report, completed by Greek Rice Jr., which became the official report in the case. The town's elected coroner would not perform the duty, so the young lawyer provided the report and testified in court in its defense.

(120) "The telephone . . ." "Convicted Slayers Removed from Jail," *Galveston (TX) Daily News*, December 21, 1925; "Lynching Freed Man Is Before Grand Jury," *Washington Post*, December 22, 1925; "Take Action Following Lynching of Negro," *Pantagraph*, Bloomington, IL, December 22, 1925; description of Brewer family home from Brewer Collection, Carnegie Public Library, Clarksdale, MS.

(120) "Brewer had never seen . . ." Quote from clipping in Earl Brewer collection, Mississippi Collection, Carnegie Public Library, Clarksdale, MS.

(120) "On the Tuesday . . ." "Women Condemn Mob Violence at Meeting," *Clarksdale Register* December 22, 1925.

(121) "The day following the lynching . . ." "Another Victory for State," *Memphis Commercial Appeal*, January 2, 1926; "Based on Third Degree," *Memphis Commercial Appeal*, January 1, 1926.

(121) "As Mrs. Brewer was . . ." "Women Condemn Mob Violence at Meeting," *Clarksdale Register*, December 22, 1925.

(122) "The next day, Brewer . . ." "Gov. Whitefield Says Preliminary Hearing Should Come Before Bond Release," *Clarksdale Register*, December 23, 1925.

(122) "Brewer jumped . . ." Ibid.

(122) "On Christmas Eve . . ." *Clarksdale Register*: "Four Indictments Returned by Grand Jury," December 24, 1925; "G. O. Cane Goes on Trial for Life Today," January 7, 1926; "Witnesses for Defense Impeach Testimony of Glass, Recused Sheriff," January 8, 1926; "Cain [sic] Case Is Now in Hands of the Jury," January 12, 1926. Note: The entire prosecution was made up of J. T. Smith, district attorney; C. S. Longino, court attorney; and Earl Brewer and Fred Montgomery as special prosecutors, but it was Brewer who wrote all the arguments and did the bulk of the questioning.

(122) "James Flowers sat . . ." Subject File: James Flowers, MDAH, Jackson, MS; Obituary, *Clarion Ledger*, Jackson, MS, May 8, 1952.

(123) "Flowers was now. . . ." Flowers, *Mississippi and the Mob*, 21.

(123) "For a man who did not . . ." Subject File: James Flowers.

(123) "'These figures patiently . . .'" Flowers, *Mississippi and the Mob*, 11–12.

(123) "Jokingly nicknamed General . . ." Subject File: James Flowers; J. T. Brown tribute to J. N. Flowers, March 1, 1965, at the unveiling of a portrait of Flowers at the circuit courthouse in Jackson, MS.

(124) "So it came as both . . ." Transcript of Record with Supporting Pleadings, Gong Lum v. Rice, US Supreme Court, 275 US 78, *The Making of Modern Law*.

(124) "Court convened at 9:30 . . ." *Clarksdale Register*: "G. O. Cane Goes on Trial for Life Today," January 7, 1926, and "Sidelights on Courtroom Scene," January 9, 1926.

(124) "Rumor was that . . ." "Cane Seized Negro, Sheriff Testifies," *Memphis Commercial Appeal*, January 8, 1926.

(124) "Glass collected his nerves . . ." Ibid.

(125) "Five days later . . ." "Cain Case Is Now in Hands of the Jury," *Clarksdale Register*, January 12, 1926.

(125) "'I am before you . . .'" Ibid.

(125) "Brewer's wife . . ." Ibid.

(125) "'Some folks enjoy . . .'" Ibid.

(126) "Following the death . . ." Williford and Strite, "Unfinished Manuscript for Biography of Earl Brewer"; Speech of Gov. Earl Brewer to the Striking Students of the A&M College, 1912, Tucker Printing House, Jackson, MS, 1912.

(127) "As Brewer came to the end . . ." "Cain Case Is Now in Hands of the Jury," *Clarksdale Register*, January 12, 1926.

(127) "'Coahoma County is being . . .'" Ibid. Note: Brewer's closing argument was also reported in the black press, but it was changed slightly: "Mob law must be overridden. . . . I come as a representative of the people of Coahoma [C]ounty to discuss the tragedy that has slapped our civilization in the face. . . . We have assumed the responsibility of carrying the burden of government for the prisoner and we must do it honestly and conscientiously. . . . If this continues,

it means anarchy." "Lynchers Acquitted of Crime," *Baltimore Afro-American,* January 23, 1926.

(127) "Judge Alcorn called . . ." "Cain Case Is Now in Hands of the Jury," *Clarksdale Register,* January 12, 1926; "Defense has Good Day in Clarksdale Trial," *Memphis Commercial Appeal,* January 10, 1926.

(127) "When it was announced . . ." *Clarksdale Register:* "G. O. Cane Goes on Trial for Life Today," January 7, 1926; "Witnesses for Defense Impeach Testimony of Glass, Recused Sheriff," January 8, 1926; "Cain's Fate Is Hanging Upon Glass Testimony," January 9, 1926; "Spectators at Court Ordered Searched," January 11, 1926; "Cain Case Is Now in Hands of the Jury," January 12, 1926; "G. O. Cain 'Not Guilty' So Say Jurymen," January 13, 1926.

(127) "Immediately following. . ." Jones v. State, 141 Miss. 894, 107 So. 8.

(127) "For more than a decade . . ." Cortner, *A "Scottsboro" Case.*

(128) "Legal scholars later noted . . ." Ibid., 75.

CHAPTER IX

(129) "James Flowers stared . . ." Full correspondence for *Gong Lum v. Rice,* Record Group 267, Records of the United States Supreme Court, Case File #31534, *Gong Lum v. Rice,* Box 7896, Location in Stacks: 17E3/06/08/01, National Archives and Records Administration, Washington, DC.

(129) "Immediately upon graduating . . ." MDAH Subject File: James Flowers; tribute to J. N. Flowers; Obituary, *Clarion Ledger,* Jackson, MS, May 8, 1952.

(129) "Flowers's greatest obstacle . . ." Westlaw database search, cases of "J. N. Flowers," http://campus.westlaw.com; *Gong Lum v. Rice* Brief, 1927.

(130) "In writing the decision . . ." Gong Lum v. Rice 275 US 78.

(130) "'Of course it is . . .'" *Gong Lum v. Rice* Brief.

(132) "As Flowers typed those . . ." Full correspondence for *Gong Lum v. Rice.*

(132) "For a successful man . . ." Roth, "The Many Lives of Louis Brandeis"; Architect of the Capitol, "History of the Supreme Court"; "Louis D. Brandeis," *Oyez,* Chicago-Kent College of Law, Illinois Institute of Technology, https:// www.oyez.org/justices/louis_d_brandeis, accessed January 13, 2015.

(132) "Brandeis had served . . ." "Louis D. Brandeis"; Architect of the Capitol, "History of the Supreme Court."

(132) "The son of Jewish immigrants . . ." Strum, *Louis D. Brandeis.*

(133) "After more than a decade . . ." Brandeis, in private conversation with Felix Frankfurter, November 30, 1922, quoted in Urofsky, "The Brandeis-Frankfurter Conversations," 310–11.

(133) "Brandeis hated the Fourteenth . . ." Strum, *Louis D. Brandeis,* 334; Brandeis in private conversation with Felix Frankfurter, July 9, 1922, quoted in

Urofsky, "The Brandeis-Frankfurter Conversations," 308; Bracey, "Louis Brandeis and the Race Question"; Bernstein, "From Progressivism to Modern Liberalism."

(134) "The case of *Gong Lum* . . ." Ng Fung Ho v. White 259 US 276.

(134) "In the brief for *Gong* . . ." *Gong Lum v. Rice* Brief, 1927; Transcript of Record with Supporting Pleadings, Gong Lum v. Rice, U.S. Supreme Court, 275 US 78, *The Making of Modern Law*.

(134) "With an effective lawyer . . ." Louis Brandeis to Felix Frankfurter, September 26, 1927, in Urofsky and Levy, *Letters of Louis D. Brandeis*, 303–4.

(134) "The news came in a telegram . . ." March 7, 1927, in full correspondence for *Gong Lum v. Rice*.

(135) "It had been less than. . ." Ibid.

(135) "A few days later . . ." Telegram from Earl Brewer and J. N. Flowers, March 11, 1927, in ibid.

(135) "Flowers now risked . . ." Telegram, March 12, 1927, in ibid.

(135) "If stipulation . . . '" Ibid.

(136) "On October 5 . . ." J.K. Young to US Supreme Court, October 5, 1927, in full correspondence for *Gong Lum v. Rice*.

(136) "The day before . . ." Telegram to the US Supreme Court, October 10, 1927, in full correspondence for *Gong Lum v. Rice*.

(137) "On November 21 . . ." *Gong Lum v. Rice*.

(138) "'*Gong Lum* is an ugly . . . '" Greene, "The Anticanon."

(138) "On the morning . . ." "Supreme Court Upholds Segregation in Schools," *Washington Post*, November 22, 1927.

(138) "It would be four days . . ." "High Court Upholds Barring of Chinese," *Bolivar County Democrat*, Rosedale, MS, November 26, 1927; "Supreme Court Upholds Segregation in Schools," *Washington Post*, November 22, 1927; "School Race Segregation Valid," *Baltimore Sun*, November 22, 1927; "Upholds Segregation of Chinese in Schools," *New York Times*, November 22, 1927; "Supreme Court Upholds Jim Crow Schools," *Philadelphia Tribune*, November 24, 1927.

(138) "Just two days after . . ." "Race Segregation," *Los Angeles Times*, November 23, 1927.

(139) "'Why can [Americans] not . . . '" "Running True to Form," *Pittsburgh Courier*, December 10, 1927.

(139) "It is the opinion of . . . '" "Some Pertinent Facts, Contradictions Mississippi," *Chicago Defender*, November 26, 1927.

CHAPTER X

(140) "Jeu Gong Lum loaded . . ." Lum, c. 1990.

(140) "It was barely dawn . . ." Ibid.

(140) "The town was nothing more . . ." Ibid.; Liao, "A Case Study of a Chinese Immigrant Community," 45.

(140) "The riches of Rosedale . . ." Chan and Gee, 1992; Yee, Poon, and Chan, 2013; Eng and Eng, 2014.

(141) "When the judgment came . . ." Chan and Gee, 1992.

(141) "Some parents made a greater . . ." Dancie Wong to Ting Kong, February 24, 1938, published in Wong and Lee, *Journey Stories*, 120–23.

(141) "For a period of twenty . . ." Wong and Lee, *Journey Stories*, xii.

(141) "It was not until the 1930s . . ." Loewen, *The Mississippi Chinese*, 68.

(142) "As for the Lum family . . ." Chan and Gee, 1992; Eng et al., 2014.

(142) "With such pressure . . ." Simpson and Dawes, "Letters from the Flood," 259–60; Lohof, "Herbert Hoover's Mississippi Valley Land Reform Memorandum," 113–14.

(142) "By May, nearly 13 . . ." Evans, *High Water Everywhere*, 4–6; Bearden, "Arkansas' Worst Disaster," 87; Hendricks, "Flood of 1927."

(142) "In total, an estimated . . ." Hendricks, "Flood of 1927"; Hobson, "Twenty-Seven Days on the Levee," 213.

(143) "Most of Jeu Gong's customers . . ." Evans, *High Water Everywhere*, 5–8.

(143) "They carried north their Bibles . . ." Ibid., 9–13.

(143) "As the waters receded . . ." Chan and Gee, 1992; C. L. "Lee" Kow to Martha Lum, July 13, 1933, courtesy of Alvin Gee.

(143) "Still, Jeu Gong gave his children . . ." Yee, Poon, and Chan, 2013.

(144) "'What evidence is there . . .'" Brown et al. v. Board of Education of Topeka et al. 345 US 972;73 S. Ct. 1114; 97 L. Ed. 1388;1953 US.

(144) "The question could not be . . ." King, *Devil in the Grove*, 336.

(144) "It was in this context that . . ." Franklin, "Behind the *Brown* Decision"; Franklin, *Mirror to America*, 156.

(144) "'What are you going . . .'" Ibid.

(145) "He threatened me in a way . . .'" Ibid.

(145) "By late August, Franklin . . ." King, *Devil in the Grove*, 336–37.

(145) "Hours before dawn . . ." Franklin, "Behind the *Brown* Decision"; King, *Devil in the Grove*, 337.

(145) "After making their arguments . . ." Franklin, "Behind the *Brown* Decision."

(145) "On the afternoon . . ." Ibid.

(145) "Have you heard what . . ." Ibid.

(145) "Franklin froze . . ." Franklin, *Mirror to America*, 159; 347 US 483 Brown v. Board of Education of Topeka (No. 1).

(146) "'We felt,' Franklin . . ." Franklin, "Behind the *Brown* Decision."

ORAL HISTORIES AND AUTHOR INTERVIEWS

Chan, Berda Lum, and Martha Lum Gee. Interview by Paul Wong. Discussion of childhood and *Gong Lum v. Rice*. Houston, August 8, 1992. Copy of original tape obtained by author.

Dong, Fay, and Juanita Dong. Interview by Kimberly Lancaster and Jennifer Mitchell. Chinese Oral Histories, Delta State University Oral History Project. May 1, 2000. http://www.deltastate.edu/academics/libraries/university-archives-museum/guides-to-the-collections/oral-histories/chinese-oral-histories/.

Eng, Sharon Lum, and Steven Eng. Interview by Adrienne Berard. Discussion of family history. Houston, September 21, 2014.

Eng, Sharon Lum, et al. Interview by Adrienne Berard. Discussion at Lum family reunion. Houston, September 20, 2014.

Gong, Kit, et al. (Bobbie Gore, Joy Gore, Amy Gore, and Billie Gore). Interview by Kimberly Lancaster and Jennifer Mitchell. Chinese Oral Histories, Delta State University Oral History Project. May 24, 2000.

Lee, Ellen Lum. Interview by Adrienne Berard. Discussion of childhood in Rosedale. Houston, March 28, 2015.

Lum, Katherine Wong. Interview by grandchildren Michael Gee and Elaine Lum. Collected for personal family oral history project. Houston, c. 1990. Copy of original tape obtained by author.

Poon, Patricia. Phone interview by Adrienne Berard. Discussion of family history, May 16, 2012.

Yee, Candy. Phone interview by Adrienne Berard. Discussion of family history, May 16, 2012.

Yee, Candy, Patricia Poon, and Charles Chan Jr. Interview by Adrienne Berard. Berda's children discuss family history. Cerritos, CA, October 15, 2013.

Anderson, Kraig. "Detroit River, MI." *Lighthouse Friends*. 2001. http://www
.lighthousefriends.com/light.asp?ID=160. Accessed August 15, 2014.

Architect of the Capitol. "History of the Supreme Court." http://www.aoc.gov
/history/supreme-court. Accessed November 7, 2015.

Armstrong, Louis. "Louis Armstrong." From *Satchmo* (1954). In *Reading Jazz: A
Gathering of Autobiography, Reportage, and Criticism from 1919 to Now*, edited by
Robert Gottlieb. New York: Pantheon Books, 1996.

Bearden, Russell E. "Arkansas' Worst Disaster: The Great Mississippi River
Flood of 1927." *Arkansas Review: A Journal of Delta Studies* 34, no. 2 (August
2003): 79–97.

Beaver, Janice Cheryl. *US International Borders: Brief Facts*. Congressional Research Service, Library of Congress. Washington, DC: Knowledge Services
Group, 2006.

Bernstein, David E. "From Progressivism to Modern Liberalism: Louis D.
Brandeis as a Transitional Figure in Constitutional Law." *Notre Dame Law
Review* 89, no. 5 (May 2014): 2029–50.

Berry, Dale. "Railroad History Story: Jackson's Evolution as a Rail Center." *RRHX:
Railroad History of Michigan*. February 1, 2001. http://www.michiganrailroads
.com/RRHX/Stories/JacksonEvolution.htm.

Bi Gan Trust. "The Origins of the Lin Family Name." Bi Gan Trust. 2010–2012.
http://bigantrust.com/index.php/lin-family-origins. Accessed April 12, 2014.

Bing, Sandra Wong Der. "To Stand Alone." *Southwest Chinese Journal* 8, no. 7
(July 1983): 12–13.

Bond, Willard Faroe. *I Had a Friend: An Autobiography*. Jackson, MS: Privately
published, 1958.

Boucher, John Newton. *Edgar Cowan, United States Senator from Pennsylvania
During the Civil War*. Somerville, NJ: American Historical Society, 1932.

Bracey, Christopher A. "Louis Brandeis and the Race Question." *Alabama Law
Review* 52, no. 3 (Spring 2001).

Cable, George Washington. *Madame Delphine*. New York: C. Scribner's Sons, 1881.

Callas, Joseph. "The Meaning of Peonage." *Colliers*, July 1909.

Cash, W. J. *The Mind of the South*. New York: Knopf, 1941.

Chao, Sheau-yueh J. *In Search of Your Asian Roots: Genealogical Research on Chinese Surnames*. Baltimore: Genealogical Publishing, 2000.

Chin, Koh Choo. "Implementing Government Policy for the Protection of Women and Girls." In *Women and Chinese Patriarchy: Submission, Servitude, and Escape*, edited by Maria Jaschok and Suzanne Miers. Hong Kong: Hong Kong University Press, 1994.

Cobb, James C. *The Most Southern Place on Earth: The Mississippi Delta and the Roots of Regional Identity*. New York: Oxford University Press, 1994.

Cohen, Lucy M. *Chinese in the Post–Civil War South: A People Without a History*. Baton Rouge: Louisiana State University, 1984.

Cold Spring Harbor Laboratory. "CIW Station for Experimental Evolution 1904–1921." *Archives at Cold Spring Harbor Laboratory*. 2015. http://library.cshl .edu/resources/library-newsletter/160–2012–10-newsletter/314-ciw-station-for -experimental-evolution. Accessed March 1, 2015.

——. "Eugenics Record Office." *Archives at Cold Spring Harbor Laboratory*. 2015. http://library.cshl.edu/special-collections/eugenics. Accessed March 1, 2015.

Commons, John Rogers, et al., eds. *A Documentary History of American Industrial Society*. Vol. 9. Cleveland: Arthur H. Clark Co., 1910.

Cortner, Richard C. *A "Scottsboro" Case in Mississippi: The Supreme Court and Brown v. Mississippi*. Jackson: University Press of Mississippi, 1986.

Daniels, Roger. *Coming to America: A History of Immigration and Ethnicity in American Life*. 2nd ed. New York: Harper Collins, 2002.

——. *Not Like Us: Immigrants and Minorities in America, 1890–1924*. Chicago: Ivan R. Dee, 1997.

Dickard, Betty Jue. *Cantonese Recipes: Class Favorites*. Clarksdale, MS: printed by author, 1978.

Dillard, James H. "Negro Migration 1916–1917." *Cayton's Weekly* (Seattle), April 26, 1919.

Dollard, John. *Caste and Class in a Southern Town*. New Haven, CT: Yale University Press, 1937.

Dumenil, Lynn. *The Modern Temper: American Culture and Society in the 1920s*. New York, NY: Hill and Wang, 1995.

Evans, David. "High Water Everywhere." In *Nobody Knows Where the Blues Come From: Lyrics and History*, edited by Robert Springer, 3–75. Jackson: University Press of Mississippi, 2006.

Ferguson, Bessie. "The Elaine Race Riot." PhD diss., George Peabody College for Teachers, Vanderbilt University, 1927.

Flemming, Anne. "Governor Earl Brewer." In *A Look at Clarksdale*, edited by Clarksdale Tourism Board, 6–22. Clarksdale, MS: City of Clarksdale, 1972.

Flowers, J. N. *Mississippi and the Mob.* Jackson, MS: Jackson Printing Company, 1926.

Fort Wayne (IN) Daily News. "Smuggle Chinks into the States." March 8, 1906.

Franklin, John Hope. "Behind the *Brown* Decision: A Conversation with John Hope Franklin." *Stetson Law Review* 34 (2005): 423–56.

———. *Mirror to America: The Autobiography of John Hope Franklin.* New York: Farrar, Straus and Giroux, 2005.

Gold, Martin. *Forbidden Citizens: Chinese Exclusion and the US Congress: A Legislative History.* Alexandria, VA: Capitol Net, 2012.

Greene, Jamal. "The Anticanon." *Harvard Law Review* 125, no. 2 (December 2011): 379–475.

Grossman, James R. "Blowing the Trumpet: The 'Chicago Defender' and Black Migration During World War I." *Illinois Historical Journal* 78, no. 2 (1985): 82–96.

Gyory, Andrew. *Closing the Gate: Race, Politics, and the Chinese Exclusion Act.* Chapel Hill: University of North Carolina Press, 1998.

Hamilton, Charles Granville. *Progressive Mississippi.* Aberdeen, MS: printed by author, 1978.

Hamilton, Mary. *Trials of the Earth: The Autobiography of Mary Hamilton.* Edited by Helen Dick Davis. Jackson: University Press of Mississippi, 1992.

Hawaiian Star. "Smuggle Chinese in Cold Storage." May 10, 1909.

Hendricks, Nancy. "Flood of 1927." *The Encyclopedia of Arkansas History & Culture.* October 23, 2014. http://www.encyclopediaofarkansas.net/encyclopedia /entry-detail.aspx?entryID=2202.

Hicks, Mary. "The Coverage of World War I by the Radical Black Press, 1917–1919." *Iowa Historical Review* 1, no. 1 (2007): 57–82.

Hobbs, Gambrell Austin. *Bilbo, Brewer, and Bribery in Mississippi Politics.* Memphis, TN: Dixon-Paul Printing, 1917.

Hobson, Edythe Simpson. "Twenty-Seven Days on the Levee: 1927." *Arkansas Historical Quarterly* 39, no. 3 (1980): 210–29.

Horn, Stanley F. *Invisible Empire: The Story of the Ku Klux Klan, 1866–1871.* Montclair, NJ: Patterson Smith, 1969.

Hsu, Madeline. *Dreaming of Gold, Dreaming of Home: Transnationalism and Migration Between the United States and South China, 1882–1943.* Stanford, CA: Stanford University Press, 2000.

———. "Trading with Gold Mountain: Jinshanzhuang and Networks of Kinship and Native Place." In *Chinese American Transnationalism: The Flow of People,*

Resources, and Ideas Between China and America During the Exclusion Era, edited by Sucheng Chan. Philadelphia: Temple University Press, 2006.

Irvin, Squire. "Autobiography of Squire Irvin." In *The American Slave: A Composite Autobiography*, edited by George P. Rawick. Supplement to series 1, vol. 8, "Mississippi Narratives," pt. 3. Westport, CT: Greenwood, 1977.

Jacobson, Matthew Frye. *Whiteness of a Different Color: European Immigrants and the Alchemy of Race*. Cambridge, MA: Harvard University Press, 1998.

Jaret, Charles. "Troubled by Newcomers: Anti-Immigrant Attitudes and Action During Two Eras of Mass Immigration to the United States." *Journal of American Ethnic History* 18, no. 3 (1999): 9–39.

King, Gilbert. *Devil in the Grove: Thurgood Marshall, the Groveland Boys, and the Dawn of a New America*. New York: Harper Perennial, 2012.

Komara, Edward M. ed. *Encyclopedia of the Blues*. 2 vols. New York: Routledge, 2004.

Kornweibel, Theodore. *Railroads in the African American Experience: A Photographic Journey*. Baltimore: Johns Hopkins University Press, 2010.

Koven, Steven G., and Frank Götzke. *American Immigration Policy: Confronting the Nation's Challenges*. New York: Springer, 2010.

Krebs, Sylvia. "The Memphis Chinese Labor Convention of 1869." *Southeast Conference Association for Asian American Studies Annals* 2 (January 1980): 112–17.

Lamar, Curt. *History of Rosedale, Mississippi, 1876–1976*. Spartanburg, SC: Rosedale Bicentennial Committee, 1976.

Lee, Erika. "Defying Exclusion: Chinese Immigrants and Their Strategies During the Exclusion Era." In *Chinese American Transnationalism: The Flow of People, Resources, and Ideas Between China and America During the Exclusion Era*, edited by Sucheng Chan. Philadelphia: Temple University Press, 2006.

———. "Enforcing the Borders: Chinese Exclusion Along the US Borders with Canada and Mexico." *Journal of American History* 89, no. 1 (June 2002): 54–86.

Liao, Pao Yun. "A Case Study of a Chinese Immigrant Community." PhD diss., University of Chicago, 1951.

Loewen, James W. *The Mississippi Chinese: Between Black and White*. 2nd ed. Prospect Heights, IL: Waveland Press, 1988.

Lohof, Bruce A., ed. "Herbert Hoover's Mississippi Valley Land Reform Memorandum: A Document." *Arkansas Historical Quarterly* 29, no. 2 (1970): 112–18.

The Making of Modern Law: U.S. Supreme Court Records and Briefs, 1832–1978. Database. Thomson Gale, 2005.

Manitoba Morning Free Press. "Customs Official Caught Smuggling." July 9, 1906.

Mann, Susan. *Local Merchants and the Chinese Bureaucracy, 1750–1950*. Stanford, CA: Stanford University Press, 1987.

Meriwether, Lee. *Jim Reed, "Senatorial Immortal": A Biography*. Webster Groves, MT: International Mark Twain Society, 1948.

Metcalf, John Calvin. *American Literature*. Richmond, VA: Johnson Publishing Co., 1921.

Mississippi Department of Archives and History, *The Official and Statistical Register of the State of Mississippi*. Jackson, MS: Democrat Printing Co., 1917.

Montgomery, Frank A. *Reminiscences of a Mississippian in Peace and War*. Cincinnati: R. Clarke, 1901.

Morganti, Leroy. "Recollections of Rosedale, the Town That Is Different." *Delta Scene* (Winter 1984): 10–14, 24.

Newton, Michael. *The Ku Klux Klan in Mississippi: A History*. Jefferson, NC: McFarland, 2010.

Ngai, Mae M. *The Lucky Ones: One Family and the Extraordinary Invention of Chinese America*. Princeton, NJ: Princeton University Press, 2012.

Oshinsky, David M. *Worse than Slavery: Parchman Farm and the Ordeal of Jim Crow Justice*. New York: Free Press, 1996.

Paul, Sir James Balfour. *The Scots Peerage; Founded on Wood's Edition of Sir Robert Douglas's Peerage of Scotland; Containing an Historical and Genealogical Account of the Nobility of That Kingdom*. Edinburgh: D. Douglas, 1904.

Percy, William Alexander. *Lanterns on the Levee: Recollections of a Planter's Son*. First published 1941 by A. A. Knopf. Baton Rouge: Louisiana State University Press, 1984.

Pereyra, Lillian A. *James Lusk Alcorn: Persistent Whig*. Baton Rouge: Louisiana State University Press, 1966.

Pfaelzer, Jean. *Driven Out: The Forgotten War Against Chinese Americans*. Berkeley: University of California Press, 2008.

Quan, Robert Seto. *Lotus Among the Magnolias: The Mississippi Chinese*. Jackson: University Press of Mississippi, 1982.

Ralph, Julian. "The Chinese Leak." *Harper's Magazine* 82, no. 490 (March 1891).

Ritchie, Donald A. *American Journalists: Getting the Story*. New York: Oxford University Press, 1997.

Roth, Larry M. "The Many Live of Louis Brandeis: Progressive-Reformer. Supreme Court Justice. Avowed Zionist. And a Racist?" *Southern University Law Review* 34, no. 2 (Summer 2007).

Santer, Richard Arthur. *A Historical Geography of Jackson, Michigan: A Study on the Changing Character of an American City, 1829–1969*. Jackson, MI: printed by author, 1970.

Shaw, Nate, and Theodore Rosengarten. *All God's Dangers: The Life of Nate Shaw*. New York: Knopf, 1974.

Shepherd, Ted. *The Chinese of Greenville, Mississippi.* Greenville, MS: Burford Brothers Printing, 1999.

Siener, William H. "Through the Back Door: Evading the Chinese Exclusion Act Along the Niagara Frontier, 1900 to 1924." *Journal of American Ethnic History* 27, no. 4 (2008).

Sillers, Florence Warfield, and Wirt A. Williams. *History of Bolivar County, Mississippi.* Jackson, MS: Hederman Brothers, 1948.

Simpson, Ethel C., and Richard Dawes. "Letters from the Flood." *Arkansas Historical Quarterly* 55, no. 3 (1996): 251–85.

Siu, Helen F. *Agents and Victims in South China: Accomplices in Rural Revolution.* New Haven, CT: Yale University Press, 1989.

Skates, John Ray. *A History of the Mississippi Supreme Court, 1817–1948.* Jackson: Mississippi Bar Foundation, 1973.

Smith, Philip Chadwick Foster. *The Empress of China.* Philadelphia: Philadelphia Maritime Museum, 1984.

Sperry, Benjamin O. "Walter Sillers and His Fifty Years Inside Mississippi Politics," Mississippi Now: The Online Publication of the Mississippi Historical Society. 2010. http://mshistorynow.mdah.state.ms.us/articles/356/walter -sillers-and-his-fifty-years-inside-mississippi-politics. Accessed February 10, 2016.

Street, James Howell. *Look Away! A Dixie Notebook.* New York: Viking Press, 1936.

Strite, Claudia Brewer. *Biography of Earl LeRoy Brewer.* Earl Brewer Family Papers, Z/0348.001/F/Folder 1. Jackson: MDAH, 1946.

Strum, Philippa. *Louis D. Brandeis: Justice for the People.* Cambridge, MA: Harvard University Press, 1984.

Thomas, R. D. *A Trip on the West River: New Going and Coming.* Guangdong Sheng: China Baptist Publication Society, 1903.

Tindall, George Brown. *The Emergence of the New South, 1913–1945.* Baton Rouge: Louisiana State University Press, 1967.

Trelease, Allen W. *White Terror: The Ku Klux Klan Conspiracy and Southern Reconstruction.* New York: Harper & Row, 1971.

United States Bureau of the Census. *Foreign Commerce and Navigation of the United States.* Part 2. Washington, DC: US Government Printing Office, 1888.

———. 1850 Federal Census. Records of the Bureau of the Census. Washington, DC: National Archives.

———. 1870 Federal Census. Records of the Bureau of the Census. Washington, DC: National Archives.

———. 1880 Federal Census. Records of the Bureau of the Census. Washington, DC: National Archives.

————. 1900 Federal Census. Records of the Bureau of the Census. Washington, DC: National Archives.

————. 1910 Federal Census. Records of the Bureau of the Census. Washington, DC: National Archives.

————. 1920 United States Federal Census. Records of the Bureau of the Census. Washington, DC: National Archives.

United States Congress. "An Act to Execute Certain Treaty Stipulations Relating to the Chinese." May 6, 1882. Enrolled Acts and Resolutions of Congress, 1789–1996. General Records of the US Government; Record Group 11. Washington, DC: National Archives.

————. *Congressional Record: Proceedings and Debates of the First Session of the Sixty-Eighth Congress of the United States of America*. Washington, DC: Government Printing Office, 1924.

Urofsky, Melvin I. "The Brandeis-Frankfurter Conversations." *Supreme Court Review* (1985): 299–339.

Urofsky, Melvin I., and David W. Levy, eds. *Letters of Louis D. Brandeis*, vol. 5, *1921–1941: Elder Statesman*. Albany: State University of New York Press, 1978.

Vancouver Daily World. "Chinese Smuggled into the States." August 19, 1907.

Vancouver Daily World. "How Orientals Are Smuggled." January 26, 1909.

Wallace, James A. "I Remember Normal." In *West Tennessee Historical Society Papers 1947–2010*, vol. 30, edited by West Tennessee Historical Society, 129–37. Memphis: West Tennessee Historical Society, 1976.

Weeks, Linton. *Clarksdale and Coahoma County: A History*. Clarksdale, MS: Carnegie Public Library, 1982.

Whitaker, Robert. *On the Laps of Gods: The Red Summer of 1919 and the Struggle for Justice That Remade a Nation*. New York: Three Rivers Press, 2009.

White, G. Edward. "The Lost Episode of *Gong Lum v. Rice*." *Green Bag* 18, no. 2 (2015): 191–205.

Whitten, Paul. *To Beulah and Back: The Right Place at the Right Time; Personal Memoirs*. Columbus, GA: Brentwood Christian Press, 1995.

Wilkerson, Isabel. *The Warmth of Other Suns: The Epic Story of America's Great Migration*. New York: Random House, 2010.

Williams, Bobby Joe. "The One They Had in 1882 Was 'The Big Flood.'" Shelby County Tennessee History and Genealogy. 2008. http://tn-roots.com/tnshelby/history/1882Flood.htm. Accessed June 20, 2014.

Williford, Martha Harrison, and Claudia Strite. "Unfinished Manuscript for Biography of Earl Brewer." Microfilm. *Miscellaneous Mississippi Statesmen's Papers*, University of Georgia Libraries, FILM F340.M580. Original material from Mississippi Department of Archives and History, Jackson, c. 1945.

Wong, Paul, and Doris Ling Lee. *Journey Stories from the Cleveland Chinese Mission School*. Cleveland, MS: privately printed, 2011.

Woodruff, Nan Elizabeth. *American Congo: The African American Freedom Struggle in the Delta*. Cambridge, MA: Harvard University Press, 2003.

INDEX